Calvin on the Death of Christ

Calvin on the Death of Christ

A WORD FOR THE WORLD

~

Paul A. Hartog

Foreword by Tony Lane

CASCADE *Books* • Eugene, Oregon

CALVIN ON THE DEATH OF CHRIST
A Word for the World

Copyright © 2021 Paul A. Hartog. All rights reserved. Except for brief quotations in critical publications or reviews, no part of this book may be reproduced in any manner without prior written permission from the publisher. Write: Permissions, Wipf and Stock Publishers, 199 W. 8th Ave., Suite 3, Eugene, OR 97401.

Cascade Books
An Imprint of Wipf and Stock Publishers
199 W. 8th Ave., Suite 3
Eugene, OR 97401

www.wipfandstock.com

PAPERBACK ISBN: 978-1-5326-8349-7
HARDCOVER ISBN: 978-1-5326-8350-3
EBOOK ISBN: 978-1-5326-8351-0

Cataloguing-in-Publication data:

Names: Hartog, Paul A., 1970, author.

Title: Calvin on the death of Christ : a word for the world / Paul A. Hartog.

Description: Eugene, OR: Cascade Books, 2021 | Includes bibliographical references and index.

Identifiers: ISBN 978-1-5326-8349-7 (paperback) | ISBN 978-1-5326-8350-3 (hardcover) | ISBN 978-1-5326-8351-0 (ebook)

Subjects: LCSH: Calvin Jean—1509–1564—Views on the atonement | Calvin Jean—1509–1564—Theology | Atonement—History of doctrines—16th century | Atonement

Classification: BX9418 H37 2021 (print) | BX9418 (ebook)

"Scripture quotations marked (ESV) are from The Holy Bible, English Standard Version® (ESV®), copyright © 2001 by Crossway, a publishing ministry of Good News Publishers. Used by permission. All rights reserved."

"Scripture taken from the New King James Version. Copyright © 1982 by Thomas Nelson, Inc. Used by permission. All rights reserved."

Dedication

I dedicate this book to my parents, who bequeathed to me a family heritage, as well as a love for the Christian heritage, and especially a love for Christ's work *extra nobis* as proclaimed in the gospel

Table of Contents

Foreword by Professor Tony Lane xi
Acknowledgements xiii

Introduction 1
Chapter One: Three General Approaches 9
Chapter Two: Twelve Issues 26
Chapter Three: Evidences for "Limited Atonement" 59
Chapter Four: Calvin and Reformed Diversity 85
Chapter Five: Epilogue 125

Bibliography 163
Name Index 189
Subject Index 193
Scripture Index 198

Foreword

THE MIDDLE L OF the infamous TULIP refers to Limited Atonement, a topic of controversy amongst Calvinists especially. While many fondly imagine that the acronym goes back to Calvin, or at least to the Synod of Dort (1618–19), Paul Hartog is well aware of its twentieth-century origin. It is not only the origin of the acronym that is problematic. There are objections to the word "atonement" and even more to the word "limited." Some prefer to talk of "definite atonement" or "particular redemption." Again, there is no one version of limited atonement (or whatever one chooses to call it) but many different ones. Hartog cites examples of theologians teaching "unlimited atonement" alongside "limited redemption," or "unlimited expiation" alongside "particular redemption." This book helpfully demonstrates the range of different views that can be gathered under the umbrella of "limited atonement."

Those arguing for one side or the other on this topic have often sought to conscript Calvin into their ranks. There has been a vigorous debate among Reformed (and other) theologians as to whether or not Calvin held to "limited atonement" (however that is understood). This is the question that lies at the heart of this book, though it is very helpfully set in the context of the wider debate in the history of Reformed theology.

Hartog argues that, for Calvin, "Christ died intentionally as a sufficient expiation and redemption for the sins of all humanity, and he died intentionally for the efficacious salvation of the elect in particular." I remember James B. Torrance telling me about a debate that he and his brother had with John Murray among others. Murray asked whether Christ's death makes our salvation certain or merely possible. The Torrances replied that our salvation is made certain, not just possible, by the combined work of Father, Son, and Holy Spirit. The structure of Calvin's *Institutes* supports their response. At the end of Book 2 he expounds the work of Christ. At the beginning of Book 3 he states that "all that [Christ] has suffered and done for the salvation of the human race" (not "for the salvation of the elect") is "useless and has no value for us" until the Holy Spirit by faith unites us to Christ (3:1:1). This is not just a random quotation from the *Institutes* but involves the very structure of the work. Book 2 is about what Christ has done for the whole human race; Book 3 is about how the Holy Spirit makes this effective for the elect.

Many books and learned articles have been written on this topic—as can be seen by perusing the twenty-six pages of bibliography. I have read a number of these and am very happy to commend the present work. Paul Hartog offers a fairly argued study that reviews the full range of evidence and that avoids the trap of expounding Calvin in isolation from the tradition to which he belongs. Also, as has already been indicated, he recognizes the complexity of the issue and avoids simplistic solutions. This book is definitely a must for anyone with an interest in the topic.

Tony Lane
Professor of Historical Theology
London School of Theology

Acknowledgements

I AM THANKFUL FOR the privilege of studying Reformation history under Raymond Mentzer, Professor of Religious Studies at the University of Iowa. Those graduate credits transferred into my M.Th. degree, and the core of the materials in this book originally began as a short excursus in my M.Th. thesis. I am grateful for Alan Clifford, as a reader of my thesis, for having motivated me to research this topic further for myself, even when I did not come to share all of his conclusions concerning Calvin, Amyraut, and others.

I especially wish to think Tony Byrne, Curt Daniel, Reid Ferguson, Martin Foord, Martha Hartog, Jonathan Kleis, Tony Lane, David Ponter, and Caleb Sturgis for proofreading drafts of this volume. David critically assisted the project through his library research. I also wish to acknowledge Amy Kramer's interlibrary loan labors. And I am grateful for the support provided by the Cascade imprint of Wipf & Stock and its editors, including Heather Carraher, Adam McInturf, Robin Parry, and Mike Surber.

Above all, my sweetheart, Alne, is to be praised for her patience during this project. I rise up and call her blessed. My children have shared in her commendable patience.

An initial draft of this work came out in electronic form in 2009 (the Calvin Quincentenary). Kevin Mungons of Regular Baptist Press labored on the formatting of that iteration. I am pleased that a variety of authors (including David L. Allen, Richard E. Clark, Paul Helm, Jeffrey Johnson, Nathan Lovell, Richard A. Muller, David Ponter, Gary L. Shultz, and Scott A. Smith) took note of that digital study and cited it, though differing in engagement and response. This published edition, however, is a completely updated and expanded revision, taking into account the recent works and critical comments of these and many other scholars.

Over the last decade, much has changed in the scholarly understanding of the relationship between Reformation and post-Reformation theology, and my own understanding has grown as well.

I trust this volume may be of some help to those interested in researching the views of John Calvin and subsequent trajectories in historical context—even readers who may differ in their interpretation of the data. My modest goal is that this brief investigation may dissipate some misunderstandings and motivate further research on the Genevan reformer and his historical influence. And so, as my work leaves my hands and enters the hands of readers, I summon a (modified) Chaucerian well-wish: "Go, litel boke! Go litel myn historie!"

—Good Friday 2021

Introduction

JOHN CALVIN'S THEOLOGY MIGHT be compared to a celebrated work of art, somewhat obscured by five hundred years of craquelure. Over the centuries, some students have added their own touch-ups upon the canvas. Others have portrayed themselves as art restorers, claiming to bring back the genuine colors of Calvin's original masterpiece. However, as experts from varying perspectives have attempted to preserve and refurbish the renowned painting, the resulting project has not been without controversy. What were the theological colors that Calvin himself initially intended? As Kevin Kennedy cautions, "if our theological forefathers are worth reading, they are worth reading without imposing theological or hermeneutical commitments on them which they themselves may not have affirmed."[1]

Historians recognize that the label "Calvinism" is problematic.[2] John Calvin definitely deserves pride of place in any discussion of the development of Reformed theology.[3] Nevertheless, Calvin was an influential thinker within a broader assemblage of influential thinkers.[4] "Calvin is one star in a much bigger galaxy."[5] As Christoph Strohm remarks, "there has been a view of the history of reformed Protestantism, which

---

1. Kennedy, "Hermeneutical Discontinuity between Calvin and Later Calvinism," 299. Kennedy's title implies that there was a rather monolithic "Later Calvinism," but the present study highlights the complexities of the phenomena. As Richard Muller insists, "No longer do we see a monolithic orthodoxy being developed in the latter half of the sixteenth century" (Muller, "*Duplex cognitio dei*," 51).

2. Stewart, *Ten Myths about Calvinism*, 11n1. Stewart maintains that "all the good historical reasons for abandoning the terminology of *Calvinist* and *Calvinism* as misrepresentative of a multifaceted, multileader and international movement still apply" (ibid., 40). See also Trueman, "Calvin and Calvinism," 225–44.

3. Gerrish, *Thinking with the Church*, 105–24.

4. Crisp, *Saving Calvinism*, 42.

5. Fesko, *Beyond Calvin*, 29.

overlooks the plurality of its beginnings due to an unhistorical fixation with placing Calvin in a central position—one which he did not occupy."[6] Kenneth Stewart insists that "Calvinism's *origins* are composite."[7] At most Calvin might be construed as *primus inter pares*, but statistical analyses of the subsequent generation reflect his relativized influence.[8] In 1898, the Dutch Reformed statesman Abraham Kuyper quipped that "no Reformed Church ever dreamed of naming a Church of Christ after a man" in Calvin's lifetime.[9] Because the Reformed movement was more of a "team effort" than an individual sport, a bounded level of diversity existed within the movement from its inception.[10]

Moreover, Reformation theology "emerged from the communal settings of universities, academies, and churches."[11] Therefore, Richard Muller has called for "the analysis of continuities and discontinuities in thought in the context of diversity and development in the Reformed tradition."[12] According to Jonathan Moore, "We need to be brave enough to face what is there: a complex interaction between continuities and discontinuities within a wide spectrum of diversity and development in the Reformed tradition, a tradition committed to Scripture alone."[13] Carl Trueman fears that even these themes ("continuity" and "discontinuity") may lead to "the surreptitious intrusion of anachronistic criteria into the historical task."[14] According to Trueman, questions of continuity or discontinuity "need to be set aside, or at least adopted in a highly qualified

---

6. Strohm, "Methodology in Discussion of 'Calvin and Calvinism,'" 79.

7. Stewart, *Ten Myths about Calvinism*, 16.

8. Strohm, "Methodology in Discussion of 'Calvin and Calvinism,'" 66; Letham, "Faith and Assurance in Early Calvinism," 358. Calvin was frequently quoted in various debates of the Westminster Assembly. See Trueman, "Reception of Calvin," 23.

9. Kuyper, "Calvinism a Life-System," 13.

10. Moore, "Calvin versus the Calvinists?" 347. "Even in the sixteenth century, Calvin was at best first among equals; his theology did not represent the entire Reformed tradition and was not the only model available to subsequent theologians" (Trueman, *Claims of Truth*, 10–11).

11. Trueman, "Reception of Calvin," 24.

12. Muller, "Calvin and the 'Calvinists,'" 158.

13. Moore, "Calvin versus the Calvinists?" 348.

14. Trueman, "Reception of Calvin," 19. Cf. Peterson, *Calvin's Doctrine of the Atonement*, 90–91. Paul Helm bemoans "the mists and fogs of anachronism" that often descend upon the discussion (Helm, "Calvin, Indefinite Language, and Definite Atonement," 99).

form."[15] Texts of historical theology should be approached as contextualized historical actions.[16]

In particular, a contemporary debate specifically rages over whether John Calvin himself emphasized (or even taught) all "five points" of so-called "five-point Calvinism."[17] The dispute centers upon whether Calvin taught the doctrine of so-called "limited atonement" (a post-Calvin

---

15. Trueman, "Reception of Calvin," 21. Trueman emphasizes that "continuity is confessional," associated with confessional and catechetical documents rather than the writings of individual authors with no official ecclesiastical status (ibid., 22). Oliver Crisp uses the confessional unity as a reflection of "a softer face to Calvinism," as "the Reformed tradition truly is a confessionalism that tolerates doctrinal plurality within certain parameters" (Crisp, *Deviant Calvinism*, 237). Crisp speaks of "the virtues of this broader confessionalism" and challenges "Reformed thinkers to look again at the wealth and diversity of the tradition to which they belong," believing that later interpreters tightened the acceptable interpretations of confessional standards (ibid., 238–40). For example, he maintains that both the Canons of Dort and the Westminster Confession allowed for a doctrine of hypothetical universalism.

16. Trueman, "Reception of Calvin," 21. See also Johnson, "New or Nuanced Perspective on Calvin?" 547.

17. Thompson, "Calvin on the Cross of Christ," 124. Sometimes the topic has been raised for polemical purposes (Geisler, *Chosen but Free*, 160–66). One acknowledges that labels such as "five-point Calvinism" and "four-point Calvinism" lack uniform definitional clarity, and therefore simply obfuscate the debate at times. For example, it should be noted that the belief that "God intended the effectual salvation of only the elect" is different from "God only intended the effectual salvation of the elect." "Whichever way the verdict goes on the extent of the atonement, Calvin certainly taught that God *effectively* wills the salvation of the elect only" (Gerrish, *Grace and Gratitude*, 171n43). The labels "four-point" Calvinist and "Amyraldian" can both be misleading. For example, the "four-point" language may imply that Jesus in no way died effectually for anyone, though even the Amyraldians distinguished between a universal redemption offered upon the condition of faith (which, however, sinful humans would not fulfill of themselves) and the decreed, efficacious application of Christ's redemption to the elect. Even the term "Calvinism" is a slippery concept (Warfield, *Calvin and Calvinism*, 353). Basil Hall comments, "Calvin himself, of course, did not use the word 'Calvinist' and did not think of himself as the founder of something called Calvinism" (Hall, "Calvin against the Calvinists," 20). According to Richard Muller, "Certain aspects of that Reformed tradition certainly can be credited to Calvin, but the tradition as a whole, as it developed from the early sixteenth century onward, was always broader than Calvin and consistently drew more strongly on other formulators for other major elements of its theology" (Muller, *Christ and the Decree*, x). "Moreover, the Reformed tradition is not defined by what John Calvin did or did not teach. It is a common but fallacious assumption that Calvin's thought should be the sole criterion of what is genuinely Reformed" (Blacketer, "Definite Atonement in Historical Perspective," 305). In sum, "strict conformity to Calvin's doctrine was no Reformed thinker's goal" (Denlinger, "Scottish Hypothetical Universalism," 99).

term).[18] As Raymond Blacketer rightly notes, "the question itself is flawed on a number of levels."[19] (1) The phrase "limited atonement" can only be discussed in relation to Calvin through anachronistic usage; (2) modern theologians will quibble about preferences of terminology between "particular redemption" or "effectual redemption" or "definite atonement" over "limited atonement"; and (3) evangelical views across a spectrum "limit" the atonement, whether in intention, sufficiency, or application.[20] Even with such qualifications, the subject "shows no signs of subsiding," to the point that some have denigrated the controversy as "a paper chase."[21] Paul Helm has compared the disputes to a "game of evidential ping-pong."[22] Nevertheless, I take heart from P. L. Rouwendal's advice: "Calvin's theology is still interesting enough to be researched further, and there is enough in his theology still to be researched."[23] Within the last

---

18. This question is part of the larger debate concerning "Calvin and the Calvinists." See Hall, "Calvin against the Calvinists"; Armstrong, *Calvinism and the Amyraut Heresy*, xvi–xx; Djaballah, "Calvin and the Calvinists," 7–20; Bell, "Was Calvin a Calvinist?" 535–40; Muller, "Calvin and the 'Calvinists'"; Trueman, *Claims of Truth*, 9–13; Lane, "Calvin versus Calvinism Revisited," 32–35; Campos, "Calvino e os Calvinistas," 11–31; Clifford, *Calvin Celebrated*; Macleod, "*Amyraldus redivivus*," 211. Martin Foord explains, "When comparing Calvin to others, it cannot be done in terms of a simple continuity and discontinuity model. This mistake helped skew the so-called 'Calvin and the Calvinists' debate in recent years" (Foord, "God Wills All People to Be Saved," 79–80).

19. Blacketer, "Blaming Beza," 121. "Studies of this issue are often plagued with wrong turns and false starts, depositing students of the question into a methodological labyrinth, to use one of Calvin's favorite terms" (ibid.).

20. Boice and Ryken, *Doctrines of Grace*, 113–14; Steele et al., *Five Points of Calvinism*, 2, 6, 39; Nicole, "Case for Definite Atonement," 200; Nicole, "Particular Redemption," 169; Carson, *Difficult Doctrine of the Love of God*, 73–74; Muller, "Tale of Two Wills," 212; Snoeberger, "Introduction," 7; Trueman, "Atonement and the Covenant of Redemption," 202. Even the usage of "atonement" in relation to Calvin's teachings is somewhat problematic (Muller, "Davenant and Du Moulin," 126).

21. Clifford, *Calvinus*. In a review of Clifford's work, Anthony Lane predicted, "The debate about Calvin's teaching on the intent of the atonement looks set to run and run" (as quoted in Clifford, *Calvinus*, 64). It is indicative that the April 1983 issue of the *Evangelical Quarterly* contained four articles debating whether later Calvinists modified Calvin, including Calvin's view of the extent of the atonement: Torrance, "Incarnation and 'Limited Atonement,'" 83–94; Bell, "Calvin and the Extent of the Atonement," 115–23; Helm, "Calvin and the Covenant," 65–81; Lane, "Quest for the Historical Calvin," 95–113.

22. Helm, "Calvin, Indefinite Language, and Definite Atonement," 100n12.

23. Rouwendal, "Calvin's Forgotten Classical Position," 335. See also Muller, *Calvin and the Reformed Tradition*, 72.

decade, several essays specifically targeting Calvin and the extent/intent of the atonement have appeared, including those authored by David L. Allen, Matthew Harding, Paul Helm, Kevin Kennedy, Thomas Nettles, and David Ponter—and with differing conclusions.[24]

It is evident that Calvin never discussed "the question of the extent of the atonement as a separate doctrinal point."[25] This present study argues that Calvin combined the language of Christ's death as in some sense a universal *provision* along with his firm emphasis upon particularist "unconditional election." Calvin's own language was not of *atonement*, of course, as "the English term *atonement* does not correspond directly to the terms that continental theologians employed."[26] Calvin rather used such terms as *satisfaction, redemption, expiation,* and *reconciliation.*[27] In Calvin, "we have a variety of biblical motifs."[28] He taught his doctrine of atonement "by drawing on the rich tapestry of metaphor present in the Old and New Testaments."[29] He did not provide a systematization of these

---

24. Allen, *Extent of the Atonement*; Harding, "Atonement Theory Revisited," 49–73; Helm, "Calvin, Indefinite Language, and Definite Atonement"; Kennedy, "Hermeneutical Discontinuity between Calvin and Later Calvinism"; Kennedy, "Was Calvin a 'Calvinist'?"; Nettles, "John Calvin's Understanding of the Death of Christ"; Ponter, "Review Essay (Part One)"; Ponter, "Review Essay (Part Two)"; See also Gatiss, "John Calvin's View."

25. Kennedy, "Was Calvin a 'Calvinist'?" 194.

26. Blacketer, "Blaming Beza," 122; cf. Belousek, *Atonement, Justice, and Peace*, 84n5.

27. In Latin, *expiatio, redemptio, reconciliatio,* and *satisfactio* (Muller, *Calvin and the Reformed Tradition*, 76). For this reason, David Ponter prefers the language of satisfaction (Ponter, "Review Essay (Part One)," 140). Blacketer acknowledges that *redemptio* can be used in "an objective indefinite sense" and in "a definite sense as applied to the elect" (Blacketer, "Blaming Beza," 122n4). Of course, one must distinguish between the concept of "atonement" and the word *atonement*, which is a word of English origin (Hesselink, "Calvin on the Atonement," 316n3). Contemporary discussions largely acquiesce to the use of the now conventional term "atonement." Nevertheless, the conventional terminology may mask anachronism or ambiguity, as the present study will also explain. On the biblical terminology of *redemption, reconciliation,* and *propitiation*, see Chafer, "For Whom Did Christ Die?" 311.

28. Hesselink, "Calvin on the Atonement," 316.

29. Sumner, "Theory and Metaphor," 49. The label of "metaphor" is considered by some to be lacking: "It is by no means clear, however, what is meant by describing biblical language on the atonement . . . as metaphorical" (Macleod, *Christ Crucified*, 102). But see Blocher, "Biblical Metaphors and the Doctrine of the Atonement," 629–45; Marshall, *Aspects of the Atonement*, 10–11. Calvin and other historic theologians were setting forth "a coherent doctrine which reflected, they believed, God's own understanding of what was transacted at Calvary; an understanding which was encapsulated

diverse motifs, but he "achieved a high degree of integration ... with the various biblical languages of atonement."[30] Calvin affirmed, "No language, indeed, can fully express the fruit and efficacy of Christ's death."[31] In a sense, although he approached the atonement with an inner consistency, "Calvin never formulated a systemic doctrine of atonement."[32] Robert Peterson has discussed six biblical atonement themes within Calvin, believing that the Genevan reformer did not thoroughly synthesize them: the obedient second Adam, the victor, the legal sacrifice, the historical sacrifice, the meritor of grace, and a cruciform example.[33]

The heart of this volume may be found in Chapter Two, "Twelve Issues," and more casual readers are encouraged to focus upon that chapter's primary source materials, but not necessarily to the neglect of the other chapters. The first chapter traces the *status quaestionis* of the research topic by examining three general approaches. Chapter Three examines the evidences for so-called "limited atonement" adduced within Calvin's writings. Chapter Four warns against a facile understanding of the options and trajectories in the Reformation and post-Reformation eras. The Reformed tradition exhibited a spectrum of diversity in the early modern period. The final Epilogue in Chapter Five reviews specific lessons and conclusions reached through the historical investigations, seeking a possible pattern *emerging* from facets in Calvin, and suggesting a non-speculative "complex-intentioned" framework for contemporary consideration.[34]

---

in a series of God-given keywords, such as expiation, propitiation and reconciliation" (Macleod, *Christ Crucified*, 106). Cf. Wells, *Cross Words*. Stephen Holmes attempts to align "five potential accounts of the extent of the atonement" with specific metaphors for the atonement (Holmes, "Nature of the Atonement and the Extent of the Atonement," 12–17).

30. Blocher, "Atonement in John Calvin's Theology," 203.

31. Calvin, Eph 5:1, *Epistle of Paul the Apostle to the Galatians, Ephesians, Philippians and Colossians*, 196.

32. Sumner, "Theory and Metaphor," 51, 57. Cf. Edmondson, *Calvin's Christology*, 112. On the inner consistency ("the stability, constancy, and consistency") of Calvin's teaching on the atonement, see Blocher, "Atonement in John Calvin's Theology," 282.

33. Peterson, *Calvin's Doctrine of the Atonement*, 85. On the incorporation of facets of a *Christus Victor* approach into Calvin's theology, see Saito, "Theory of the Atonement," 9–10, 76–82, 106–7; Sumner, "Theory and Metaphor in Calvin's Doctrine of the Atonement"; Treat, "Expansive Particularity," 46, 54–55; Estes, "Reincorporating Christus Victor in the Reformed Theology of Atonement."

34. Obviously, Calvin himself never used such a phrase.

Admittedly, this brief study will not fully exhaust the complicated issue of Calvin's view of the so-called "extent of the atonement."[35] Nor am I so brash as to believe that this investigation will solve the conundrum to the satisfaction of all. Moreover, one should keep in mind the purpose of this work: it is a study in *historical theology* that examines John Calvin's own perspectives, along with an overview of interpretations and trajectories into the post-Reformation period. Only the final chapter (the Epilogue) extends "toward" a more *constructive task, and even then only in framework form, suggesting a possible pattern emerging from facets in Calvin*.[36] If nothing else, perhaps this small volume will spur on further study and even further adaptation and refinement.

---

35. Cf. Kennedy, "Was Calvin a 'Calvinist'?" 212.

36. Rouwendal cautions, "A church historian needs to disengage his own doctrinal position from the position of the person he is researching" (Rouwendal, "Calvin's Forgotten Classical Position," 334). Cf. the dispositions found in Hastie, "Straight Talk on John Calvin." Roger Nicole relates, "Correspondence with Dr. [Curt] Daniel has elicited the fact that he originally held to definite atonement and thought that Calvin also held that view. His further studies have led him to the opposite conclusion both as to Calvin's position and as to his own understanding of Scripture" (Nicole, "John Calvin's View of the Extent of the Atonement," 208n46).

CHAPTER ONE

Three General Approaches

ROBERT PETERSON, A REFORMED theologian, acknowledges that John Calvin's view of the so-called "extent of the atonement" has been a "matter of considerable debate."[1] Faced with the diverse (and seemingly conflicting) evidence within Calvin's corpus, scholars have reached differing conclusions by means of varying (and sometimes overlapping) approaches.[2] The following three approaches should be construed merely as heuristic constructions to understand the basic "lay of the land," giving a sense of the terrain as one maps out the contours of the present topography. The approaches represent "family resemblances" but are not boxed-in categories.[3]

---

1. Peterson, "Calvin on Christ's Saving Work," 246. Peterson adds, "The position of Calvin has been hotly disputed" (ibid., 247). Cf. Peterson, *Calvin's Doctrine of the Atonement*, 90.

2. For an overview, see Allen, *Extent of the Atonement*, 48–96; Allen, "Calvin and the Extent of the Atonement," 1–20; Allen interacts with my research in Allen, *Extent of the Atonement*, 76, 83–85; Allen, "Calvin and the Extent of the Atonement," 1, 10–11.

3. Cf. Partee, "Phylogeny of Calvin's Progeny," 23. The normal caveats of the socially situated nature of knowledge apply. Partee explains, "Additionally, selecting and enumerating similarities and differences is greatly complicated by one's own standpoint, and one's point of standing is reciprocally affected personally and professionally by the community in which one is comfortable" (ibid., 24). Partee is not discussing views of Calvin and the so-called "extent of the atonement," but his construction of Conservative, Liberal, and Evangelical Calvinists. His categorical nomenclature remains problematic, with the "Evangelical Calvinists" being Barth and his sympathizers.

Approach 1: Calvin believed in "limited atonement"

In a *first* approach, some scholars conclude that Calvin believed in a strictly "limited" atonement, even though he did not emphasize the doctrine in an explicit manner.[4] In such a view, so-called "limited atonement" is a logical inference standing as a necessary corollary of his other teachings.[5] The complexities of the evidence caused Roger Nicole to concede that sometimes Calvin sounds *as if* he believed in "unlimited atonement." However, after "examining the data," the "balance of evidence" favors the view that Calvin upheld limited atonement.[6] Nicole rigorously opposed the possibility that Calvin's descriptions of a "for-all" gospel could include a for-all sacrificial provision as well, even if sovereignly and efficaciously applied to the elect alone.[7] Nicole argued that "the proposition that the prerequisite for an indiscriminate call is a universal provision, which is the base of the whole argument, appears to us palpably and demonstrably false."[8] He denied that the general offer "extended to all humans" must be accompanied by any notion of a universal provision.[9]

Within the general disposition of this "first approach," some argue that Calvin's *overall system* points toward a limited-atonement view, although he himself never explicitly stated this specific conclusion.[10] Andrew McGowan acknowledges the tensions and ambiguity in Calvin's materials, but he concludes that the overall tenor of his theology points toward limited atonement. "In the case of the doctrine of atonement it will be recognized that Calvin's position was ambiguous but that the doctrine of limited atonement is a reasonable theological development

---

4. Murray, "Calvin on the Extent of the Atonement," 20–22; Rainbow, "*Redemptor Ecclesiae, Redemptor Mundi*"; Rainbow, *Will of God and the Cross*; Nicole, "John Calvin's View of the Extent of the Atonement," 197–225; Leahy, "Calvin and the Extent of the Atonement," 54–64; Helm, *Calvin and the Calvinists*; Helm, "Calvin and the Covenant," 65–81.

5. Kevin Kennedy has offered "an attempt to show that it is not unreasonable to claim that Calvin held to a universal atonement" (Kennedy, "Was Calvin a 'Calvinist'?" 196). One appreciates his tenor, while also noting the contested or ambiguous meaning of "universal atonement" (even apart from Calvin studies).

6. Nicole, "John Calvin's View of the Extent of the Atonement," 207–8.

7. See also Helm, *Calvin and the Calvinists*; Nicole, "John Calvin's View of the Extent of the Atonement," 197–225; Rainbow, *Will of God and the Cross*.

8. Nicole, "John Calvin's View of the Extent of the Atonement," 213.

9. Cf. also Leahy, "Calvin and the Extent of the Atonement," 59.

10. Blocher, "Atonement in John Calvin's Theology," 280–82. Basil Hall argues the opposite in Hall, "Calvin against the Calvinists," 27.

from his position."[11] W. Robert Godfrey agrees with Nicole that "definite atonement" fits better "into the total pattern of Calvin's teaching."[12] Godfrey highlights Calvin's "pervasive particularism."[13] According to Thomas Nettles, "limited atonement may be inferred from several pivotal exegetical/doctrinal discussions and is more consistent with his overall theological view than is general atonement."[14]

Already in the nineteenth century, William Cunningham asserted, "The truth is, that no satisfactory evidence has been or can be derived from his writings that the precise question upon the extent of the atonement . . . ever exercised Calvin's mind, or was made by him the subject of any formal or explicit deliverance."[15] "We admit, however, that he [Calvin] has not usually given any indication, that he believed in any limitation as to the objects of the atonement; . . . and that upon a survey of all that has been produced from his writings, there is fair ground for a difference of opinion as to what his doctrine upon this point really was."[16] Cunningham himself maintained, "It is likewise true, that no sufficient evidence has been produced that Calvin believed in a universal or unlimited atonement."[17] Nevertheless, Cunningham argued that unlimited atonement is "somewhat alien, to say the least, in its general spirit and complexion, to the leading features of his [Calvin's] theological system."[18] Cunningham therefore concluded that systematic considerations provided "sufficient evidence" that Calvin must have held to limited atonement.[19]

---

11. McGowan, "Was Westminster Calvinist?" 48–49.

12. Godfrey, "Reformed Thought on the Extent of the Atonement," 138; cf. Nicole, "John Calvin's View of the Extent of the Atonement," 225.

13. Godfrey, "Reformed Thought on the Extent of the Atonement," 138.

14. Nettles, "John Calvin's Understanding of the Death of Christ," 295.

15. Cunningham, *Reformers and the Theology of the Reformation*, 396–97.

16. Cunningham, *Reformers and the Theology of the Reformation*, 396.

17. Cunningham, *Reformers and the Theology of the Reformation*, 396.

18. Cunningham, *Reformers and the Theology of the Reformation*, 398. At the same time, Cunningham acknowledged that "it is certain that some men of distinguished ability and learning, such as Amyraut and Daillée, Davenant and Baxter, have held both these doctrines of universal atonement and universal grace, and at the same time have held the Calvinistic doctrine of election" (ibid., 399). Many more examples, of course, could be added, such as James Ussher, Edmund Calamy, J. C. Ryle, Millard Erickson, Bruce Ware, etc. See the compilations of primary sources available online at Ponter, "Calvin and Calvinism" and in print in Allen, *Extent of the Atonement*.

19. Cunningham, *Reformers and the Theology of the Reformation*, 398–402.

Paul Helm nuances and qualifies his similar claims: "Overall, Calvin's remarks are not consistent with universal atonement but they are with limited, definite atonement."[20] Helm posits that Calvin "could be said to *be committed* to definite atonement, even though he does not *commit himself* to definite atonement."[21] Helm adds, "There was no occasion for Calvin to enter into argument about the matter, for before the Arminian controversy the extent of the atonement had not been debated expressly within the Reformed churches."[22] "But it is impossible to settle what Calvin's view was from his own somewhat underdeveloped language over the precise question of the atonement, or indeed to make such progress, without undertaking a wider examination of Calvin's thought."[23] Helm concludes that definite atonement fits better into the totality of Calvin's theology. "The case for Calvin's being committed to definite atonement is a cumulative one, embracing his unitary, singular view of the divine decree; his beliefs in substitutionary atonement, unconditional election, and effectual grace; and his denial of bare foreknowledge, as well as his explicit statements regarding the definite scope of the atonement."[24]

Approach 2: Calvin believed in a form of "unlimited atonement"

In a *second* approach, some scholars maintain that Calvin held a form of so-called "unlimited atonement," which he espoused in combination with his definite view of "unconditional election."[25] The introductory

20. Helm, "Calvin, English Calvinism and the Logic of Doctrinal Development," 180.

21. Helm, *Calvin and the Calvinists*, 18; italics original. See also Helm, "Calvin, Indefinite Language, and Definite Atonement," 98, 111; Letham, "Saving Faith and Assurance in Reformed Theology," vol. 1, 125.

22. Helm, *Calvin and the Calvinists*, 18; cf. Helm, "Calvin, Indefinite Language, and Definite Atonement," 98.

23. Helm, "Calvin, Indefinite Language, and Definite Atonement," 98.

24. Helm, "Calvin, Indefinite Language, and Definite Atonement," 119. Later Reformed theologians came to see limited atonement as a necessary logical corollary of the doctrine of election and the penal theory of the atonement (McDonald, *Atonement of the Death of Christ*, 192; Williams, "Definite Atonement of Penal Substitutionary Atonement," 461, 481). John Murray argued that all those for whom Christ died also died with Christ, and his heavenly activity is co-extensive with his once-for-all redemption (Murray, *Redemption Accomplished and Applied*, 70–71).

25. Anderson, "Grace of God and the Non-Elect"; Armstrong, *Calvinism and the*

sentences to R. T. Kendall's first chapter of his 1979 monograph announced, "Fundamental to the doctrine of faith in John Calvin (1509–64) is his belief that Christ died indiscriminately for all men. Equally crucial, however, is his conviction that, until faith is given, 'all that he has suffered and done for the salvation of the human race remains useless and of no value.'"[26] Charles Bell explains, "For this reason, he [Calvin] is able to teach a doctrine of predestination in which faith is limited to the elect, and, at the same time, to give proper consideration to Scripture passages which clearly teach universal atonement."[27] "In my view," declares Anthony Lane, "there is no doubt that the thrust of Calvin's teaching points in the direction of Christ's death for all without exception . . . there can be little doubt that the overwhelming emphasis in Calvin is that Christ died for all."[28] Curt Daniel has asserted "the evidence is overwhelming"

Amyraut Heresy; Bell, "Calvin and the Extent of the Atonement," 115–23; Clifford, "Calvin & Calvinism"; Clifford, *Calvinus*; Daniel, "Hyper-Calvinism and John Gill," 777–828; Douty, *Did Christ Die Only for the Elect?*; Kendall, "Puritan Modification of Calvin's Theology"; Kennedy, *Union with Christ and the Extent of the Atonement*; Lane, "Calvin's Doctrine of Assurance Revisited," 306–7; Lane, "Quest for the Historical Calvin," 109–11; van Stam, *Controversy over the Theology of Saumur*.

26 . Kendall, *Calvin and English Calvinism to 1649*, 13. Kendall connected the issue of the extent of the atonement with the issue of assurance. For a critical summary, see Helm, *Calvin: A Guide for the Perplexed*, 144–47; Helm, *Calvin and Calvinism*, 23–31. Kendall's thesis concerning a shift in the doctrine of assurance within early Calvinism has been opposed by Joel Beeke and others. See Beeke, *Assurance of Faith*; Beeke, "Does Assurance Belong to the Essence of Faith," 43–71; Beeke, *Quest for Full Assurance*. Cf. Thorson, "Tensions in Calvin's View of Faith," 413–26; Wolterstorff, "Assurance of Faith," 305–8. But see also Bell, *Calvin and Scottish Theology*; Lane, "Calvin's Doctrine of Assurance," 32–54; Bond, "Amyraldianism and Assurance," 92–108. Kendall's understanding of the role of Christ's intercession has also been criticized. See Bell, "Calvin and the Extent of the Atonement," 121–23; Bell, *Calvin and Scottish Theology*, 18–19; Archbald, "Comparative Study of John Calvin and Theodore Beza," 187–88; Thomas, "Calvin and English Calvinism," 120. See also Thomas, *Extent of the Atonement*, 33–34. For empathetic assessments critical of Kendall, see Lane, "Review of *Calvin and English Calvinism to 1649*," 29–31; Moore, *English Hypothetical Universalism*, x, 220–22. In an article, Moore argues that Kendall was ironically wrong in his analysis of John Preston, who was actually a hypothetical universalist (Moore, "Calvin versus the Calvinists?" 327–48).

27. Bell, "Was Calvin a Calvinist?" 536.

28. Lane, "Calvin's Doctrine of Assurance Revisited," 307. Lane points especially to the structure of the *Institutes*, flowing from the end of book 2 on Christ's work to the beginning of book 3: "First, we must understand that as long as Christ remains outside of us, and we are separated from him, all that he has suffered and done for the salvation of the human race remains useless and of no value for us" (ibid.). Elsewhere, Lane explains, "There has been considerable controversy about Calvin's relation to the later

that Calvin believed "Christ died for all."[29] David L. Allen has declared that Calvin's writings "indicate" that Christ died for the sins of all people, though the benefit of the atonement is applied to the elect alone.[30]

Some then take a further step of nomenclature, concluding that Calvin was similar to an "Amyraldian" or so-called "four-point Calvinist" model (both anachronistic labels as applied to Calvin), while others may seek a lesser degree of systematization.[31] Alan Clifford has led the Amyraldian Association in the United Kingdom and has done extensive writing on Calvin's view of the extent of the atonement.[32] Clifford argues, "Notwithstanding the rationally-challenging paradox involved, Calvin maintained the doctrines of universal atonement and divine election side by side. Faced by clear biblical evidence for both, he refused to tamper with the scriptural texts."[33] Clifford contends that "the 'Calvin-Amyraut' outlook best reflects the Gospel of the grace of God according to the Scriptures."[34] Matthew Harding has traced Calvin's theological trajectories into Theodore Beza and Moïse Amyraut, and he concludes that "there is sufficient evidence among textual comparisons to conclude that Amyraut appears closer to Calvin as it relates to the universal language of the atonement than does his successor Beza."[35] Others have found a universal provision in Calvin and have spoken of a "real affinity" with

---

idea of limited atonement. He does not address the question directly, but the thrust of his teaching points to universal rather than limited atonement" (Lane, *Reader's Guide to Calvin's Institutes*, 98n1).

29. Daniel, *History and Theology of Calvinism*, 360. Daniel stresses Christ died specially for the elect, not equally for all. His rev. ed. arrived post final edits.

30. Allen, *Extent of the Atonement*, 96.

31. Still others have been influenced by Barthian critiques of developed Calvinism. See Grebe, *Election, Atonement and the Holy Spirit*. For more context to views combining a so-called "unlimited atonement" with "unconditional election," see Kendall, *Calvin and English Calvinism to 1649*, 13–28; Kendall, "Puritan Modification of Calvin's Theology," 199–214; Torrance, "Incarnation and 'Limited Atonement,'" 82–94; Bell, *Calvin and Scottish Theology*, 13–40; Daniel, "Hyper-Calvinism and John Gill," 777–829; Anderson, "Grace of God and the Non-Elect." For a popular-level equating of "Amyraldianism" with "four-point Calvinism," see Pugh, *Atonement Theories*, 81.

32. See especially Clifford, *Amyraut Affirmed*; Clifford, *Atonement and Justification*; Clifford, *Calvinus*; Clifford, "Calvin & Calvinism." Clifford himself disputes the normal explanation of the "five-point" nomenclature (Clifford, *Calvinus*, 11).

33. Clifford, "Calvin & Calvinism," 37–38.

34. Clifford, "Calvin & Calvinism," 37–38. Moïse Amyraut was also known by the Latinized name of Amyraldus, hence the terms Amyraldian and Amyraldianism.

35. Harding, "Atonement Theory Revisited," 55.

Amyraut's later views, yet distance his perspective from Amyraut's developed doctrine.[36]

Approach 3:
Calvin's theology contains unresolved tensions

In a *third* approach, scholars emphasize the conflicting tensions or inconsistent elements (or even "contradictions") in Calvin, or at least the insurmountable anachronisms or ambiguities, such that our questions ultimately remain unanswerable, given the available evidence.[37] Hans Boersma claims, "It seems a fair conclusion that the groundwork of Calvin's theology does not allow for a theory of universal atonement."[38] Nevertheless, Boersma acknowledges: "There is a line of thought in Calvin which wants to maintain that God wills the salvation of all people, that God extends his love and grace to all people, and in particular to those whom he has chosen as his people in a more general sense. At the same time this line of thinking causes a certain tension."[39] Boersma proposes

---

36. Williams, *Heart of Piety*, 189.

37. See Boersma, "Calvin and the Extent of the Atonement," 333–55. Archibald Alexander Hodge, a nineteenth-century pillar of American Presbyterian theology, declared, "Let the fact be well noted, therefore, that Calvin does not appear to have given the question we are at present discussing a deliberate consideration, and has certainly not left behind him a clear and consistent statement of his views" (Hodge, *Atonement*, 88). Hodge argued that one should look beyond Calvin to the seventeenth-century Reformed creeds (and their representative theologians) as "the standard of Calvinism," and their view was "of the Atonement as definite and personal" (ibid., 392).

38. Boersma, "Calvin and the Extent of the Atonement," 344. Boersma criticized both Kendall and (to a lesser degree) Nicole. He also expressed his gratitude toward Alan Clifford, who had been of assistance through his critiques (ibid., 333n1).

39. In Boersma's perspective, "Calvin does not always attempt to dissolve it [the tension], but when he does so, he never solves it at the cost of God's purpose as laid down in his decree. . . . Where Calvin does move toward a solution he always does so at the cost of the universal aspect, at the cost of the notion of God's will that all people be saved, at the cost of common grace" (ibid., 351; contrast Daniel, "Hyper-Calvinism and John Gill," 813n83). Boersma adds, "They [relevant passages from Calvin] indicate a desire on God's part that all people be saved. In terms of the extent of the atonement this means that Calvin in effect argues that Christ died for all people, *i.e.*, with the intent that all be saved. The question as to whether Christ really atoned for someone's sins of course depends on the Holy Spirit's efficacious working of faith. Moreover, sensing the tension which this brings into his theology, Calvin at times limits this universal intent of the atonement, in order to bring its extent in line with his emphasis on the unity of God's work due to his decree" (Boersma, "Calvin and

a solution to this "certain tension" by distinguishing between God's revealed will and his secret decree:

> A clear overall picture has emerged: there is a distinction between God's revealed will and secret decree. The former is normative, the latter for wonderment and adoration. The distinction does not mean a dual will in God. To maintain this seeming contradiction Calvin refers to the concept of *accommodation*, while denying that God's revealed will is in any way deceptive. One cannot avoid the impression of a certain ambiguity at this point.[40]

Boersma pronounces, "The picture which emerges from this study is not consistent. Perhaps it is one of the weaknesses of the discussion of Calvin's view on the extent of the atonement that one expects to find an overall, coherent, and consistent picture."[41] "This means," concludes

---

the Extent of the Atonement," 351). See also Thomas, *Extent of the Atonement*, 12–40. Like Boersma, Thomas describes the "tension" in Calvin's theology. Cf. the response in Rouwendal, "Calvin's Forgotten Classical Position," 325–26.

40. Boersma, "Calvin and the Extent of the Atonement," 348–49 (cf. Calvin, Rom 11:34). Boersma continues, "It seems that Calvin's reverence for God's revelation demands an insistence on the unity and immutability of God as well as an acceptance of the testimony of Scripture regarding God's revealed will of universal salvation. Without wanting to infringe on God's veracity, Calvin must nevertheless use the dogmatic concept of accommodation to rid himself of his dilemma. It seems clear that this does not go at the expense of the decree of predestination, but tends to take away somewhat from God's universal will of salvation" (ibid., 349; cf. Lane, "Quest for the Historical Calvin," 110; contrast Doyle, "Context of Moral Decision Making," 281–84). According to Boersma, the "revealed will" is "God's normative, prescriptive will" and "is connected to the gospel offer" (Boersma, "Calvin and the Extent of the Atonement," 354). "The point is that though 'God's will is . . . not at war with itself,' God speaks according to our *imbecillitas*, the *hebetudo* of our understanding. God accommodates himself to it when presenting us with his will" (ibid., 345). Although Calvin speaks of a *duplex persona* ("twofold character") of God in regard to Ezek 18:32, he denies that there are "two contrary wills" in God (Calvin, Ezek 18:32; *Institutes* I.18.3). "God 'conforms' (*conformet*) himself to our ignorance, he descends (*descendat*) to us in a certain way. God adapts his speech, speaks *metaphorice*. It is clear that the real will of God lies in his *arcane consilia*" (Boersma, "Calvin and the Extent of the Atonement," 348). At the same time, "Calvin argues that God does not act deceitfully (*falliciter*) when inviting all while not touching the hearts of all" (ibid., 348n54; cf. Calvin, *Institutes* III.24.15). See also Calvin, *Concerning the Eternal Predestination of God*, 105–6.

41. Boersma, "Calvin and the Extent of the Atonement," 350. Peter Toon has reasoned, "It is perhaps fair to state that the extent of the atonement does not seem to have been a problem which agitated the mind of Calvin" (Toon, *Emergence of Hyper-Calvinism in English Nonconformity*, 15).

Boersma, "that it is not possible to speak of a consistent, precise Calvinian view on the extent of the atonement. A lack of precision will remain. . . . Calvin is not always consistent on the point, at times accepting a universal intent, while more often asserting that this is not the real way of speaking."[42] Nevertheless, Boersma insists, "The dilemma must not be overcome by weakening either God's will for universal salvation or his decree of predestination."[43]

G. Michael Thomas argues that "the reformer left to his successors a theology that was . . . inherently unstable."[44] Thomas explains that "as a rule, Calvin spoke of the atonement as universal when he was dealing with the promise of the gospel, and particular in the context of eternal election. Whether or not this is the best analysis, it seems that a more nuanced treatment than claiming Calvin as a supporter of either universal or limited atonement is required."[45] Thomas adds, "Calvin's approach is that when universal saving will and particular predestination seem to be in conflict, particular predestination must take precedence."[46]

A modification of this third approach is exemplified by P. L. Rouwendal's article in the *Westminster Theological Journal*, which argued that our question is ultimately unanswerable because of its anachronistic imposition.[47] He concludes that Calvin espoused neither limited atone-

42. Boersma, "Calvin and the Extent of the Atonement," 354–55.
43. Boersma, "Calvin and the Extent of the Atonement," 349.
44. Thomas, *Extent of the Atonement*, 34.
45. Thomas, "Calvin and English Calvinism," 120. Contrast Lane, "Calvin's Doctrine of Assurance Revisited," 306.
46. Thomas, "Calvin and English Calvinism," 122; cf. Thomas, *Extent of the Atonement*, 214. Contrast Kennedy, *Union with Christ and the Extent of the Atonement*, 10–11.
47. Cf. Andrew McGowan's construction of three positions concerning Calvin's understanding of the extent/intent of the atonement (McGowan, "Was Westminster Calvinist?" 47). McGowan acknowledges, "Now clearly these are generalizations and there are scholars who have contributed to the debate who cannot be conveniently fitted into one of these three 'camps'" (ibid., 47). McGowan describes Anthony Lane as one of those who does not conveniently fit into one of the groupings. In previous work, I distinguished four approaches to the evidence. However, Anthony Lane (in personal correspondence) suggested that my "fourth approach" (exemplified by Rouwendal) was a rather superfluous category, because of affinities with the "third approach." David Allen concurred with this assessment: "This categorization is helpful, though it does appear that the fourth general approach is not much different from the third" (Allen, *Extent of the Atonement*, 84). By merging my discussion of the fourth approach into that of the third, here I distinguish only three general "families" within a new structuring.

ment nor unlimited atonement, but simply the "classic view," which modestly stated that "Christ died sufficiently for all but efficiently only for the elect."[48] According to Rouwendal, the classical view left the question—"For whom did Christ die?"—rather open-ended.[49] Rouwendal concludes, "(1) Calvin did not teach universal atonement; (2) Calvin did not teach limited atonement."[50] Rouwendal argues that the attempt to

48. In Latin, sometimes simply stated as *sufficienter pro omnibus, efficaciter pro electis* or more completely as *pro omnibus quantum ad pretii sufficientiam, sed pro electis tantum quantum ad efficaciam*. According to Peter Lombard, Jesus Christ offered himself "for all, with respect to the sufficiency of the ransom, but for the elect alone with regard to the efficiency, because it effects salvation for the predestined alone" (Peter Lombard, *Sententiae in IV Libris Distinctae* 3.20.5). Thomas Aquinas declared, "Christ's Passion sufficed for all; while as to its efficacy it was profitable for many" (Thomas Aquinas, *Summa Theologiae* 3, quest. 78, art. 8, obj. 8). See quotations in Blacketer, "Definite Atonement in Historical Perspective," 311–12. Blacketer repeats Rainbow's fallacious understanding of Luther (ibid., 313; Rainbow, *Will of God and the Cross*, 181). In his comments on 1 John 2:2, Calvin claims that the Lombardian formula is not applicable to the text at hand, although he allows the classic formula's truthfulness (Calvin, 1 John 2:2, *Gospel according to St John 11–21 and the First Epistle of John*, 244). For Gisbertus Voetius's categories, see Kang, "John Davenant," 5–6.

49. Rouwendal, "Calvin's Forgotten Classical Position," 317–35. Rouwendal theorizes, "It is plausible that the Saumur theologians annexed the classical formula of the aforementioned distinction, and hence all who held the classical position" (ibid., 321). However, theologians such as Kimedoncius, Paraeus, Ursinus, and Bucanus continued to use the "classical" formula without espousing a full Amyraldian system. On the continued use of the formula (even with different emphases), see Godfrey, "Reformed Thought on the Extent of the Atonement," 133–71; Godfrey, "Tensions within International Calvinism." Ursinus will serve as one example (see Daniel, "Hyper-Calvinism and John Gill," 531n104). He proclaimed that Christ suffered "the keenest and most bitter anguish of soul, which is doubtless a sense of the wrath of God against the sins of the whole human race." When faced with the counterargument, "If Christ made a satisfaction for all, then all ought to be saved. But all are not saved. Therefore he did not make a perfect satisfaction," Ursinus responded, "Christ satisfied for all, as it respects the sufficiency of the satisfaction which he hath made, but not as it respects the application thereof" (Ursinus, *Commentary of Dr. Zacharius Ursinus on the Heidelberg Catechism*, 213–15). While Rouwendal cites three instances where Calvin explicitly mentioned the "classical" view, Clifford refers to two others as well (Clifford, "Calvin & Calvinism," 57; cf. Daniel, "Hyper-Calvinism and John Gill," 801–2). Thomas concludes, "Thus Calvin found the formula insufficiently clear about the very issue at stake between himself and his opponents: whether the acceptance or rejection of the benefits of Christ's death is to be attributed ultimately to human or divine will" (Thomas, *Extent of the Atonement*, 31).

50. Rouwendal, "Calvin's Forgotten Classical Position," 333. One might seek more explanation from Rouwendal concerning these two assertions side-by-side, considering Rouwendal's statements concerning the lack of contradictions in Calvin (ibid., 334). Perhaps Rouwendal meant that Calvin did not teach *only* an understanding of

fit John Calvin himself within post-Calvin debates is an "anachronism" and therefore a poor example of historical scholarship.⁵¹ Moreover, "the apparent paradoxical and contradictory statements in Calvin regarding the atonement are proven to dovetail with the classical position."⁵² "Contradictions and paradoxes only appear when Calvin is read with post-Calvinian paradigms in mind."⁵³

> Unlike Boersma and Thomas, it is my opinion that Calvin's doctrine of the atonement, when examined in Calvin's own theological context, is actually consistent. Those questions asked at a later stage of Reformed history were not asked by Calvin. . . . As soon as one interprets Calvin in terms of later terminology, tensions, inconsistencies, and contradictions seems to abound in his works; however, this should not be attributed to Calvin, but rather to the reader who is reading him anachronistically.⁵⁴

One notes Rouwendal's insistence that Calvin's view was "actually consistent" (when contextualized), thereby differing from those who find "inconsistencies" or even "contradictions" in the reformer's thought. Rouwendal explicitly distinguishes his interpretations from those of Boersma and Thomas, who spoke of Calvin's view as "not consistent" and "inherently unstable."

"unlimited atonement" that made salvation only *possible* for all, nor did he teach *only* a "limited atonement" that left out the "sufficiency" side of the "classic" formula?

51. Frederick Leahy agrees, "It is true that Calvin does not deal explicitly with the extent of the Atonement, but this was not the issue in his day" (Leahy, "Calvin and the Extent of the Atonement," 61). Rouwendal adds, "The classical formula was neither a point of difference between Catholics, Lutherans, and the Reformed in Calvin's day, nor a disputed subject among the Reformed. Attention was given to other subjects. The extent of the atonement first became a point of difference approximately a quarter century after Calvin's death" (Rouwendal, "Calvin's Forgotten Classical Position," 326). Of course, related debates had been flaring up centuries before Calvin.

52. Rouwendal, "Calvin's Forgotten Classical Position," 334.

53. Rouwendal, "Calvin's Forgotten Classical Position," 334.

54. Rouwendal, "Calvin's Forgotten Classical Position," 325–26. Jeremy Treat has argued that Calvin, in general, apart from the so-called "extent of the atonement," was inclined "to uphold seemingly contradictory truths (a paradox)" by finding a biblical *via media* (Treat, "Expansive Particularity," 50). "For Calvin, expansive particularity is a methodological key that avoids 'either/or reductionism' and 'both/and' homogeneity in order that the 'whole counsel of God' be maintained while upholding the 'first importance' of particular truths" (ibid., 59).

To establish consistency, Rouwendal seeks to bring God's "revealed will" and "secret will" together.[55]

> Calvin used the conditionality of gospel-preaching to show that the universal call or promise of the gospel and God's secret decree are not contradictory. The universal call or promise is conditional: Everybody is invited (universal) to faith and repentance (condition), and all those who believe and repent will be saved (promise). In this conditional sense one could say, according to Calvin, that God indeed wills the salvation of all men. But since God himself fulfills the condition in his elect, there is no contradiction between his revealed and his secret will.[56]

In this harmonization and removal of any "contradiction," Rouwendal blends a universality of promised availability in the revealed will (in a "conditional sense") into Calvin's "classical" view.[57]

---

55. Rouwendal adds, "Now Clifford suggests that Calvin spoke about two different wills or even decrees in God. But Calvin did not say that it is God's will to save all men without adding any declaration or condition" (Rouwendal, "Calvin's Forgotten Classical Position," 330). For Clifford's response, see his "Calvin & Calvinism," 57–62.

56. Rouwendal, "Calvin's Forgotten Classical Position," 330.

57. The Amyraldians continued to use the "classical" maxim, though they were not alone. According to John Quick's *Synodicon in Gallia Reformata* (1692): "They [the Amyraldians] declared that Jesus Christ died for all men sufficiently, but for the elect only effectually: and that consequently his intention was to die for all men in respect of the sufficiency of his satisfaction, but for the elect only in respect of its quickening and saving virtue and efficacy; which is to say, that Christ's will was that the sacrifice of his cross should be of infinite price and value, and most abundantly sufficient to expiate the sins of the whole world; yet nevertheless the efficacy of his death appertains only unto the elect; so that those who are called by the preaching of the gospel, to participate by faith in the effects and fruits of his death, being invited seriously, and God vouchsafing them all eternal means needful for their coming to him, and showing them in good earnest, and with the greatest sincerity by his Word, what would be well-pleasing to him, if they should not believe in the Lord Jesus Christ, but perish in their obstinacy and unbelief; this cometh not from any defect of virtue or sufficiency in the sacrifice of Jesus Christ, nor yet for want of summons or serious invitations unto faith or repentance, but only from their own fault. And as for those who do receive the doctrine of the gospel with the obedience of faith, they are according to the irrevocable promise of God, made partakers of the effectual virtue and fruit of Christ Jesus's death; for this was the most free counsel and gracious purpose both of God the Father, in giving his Son for the salvation of mankind, and of the Lord Jesus Christ, in suffering the pains of death, that the efficacy thereof should particularly belong unto all the elect, and to them only, to give them justifying faith, and by it to bring them infallibly unto salvation, and thus effectually to redeem all those and none other, who were from all eternity from among all people, nations, tongues, chosen unto salvation" (as quoted in Nicole, "Moyse Amyraut," 110; English spelling updated).

A key component of Rouwendal's "classical" argument is his opposition to anachronistic imposition upon Calvin. Myron Penner also opposes such imposition. He acknowledges that "Calvin makes statements in his writings that provide fuel for both sides of the debate."[58] He explains, "The distinction itself is somewhat anachronistic, though, as there was no real controversy over limited atonement during (or prior to) Calvin's life and he was therefore not compelled to reach a definitive conclusion on it."[59] Penner continues, "the situation may well be that Calvin never settled in his own mind exactly what is the best way of characterizing the extent of the atonement. This does not mean that one cannot or should not attempt to deem which position is the most consistent with Calvin's theology, but I do not find it especially helpful to try to reconstruct Calvin's personal position on the matter."[60]

Robert Peterson seems to combine characteristic elements of the "third approach" with a refined "first approach." He declares, "I hold to a position of limited atonement, but continue to think that the evidence is too ambiguous to allow a definitive answer to the question of what Calvin thinks on the matter."[61] Peterson acknowledges, "I confess uncertainty concerning Calvin's position on the extent of the atonement."[62] Elsewhere, Peterson moves beyond the language of being "ambiguous" to being possibly "contradictory." He agrees with Robert Letham's sentiment: "My position is that Calvin was ambiguous or contradictory on the question but that he maintained the intrinsic efficacy of the atonement."[63] He con-

---

58. Penner, "Calvin, Barth, and the Subject of Atonement," 133.

59. Penner, "Calvin, Barth, and the Subject of Atonement," 133. Penner compares Muller, *Unaccommodated Calvin*, 6. Some claim that Calvin would have clearly defended so-called "limited atonement" if the matter had been contested (see Helm, *Calvin and the Calvinists*, 18; Leahy, "Calvin and the Extent of the Atonement," 54–64). For a contrary perspective, see Shultz, *Multi-Intentioned View of the Atonement*, 23n58, 26).

60. Penner, "Calvin, Barth, and the Subject of Atonement," 133. He adds, "Perhaps the strongest claim of this sort we may make is that Calvin apparently was familiar with and gave his limited acceptance to the scholastic formulation, 'Christ's death was sufficient for all but efficient for only those who believe.' I will say, however, that the concept of limited atonement seems to fit more easily into Calvin's logic of atonement as I have developed it here, because it entails an atonement that is particular in both its implementation (one at a time) and its application (for the elect only)" (ibid.).

61. Peterson, *Calvin and the Atonement*, 118.

62. Peterson, *Calvin and the Atonement*, 118.

63. See Peterson, "Calvin on Christ's Saving Work," 247 (cf. Letham, *Work of Christ*, 266n5). See also Letham, "Faith and Assurance in Early Calvinism," 355–84. "Despite his pronounced emphasis on the efficacy of Christ's atoning death, Calvin does not

cludes that Calvin was "noncommittal on the extent of the atonement,"[64] although systematically "the position of limited atonement is a logical extension of Calvin's thought."[65]

During his extended writing career, Peterson has adjusted his own understanding of the "anachronism" in question. Peterson's 1983 study acknowledged that Calvin did not emphasize a limited atonement, but then added that this topic was not yet a subject of debate.[66] "The conclusion must be that it is uncertain what position Calvin would have taken if he were living at the time of the debates over the extent of the atonement."[67] Peterson argued, "it is unfair to ask for a man's position on a matter that became an issue only after his death."[68] Peterson, however, later qualified these assessments in his 1999 work:

---

commit himself on the question of the extent of the atonement" (Letham, "Saving Faith and Assurance in Reformed Theology," vol. 1, 125). According to Letham, Calvin followed Scripture "even where there is apparent contradiction. Consequently, he can make statements that seem contradictory" (ibid.). I. John Hesselink concurs with Letham's judgment (Hesselink, "Calvin on the Atonement," 316). Hesselink concludes, "There are passages in Calvin that indicate both a universal atonement and a limited atonement, but the latter predominate" (ibid.).

64. Peterson, "Calvin on Christ's Saving Work," 247. Peterson notes, "It is significant that the *Institutes* is silent on this question" (ibid., 246; though cf. Calvin, *Institutes* III.1.1). "However," Peterson adds, "appeal can be made to Calvin's commentaries to argue for limited atonement." Peterson cites Calvin on 1 John 2:2 (see below). Cf. Peterson, *Calvin's Doctrine of the Atonement*, 90. According to Clifford, "The answer to [the] question 'why does the doctrine of limited atonement not appear clearly in the *Institutes*?' can only be: 'The author never believed it'" (Clifford, *Calvinus*, 52).

65. Peterson, "Calvin on Christ's Saving Work," 247. At the same time, Peterson praises Calvin's example "as a theologian in two areas: his eschewing speculation and seeking to base his theology on the exposition of Holy Scripture" (ibid.). See also Hill, *History of Christian Thought*, 203.

66. Cf. Peterson, *Calvin's Doctrine of the Atonement*, 90-91. This is how Joel Beeke construes the issue (Beeke, "William Perkins and His Greatest Case of Conscience," 277). Paul Helm, who was trying to counter Kendall, nevertheless acknowledged, "There are, of course, theological differences between John Calvin and later Calvinism, for example the explicit doctrine of limited atonement, covenant theology, and the careful discrimination between faith and assurance" (Helm, "Calvin, English Calvinism and the Logic of Development," 185). See the later qualifications in Peterson, *Calvin and the Atonement*, 119-20. Cf. Orr, *Progress of Dogma*, 292-97; Lane, "Quest for the Historical Calvin," 101; Daniel, "Hyper-Calvinism and John Gill," 514, 814; Thomas, *Extent of the Atonement*, 12.

67. Peterson, *Calvin's Doctrine of the Atonement*, 91. Cf. a similar recognition in Thomas, *Extent of the Atonement*, 12.

68. Peterson, *Calvin's Doctrine of the Atonement*, 90.

Although I reject his major thesis, that Calvin clearly taught limited atonement, [Jonathan] Rainbow's work has changed my thinking. I can no longer maintain, as I did in 1983, that the extent of the atonement was not an issue until after Calvin. Rainbow convinces me that Gottschalk and Bucer (in debates with Anabaptists) taught limited atonement before Calvin. I must modify my judgment, therefore, and argue that limited/unlimited atonement was not a debated issue within *reformed* circles until the time of Calvin's successor, Beza. I thus agree with Robert Letham that the extent of the atonement "only became a major issue in the next generation." The debate over this matter waited until Moses Amyrald and John Cameron began promoting unlimited atonement and thereby precipitated responses from the defenders of reformed orthodoxy. Hence the question of Calvin's view of the extent of the atonement is somewhat anachronistic.[69]

Peterson reasons, "The very fact that scholars have to appeal to systematic theology hints at a paucity of actual statements in Calvin on the issue of the extent of the atonement and should serve to make us examine whether or not Calvin answers the questions that we ask."[70] Peterson concludes: "One more point needs to be made. I am persuaded that it is fair to say that limited atonement fits better with the system of Calvin's thought than does unlimited atonement.... But I still maintain that it is unwise to ask what is Calvin's view on the extent of the atonement, because it was a question that he did not address."[71]

In sum, scholars have developed multiple approaches to the study of Calvin on the extent of the atonement.[72] In one sense, merely the

---

69. Peterson, *Calvin and the Atonement*, 119–20; italics original. Cf. Rainbow, *Will of God and the Cross*; Harding, "Atonement Theory Revisited," 52. For a critique of Rainbow's assessment of Bucer (which Peterson relies upon), see Allen, *Extent of the Atonement*, 40–42.

70. Peterson, *Calvin and the Atonement*, 118.

71. Peterson, *Calvin and the Atonement*, 120. Peterson reiterates, "I would go so far as to conclude that limited atonement, as framed by Calvin's successors, is a valid theological extension of his own theology" (ibid.). While Peterson claims that Calvin "did not address" the extent of the atonement, Daniel responds, "we are rather surprised that some of those who have commented on the subject have asserted that Calvin did not address himself to the subject" (Daniel, "Hyper-Calvinism and John Gill," 778).

72. "Determining Calvin's position on the extent of the atonement proves to be a bit more difficult, and Calvin scholars themselves have something of a dispute about the matter.... As far as I can tell, this dispute remains among Calvin scholars to this day" (Nelson, "Design, Nature, and Extent of the Atonement," 123). "First, I should

recognition that Calvin's stance has been vigorously contested is itself noteworthy, since this alone demonstrates that Calvin could not have emphasized limited atonement as explicitly or unambiguously as many later "high orthodox" Calvinists did, such as William Perkins, William Ames, and John Owen.[73] For example, no one has published an academic monograph or refereed article that debates whether John Owen believed in a strict "particular redemption"!

At the very least, such scholarly disputations concerning Calvin's views demonstrate that a developed doctrine of limited atonement was not an emphasis that was explicitly or patently central to Calvin's own theology.[74] William Cunningham mused that "there is fair ground for a

---

make reference to the fact that there is some debate whether Calvin himself taught limited atonement. Even among his followers there are differences of opinion on this subject. . . . This leaves one less than dogmatic" (Picirilli, *Grace, Faith, Free Will*, 87).

73. Kennedy, "Was Calvin a 'Calvinist'?" 211. See also Archbald, "Comparative Study of John Calvin and Theodore Beza," 273, 372, 381-83. "It is often stated—and with considerable propriety—that Calvin did not write an explicit treatment concerning the extent of the atonement, in fact did not deal with this precise issue in terms to which Reformed theology has been accustomed" (Nicole, "John Calvin's View of the Extent of the Atonement," 197). Nicole concludes that "definite atonement fits better than universal grace into the total pattern of Calvin's teaching" (ibid., 225). Nevertheless, he acknowledges that "full discussion of the scope of the atonement is not found in Calvin's writings, and the assessment of his position in this area has been varied" (ibid., 197-98). I use "high orthodox" Calvinism of coalescing scholastic Calvinist orthodoxy in the late sixteenth and seventeenth centuries. The high orthodox were increasingly fascinated with federalism and lapsarianism. On the other hand, "scholastic" tendencies could be found in various constructions of both Reformation and Post-Reformation theology (see Moore, *English Hypothetical Universalism*, 221-22). See also Trueman and Clark, *Protestant Scholasticism*; van Asselt and Dekker, *Reformation and Scholasticism*. Also, contrast Moltmann, "Zur Bedeutung des Petrus Ramus," 295-318; Muller, *Calvin and the Reformed Tradition*.

74. In this regard, it may be instructive to consider Calvin's own polemical writing against the earlier sessions of the Council of Trent. The council's fourth chapter of the sixth session contained an explicit declaration that Christ died for all ("Him God set forth to be a propitiation through faith in his blood for our sins, and not only for ours, but also for the sins of the whole world. . . . But though He died for all, all do not receive the benefit of His death, but only those to whom the merit of his passion is communicated"), and Calvin benignly commented without any critique, *tertium et quartum caput non attingo* ("I do not touch upon the third and fourth chapters"). Cf. Thomas, *Extent of the Atonement*, 28; Kennedy, "Was Calvin a 'Calvinist'?" 208; Archbald, "Comparative Study of John Calvin and Theodore Beza," 304. Would later, high orthodox Calvinists, in writing a formal response to such a document, have replied to such statements in the same benign manner as their namesake, without even "touching upon" it? P. L. Rouwendal claims, "For the theologians of Trent, as well as Calvin, taught the classical, commonly acknowledged view on the extent of the

difference of opinion as to what his doctrine upon this point really was."[75] We fittingly focus upon Calvin's own words in the following chapter.

---

atonement. There was no difference concerning this question between Catholics and the Reformed" (Rouwendal, "Calvin's Forgotten Classical Position," 330). At the same time, we have no evidence that Calvin objected to Beza's emphasis upon so-called "limited atonement" (Thomas, "Calvin and English Calvinism," 123; Thomas, *Extent of the Atonement*, 41–65; Blacketer, "Blaming Beza," 123). The matter of continuity and discontinuity between Calvin and Beza is much debated. For examples, see Dantine, "Das christologie Problem in Rahmen der Prädestinationslehre," 81–96; Dantine, "Les Tabelles sur la doctrine de la predestination," 365–67; Kickel, *Vernunft und Offenbarung bei Theodor Beza*; Bray, *Theodore Beza's Doctrine of Predestination*, 111–18; McPhee, "Conserver or Transformer of Calvin's Theology?"; Jinkins, "Theodore Beza," 131–54; Holtrop, *Bolsec Controversy on Predestination*; Archbald, "Comparative Study of John Calvin and Theodore Beza"; Blacketer, "Blaming Beza."

75. Cunningham, *Reformers and the Theology of the Reformation*, 396. "The truth is," added Cunningham, "that no satisfactory evidence has been or can be derived from his writings, that the precise question upon the extent of the atonement which has been mooted in more modern times . . . ever exercised Calvin's mind, or was made by him the subject of any formal or explicit deliverance."

CHAPTER TWO

Twelve Issues

I NOW WISH TO elucidate what I perceive to be the complex structure of Calvin's theology through a series of twelve issues and how he seems to address them through his own writings.[1] Admittedly, one can structure such a topical framework of questions to fit one's own purposes, but the attempt here is to let Calvin's own materials speak for themselves within a topical framework. To borrow from a play on words, the intent is to frame the conversation without the conversation "feeling framed." Moreover, while one can cull various comments from Calvin's works, one cannot develop a full-scale, developed doctrine of the so-called "extent of the atonement" from them.[2] "Putting all his statements together into a satisfying, coherent whole is genuinely challenging."[3] At the same time, Calvin did accept some rather specific and relevant tenets, as illustrated by the assemblage of primary source quotations below, gathered from his extant writings.[4]

---

1. These dozen issues obviously do not exhaust Calvin's thought on the death of Christ. For example, Calvin emphasized the exclusivity of Christ's work, the only way to God. "Our sins were thrown upon Christ in such a manner that he alone bore the curse. . . . Hence it follows that nowhere but in Christ is found expiation and satisfaction for sin. . . . Consequently, we must come to the death of Christ; for in no other way can satisfaction be given to God" (Calvin, Isa 53:10, *Commentary on the Book of the Prophet Isaiah*, vol. 4, 124–25). See Ascol, "Redemption Defined," 165–66.

2. Muller, *Unaccommodated Calvin*, 6.

3. Gatiss, *For Us and for Our Salvation*, 74.

4. Keeping in mind that some of his writings may not have been as "considered" as others, and that he did not necessarily check the sermon texts scribbled down and published in his name (Gatiss, *For Us and for Our Salvation*, 72).

I

First, will all individuals ultimately be saved? Calvin responds with a firm negative. He labeled the heretical "universalist" view an "absurdity."⁵ "I pass over the dreams of the fanatics, who make this a reason to extend salvation to all the reprobate and even to Satan himself. Such a monstrous idea is not worth refuting."⁶ Calvin argues that "no one unless deprived of sense and judgment can believe that salvation is ordained in the secret counsel of God equally for all."⁷ "Hence it is clear that the doctrine of salvation, which is said to be reserved solely and individually for the sons of the church, is falsely debased when presented as effectually profitable to all."⁸ As Robert Peterson avers, "It is clear that Calvin denied universalism, the teaching that all would ultimately be saved."⁹

II

Second, who is beckoned in the offer of the gospel? Calvin firmly supports the general offer of the gospel with its universal promises.¹⁰ Christ "offers salvation to all indiscriminately and stretches out His arms to embrace all, that all may be the more encouraged to repent."¹¹ God "offers

---

5. Calvin, 1 John 2:2, *Gospel according to St John 11-21 and the First Epistle of John*, 244.

6. Calvin, 1 John 2:2, *Gospel according to St John 11-21 and the First Epistle of John*, 244. Cf. Calvin, *Second Epistle of Paul the Apostle to the Corinthians and the Epistles to Timothy, Titus and Philemon*, 373. In his *Sermon* on Titus 2:11, Calvin compares the import to that found in 1 Tim 2:6. The good news of the gospel is to be preached to all classes and orders, both to the great and to the despised ("all classes of men with their diverse ways of life"). If salvation was universally granted to all the reprobate, that would include deceased unbelievers, leading to compounded theological problems.

7. Calvin, *Concerning the Eternal Predestination*, 109.

8. Calvin, *Institutes* III.22.10. Throughout this study, English translations of the *Institutes* come from Calvin, *Institutes of the Christian Religion*, ed. John T. McNeill and trans. Ford Lewis Battles (Philadelphia: Westminster, 1960), unless otherwise noted.

9. Peterson, *Calvin's Doctrine of the Atonement*, 90.

10. The universal promises are presented in the general offer. Calvin elsewhere distinguishes between objective availability and gospel presentation (not all hear the gospel).

11. Calvin, John 12:47, *Gospel according to St John 11-21 and the First Epistle of John*, 52. Cf. Calvin on Matt 18:12, where he notes the differences between the Matthean and Lukan parables concerning the one lost sheep and the ninety-nine. Calvin recognizes that the Matthean parable appears in a wider context concerning the

salvation to all. . . . All are equally called to penitence and faith; the same mediator is set forth for all to reconcile them to the Father."[12] Therefore, "the crime of rejecting an invitation so kind and gracious" is culpable, and "no man is condemned for despising the Gospel save he who spurs the lovely news of salvation and deliberately decides to bring destruction on himself."[13] "The gospel invites all to partake of salvation without any difference," for "Christ is there offered."[14]

Therefore, "it is certain that all those to whom the Gospel is preached are invited to a hope of eternal life."[15] "So however much a man may be overwhelmed in the gulf of misery there is yet set before him a way of escape. . . . Therefore since no man is excluded from calling upon God the gate of salvation is open to all. There is nothing else to hinder us from entering, but our own unbelief."[16] Peterson rightly concludes, "It is equally plain that Calvin held to a universal and free offer of the gospel."[17] Another corollary in Calvin concerns prayer: "The Holy Spirit bids us pray for all, because our one Mediator bids all to come to Him, since by His death He has reconciled all to the Father."[18]

---

restoration of a disciple, "because they are sheep over whom God made His Son the shepherd." "Luke's account," continues Calvin, "has a rather different object: because the whole human race belongs to God, those who are estranged are to be gathered in, and it is as much cause for rejoicing when the lost reform as when someone finds something precious which he had given up for lost" (Calvin, Matt 18:12, *Harmony of the Gospels*, vol. 2, 219).

12. Calvin, *Concerning the Eternal Predestination of God*, 103.

13. Calvin, John 12:47, *Gospel according to St John 11–21 and the First Epistle of John*, 52–53.

14. Calvin, Rom 1:16, *Epistles of Paul the Apostle to the Romans and to the Thessalonians*, 27.

15. Calvin, 1 Tim 2:3, *Second Epistle of Paul the Apostle to the Corinthians and the Epistles to Timothy, Titus and Philemon*, 208.

16. Calvin, Acts 2:21, *Acts of the Apostles 1–13*, 62.

17. Peterson, *Calvin's Doctrine of the Atonement*, 90. Cf. Murray, "Atonement and the Free Offer of the Gospel," 59–85; Beach, "Calvin's Treatment of the Offer of the Gospel," 55–76.

18. Calvin, 1 Tim 2:5, *Second Epistle of Paul the Apostle to the Corinthians and the Epistles to Timothy, Titus and Philemon*, 211. Cf. Calvin, Jer 14:22, *Commentary on Jeremiah*, vol. 1, 244. See Rom 10:1–3, which includes Paul's earnest prayer for his fellow Jews "that they may be saved" (ESV), on the heels of his discussions in chapter 9.

III

Third, why is it that not everyone believes? According to Calvin, not everyone is efficaciously drawn by the Holy Spirit. "Paul makes grace common to all men, not because it in fact extends to all, but because it is offered to all. Although Christ suffered for the sins of the world, and is offered by the goodness of God without distinction to all men, yet not all receive him."[19] Calvin recognized that not all receive the grace offered to them, since many remain in their unbelief. While commenting upon Heb 9:27 and 28, Calvin noted, "It is of course certain that not all enjoy the fruits of Christ's death, but this happens because their unbelief hinders them."[20]

Calvin believed that humans are so affected by sin that they will not believe of their own accord. "We are so contrary in our nature, and such enemies to God, that we cannot but resist him."[21] We cannot and will not become partakers of salvation "unless God draw us to it by his Holy Spirit."[22] Therefore, for any individual to trust in Christ as he is freely offered in the gospel, a special work of God is required.[23] Through a particular, efficacious work within specific individuals, the Holy Spirit forms faith in the all-sufficient work of Christ.[24] "Because God does not work effectually in all men, but only when the Spirit shines in our hearts as the inward teacher, [Paul] adds *to everyone who believes*. The Gospel

---

19. Calvin, Rom 5:18, *Epistles of Paul the Apostle to the Romans and to the Thessalonians*, 117–18.

20. Calvin, Heb 9:27, *Epistle of Paul the Apostle to the Hebrews and the First and Second Epistles of St Peter*, 131. In the immediate context, the sentence before states, "He says *many* meaning all, as in Rom. 5:15." The succeeding sentences affirm, "The question is not dealt with here because the apostle is not discussing how few or how many benefit from the death of Christ, but meant simply that he died for others, not for himself. He therefore contrasts the many to the one." See Kennedy, "Was Calvin a 'Calvinist'?" 203–4.

21. Calvin, Sermon on 1 Tim 2:3–5, *Selection of the Most Celebrated Sermons of John Calvin*, 99.

22. Calvin, Sermon on 1 Tim 2:3–5, *Selection of the Most Celebrated Sermons of John Calvin*, 99.

23. Calvin, Matt 15:13; Calvin, *Institutes*, III.3.21.

24. "For the present question is not how great the power of Christ is or what efficacy it has in itself, but to whom He gives Himself to be enjoyed. If possession lies in faith and faith emanates from the Spirit of adoption, it follows that only he is reckoned in the number of God's children who will be a partaker of Christ" (Calvin, *Concerning the Eternal Predestination*, 149).

is indeed offered to all for their salvation, but its power is not universally manifest."[25]

IV

Fourth, what distinguishes these specific individuals (whom the Spirit efficaciously draws) from all others? Calvin responds that the gracious, eternal, unconditional election of God sets them apart.[26] "The general nature of the promises does not alone and of itself make salvation common to all. Rather, the peculiar revelation which the prophet [Isaiah] has mentioned restricts it to the elect."[27] "Hence, we conclude that, though reconciliation is offered to all through Him, yet the benefit is peculiar to the elect, that they may be gathered into the society of life. However, while I say it is offered to all, I do not mean that this embassy, by which on Paul's testimony (II Cor 5.18) God reconciles the world to Himself, reaches to all, but that it is not sealed indiscriminately on the hearts of all to whom it comes so as to be effectual."[28]

Calvin's commentary on John 3:16 explains: "Moreover, let us remember that although life is promised generally to all who believe in Christ, faith is not common to all. Christ is open to all and displayed to all, but God opens the eyes only of the elect that they may seek Him by faith."[29] Calvin notes that although "all are equally called to penitence and faith," "God honours with illumination none but those whom He will."[30]

---

25. Calvin, Rom 1:16, *Epistles of Paul the Apostle to the Romans and to the Thessalonians*, 27; italics original; English spelling updated.

26. Thomas, *Extent of the Atonement*, 33.

27. Calvin, Rom 10:16, *Epistles of Paul the Apostle to the Romans and to the Thessalonians*, 232.

28. Calvin, *Concerning the Eternal Predestination*, 149. "Such is the significance of the term 'world' which He had used before. For although there is nothing in the world deserving of God's favour, He nevertheless shows He is favourable to the whole world when He calls all without exception to the faith of Christ, which is indeed an entry into life" (Calvin, John 3:16, *Gospel according to St John 1–10*, 74). "The draught appointed to Christ was to suffer the death of the cross for the reconciliation of the world" (Calvin, John 18:11, *Gospel according to St John 11–21 and the First Epistle of John*, 157).

29. Calvin, *Gospel according to St John 1–10*, 75.

30. Calvin, *Concerning the Eternal Predestination*, 103. Thus God's eternal decree of election and his universal offer of salvation are not inconsistent: "I maintain that these statements agree perfectly with each other. For by so promising he merely means that his mercy is extended to all, provided they seek after it and implore it. But only those whom he has illumined do this. And he illumines those whom he has predestined to

Calvin declares, "Even those opposed to me will concede that the universality of the grace of Christ is not better judged than from the preaching of the Gospel. But the solution of the difficulty lies in seeing how the doctrine of the Gospel offers salvation to all. That it is salvific for all I do not deny. But the question is whether the Lord in His counsel here destines salvation equally for all."[31] Calvin affirms, "God's election will be sure and nothing will perish that He wishes to be saved. For the secret purpose of God by which men were ordained to life is at length manifested in His own time by the calling."[32] Faith does not arise of one's "own impulse and free will," rather "faith is a fruit of election."[33] On the other hand, Calvin counsels in the same passage of comments on Ephesians 1: "How do we know that God has elected us before the creation of the world? By believing in Jesus Christ."[34]

---

salvation. . . . Therefore, since God's mercy is offered to both sorts of men through the gospel, it is faith—the illumination of God—that distinguishes between pious and impious, so that the former feel the working of the gospel, while the latter derive no profit from it. Illumination itself also has God's eternal election as its rule" (Calvin, *Institutes* III.24.17). The Beveridge translation (Eerdmans, 1964) has, "I hold that they are perfectly consistent, for all that is meant by the promise is, just that his mercy is offered to all who desire and implore it, and this none do, save those whom he has enlightened. Moreover, he enlightens those whom he has predestinated to salvation. . . . Therefore, since by the Gospel the mercy of God is offered to both, it is faith, in other words, the illumination of God, which distinguishes between the righteous and the wicked, the former feeling the efficacy of the Gospel, the latter obtaining no benefit from it. Illumination itself has eternal election for its rule." On Calvin's notion of illumination, see Shepherd, *Nature and Function of Faith*, 20-21.

31. Calvin, *Institutes* III.24.17.

32. Calvin, John 10:16, *Gospel according to St John 1-10*, 267. The elect were given to Christ "to give eternal life to all his people," so that "he limits this grace to those who have been given to him," and he "brings salvation to none but the elect" (Calvin, John 17:2, *Gospel according to St John 11-21 and the First Epistle of John*, 136).

33. Calvin, *Sermons on the Epistle to the Ephesians*, 44. Cf. Calvin, Eph 1:4-6, *Epistles of Paul the Apostle to the Galatians, Ephesians, Philippians and Colossians*, 124-27. "The efficient cause is the good pleasure of the will of God; the material cause is Christ; and the final cause is the praise of His grace. . . . Hence the cause of our salvation did not proceed from us, but from God alone" (ibid., 126).

34. Calvin, *Sermons on the Epistle to the Ephesians*, 47. Cf. Ponter, "Review Essay (Part Two)," 269; Bell, *Calvin and Scottish Theology*, 15-16.

V

Fifth, does this mean that the elect are saved by Christ's work in the cross even prior to their belief? No, replies Calvin. God, through his Spirit, effectually applies Christ's work to the elect when they believe, but they are not saved until they believe.[35] Calvin insists, "*For me* is very emphatic. It is not enough to regard Christ as having died for the salvation of the world; each man must claim the effect and possession of this grace for himself personally."[36] "Yet it is one thing to be offered, another to be received."[37] "For it is nothing if the fruit of this redemption, which was purchased for us, does not show itself by faith: for otherwise, it will become a thing of naught, and for our parts utterly perish."[38] "For it is faith that puts us in possession of this salvation: although we find it not but in the person of our Lord Jesus Christ, and we must needs come thither, yet if we have

---

35. Cf. Eph 2:1–7; Lynch, "*Quid Pro Quo* Satisfaction?" 66. See also Calvin's relevant comments in his fourth sermon on Ephesians, as quoted in Blocher, "Atonement in John Calvin's Theology," 281n8. Furthermore, Calvin speaks of an "accommodation" in the manner of speaking, reflected in the inherent tension between God being our enemy until we were reconciled in Christ and God already embracing us with his free favor (see Penner, "Calvin, Barth, and the Subject of Atonement," 130–31; Helm, "Faith, Atonement, and Time," 394; Duby, "Cross and the Fullness of God," 173–75; Hay, "Heart of Wrath," 361–78). "For, in some ineffable way God loved us and yet was angry toward us at the same time until he became reconciled to us in Christ" (Calvin, *Institutes* II.17.2). "Therefore, he loved us even when we practiced enmity toward him and committed wickedness. Thus in a marvelous and divine way he loved us even when he hated us" (Calvin, *Institutes* II.16.4). According to Calvin, this divine love was rooted in God's own creative work, that we still reflected vestiges of what he had made. "For he hated us for what we were that he had not made; yet because our wickedness had not entirely consumed his handiwork, he knew how, at the same time, to hate in each one of us what we had made, and to love what he had made" (Calvin, *Institutes* II.16.4). Cf. Hesselink, "Calvin on the Atonement," 305; Ware, "Extent of the Atonement," 5. For Calvin's thoughts on God's love for all humanity, see his comments on Ps 81:13; Lam 3:33; Matt 23:37; John 3:16–17; 2 Pet 3:9.

36. Calvin, Gal 2:20, *Epistles of Paul the Apostle to the Galatians, Ephesians, Philippians and Colossians*, 44. In this instance, Calvin does not deny that Christ died "for the salvation of the world," but insists that "this grace" must be personally applied. "It is not enough, then, that our Lord Jesus Christ has suffered, but the good which He acquired for us must be communicated, and we must be put in possession of it. That is done when we are drawn to Him by faith" (Calvin, *Deity of Christ and Other Sermons*, 95).

37. Calvin, *Institutes* IV.17.33.

38. Calvin, *Sermons on the Epistles to Timothy and Titus*, 612; English spelling updated. The preceding sentence asserts that "when Jesus Christ had suffered for the sins of the world, he went up into heaven."

not this key of faith, Jesus Christ shall be (as it were) strange to us, and all that he has suffered, shall not profit us one whit, as indeed it belongs not to us."[39] Concerning Paul's statements in Rom 3:25, Calvin explains, "Having just stated that God has been reconciled in Christ, he now adds that this reconciliation is brought to pass by faith, at the same time stating what should be the chief object of our faith in looking to Christ."[40]

Calvin affirms, "First, we must understand that as long as Christ remains outside of us, and we are separated from him, all that he has suffered and done for the salvation of the human race remains useless and of no value for us."[41] This statement appears at the beginning of the third book of the *Institutes*. Anthony Lane notes, "Having in Book II expounded the work of Christ on the cross, Calvin begins Book III by stating that what Christ has achieved for the human race is of no use unless it is applied to us by the Holy Spirit."[42] Calvin explains, "St. Paul also shows us that faith is essential or Christ will profit us nothing. Although, then,

---

39. Calvin, *Sermons on the Epistles to Timothy and Titus*, 178; English spelling updated. Rainbow cautions that such statements should be read with faith as the *causa instrumentala* in mind (Rainbow, *Will of God and the Cross*, 94).

40. Calvin, Rom 3:25, *Epistles of Paul the Apostle to the Romans and the Thessalonians*, 76.

41. Calvin, *Institutes* III.1.1; cf. Calvin, 2 Cor 5:18. Unlike some later authors, such as Tobias Crisp and John Eaton, Calvin did not espouse a notion of "eternal justification" (Helm, "Faith, Atonement, and Time," 408n47). There is, in fact, "an important logical distinction between recognition and appropriation" (ibid., 409). According to Calvin, until one is united with Christ by faith (which the Spirit efficaciously forms in the elect through the Word), one is not justified. See Kennedy, *Union with Christ and the Extent of the Atonement*; Hammett, "Multiple-Intentions View of the Atonement," 164. "It is not easy to harmonize all of Calvin's thoughts on the work of Christ, partly because he holds to a substitutionary atonement that is nonetheless ineffectual until we are united with Christ" (Gerrish, *Grace and Gratitude*, 56n17). Cf. Gerrish, "Atonement and 'Saving Faith,'" 181–91; Billings, *Calvin, Participation, and the Gift*; Garcia, *Life in Christ*, 3: "Calvin insists on the indispensability of this union with Christ perhaps most emphatically when he makes the 'profitability' of Christ's redemptive work to depend wholly upon it." One should distinguish between an incarnational union and a spiritual union with Christ in Calvin's thought (see Gatiss, *For Us and for Our Salvation*, 73). See also Partee, "Calvin's Central Dogma Again," 191–99; Hart, "Humankind in Christ and Christ in Humankind," 67–84; Tamburello, *Union with Christ*; Gatiss, "Inexhaustible Fountain of All Good Things," 194–206; Venema, "Union with Christ," 91–114; Horton, "Calvin's Theology of Union with Christ and the Double Grace," 72–94; Billings, "Union with Christ and the Double Grace," 49–69.

42. Lane, "Calvin versus Calvinism Revisited," 35. Cf. Lane, "Calvin's Doctrine of Assurance Revisited," 306; Lane, *Reader's Guide to Calvin's Institutes*, 98: "Calvin appears to teach that Christ's work is for all, but the application of it is only for some."

Christ is in a general view the Redeemer of the world, yet his death and passion are of no advantage to any but such as receive that which St Paul shows here. And so we see that when we once know the benefits brought to us by Christ, and which he daily offers us by his gospel, we must also be joined to him by faith."[43]

> Thus you see in effect, whereunto we should refer this saying, where Saint Paul tells us expressly, that the Son of God gave himself. And he contents not himself to say, that Christ gave himself for the world in common, for that had been but a slender saying: but [shows that] every one of us must apply to himself particularly, the virtue of the death and passion of our Lord Jesus Christ. Whereas it is said that the Son of God was crucified, we must not *only* think that the same was done for the Redemption of the world: but *also* every of us must on his own behalf join himself to our Lord Jesus Christ, and conclude, It is for me that he has suffered.[44]

VI

Sixth, does this mean that the provision of Christ's sacrifice is limited to the elect alone, since God eternally intended to apply Christ's work ultimately to the elect alone? Apparently no, because Calvin seems in some sense to coordinate a universal provision of Christ's sacrifice with the general call of the gospel: "God commends to us the salvation of all men without exception, even as Christ suffered for the sins of the whole world."[45] Calvin declares, "Although Christ *suffered* for the sins of the

---

43. Calvin, *Sermons on Ephesians*, 55. "In order that the redemption of Christ may be effectual and useful to us, we must renounce our former life" (Calvin, 1 Pet 1:18, *The Epistle of Paul the Apostle to the Hebrews and the First and Second Epistles of St Peter*, 248). "He must be the redeemer of the world. He must be condemned, indeed, not for having preached the Gospel, but for us He must be oppressed, as it were, in the person of all cursed ones and of all transgressors, and of those who deserved eternal death" (Calvin, *Deity of Christ*, 95, CO 46.870; cf. Calvin, *Deity of Christ*, 156, CO 46.919; English translation from Kennedy, "Hermeneutical Discontinuity between Calvin and Later Calvinism," 306).

44. Calvin, *Sermons on Galatians*, 299–300; italics added. According to Calvin, "outward teaching will always be coldly received, unless His Spirit is teaching within" (Calvin, Acts 26:28, *The Acts of the Apostles 14–28*, 284).

45. Calvin, Gal 5:12, *Epistles of Paul the Apostle to the Galatians, Ephesians, Philippians and Colossians*, 99. See Daniel, "Hyper-Calvinism and John Gill," 788. Contrast Calvin's own words with Leahy: "For Calvin, with Bible in hand, Christ died for all

world, *and is offered* by the goodness of God without distinction to all men, yet not all receive him."[46] Citing the Lukan genealogy of Jesus, Calvin notes that "the salvation provided by Christ is common to all mankind. For Christ, the Author of salvation, was begotten of Adam, the common father of us all."[47] Jesus is "Redeemer of the world . . . since He was there, as it were, in the person of all cursed ones and of all transgressors, and of those who had deserved eternal death . . . and bears the burdens of all those who had offended God mortally."[48] Calvin's "Last Will" refers to "the blood of our great Redeemer, as it was shed for all poor sinners."[49]

Calvin insists, "But this does not alter the fact that the reprobate are mixed up with the elect in the world. It is incontestable that Christ came for the expiation of the sins of the whole world."[50] He declares, "This redemption was procured by the blood of Christ, for by the sacrifice of His death all the sins of the world have been expiated."[51] Calvin reiterates that the Lord Jesus suffered "for the redemption of the whole world."[52] Multiple other examples can be assembled: "Indeed the death of Christ was life for the whole world, and that is surely supernatural."[53] Jesus, who was "sent to be the Redeemer of the human race" was "burdened with the

---

without distinction, not all without exception" (Leahy, "Calvin and the Extent of the Atonement," 62).

46. Calvin, Rom 5:18, *Epistles of Paul the Apostle to the Romans and to the Thessalonians*, 118; italics added. See Beach, "Calvin's Treatment of the Offer of the Gospel," 63.

47. Calvin, *Institutes* II.13.3.

48. Calvin, *Deity of Christ and Other Sermons*, 95.

49. Translation of the French version, as quoted in Clifford, *Calvinus*, 37. The Latin version (in *Calvin's Life* by Beza) has "the great Redeemer's blood, shed for the sins of the human race." Cf. Nicole, "John Calvin's View of the Extent of the Atonement," 203.

50. Calvin, *Concerning the Eternal Predestination*, 148. Calvin continues, "But the solution lies close at hand, that whosoever believes in Him should not perish but should have eternal life."

51. Calvin, Col 1:14, *Epistle of Paul the Apostle to the Galatians, Ephesians, Philippians and Colossians*, 308.

52. Calvin, *Deity of Christ and Other Sermons*, 55.

53. Calvin, Heb 8:2, *Epistle of Paul the Apostle to the Hebrews and the First and Second Epistles of St Peter*, 105.

sins of the world,"[54] and "on him was laid the guilt of the whole world."[55] Jesus "bore all the wickednesses of all the iniquities of the world," and God "took Him as being there in the place of all sinners."[56]

Calvin affirms that Jesus "willed in full measure to appear before the judgment seat of God His Father in the name and in the person of all sinners, being then ready to be condemned, inasmuch as He bore our burden."[57] "But though our Lord Jesus by nature held death in horror and indeed it was a terrible thing to Him to be found before the judgment seat of God in the name of all poor sinners (for He was there, as it were, having to sustain all our burdens), nevertheless He did not fail to humble Himself to such condemnation for our sakes."[58] "Now, then, the blame lies solely with ourselves, if we do not become partakers of this salvation; for he *calls* all men to himself, without a single exception, and *gives* Christ to all, that we may be illuminated by him. Let us only open our eyes, he alone will dispel the darkness, and illuminate our minds by the 'light' of truth."[59]

In this manner, a universal provision of Christ's death seems to undergird the general call of the gospel promises. Calvin's commentary on 2 Corinthians correlates Christ's "sufferings" with the proclamation of the gospel "which He has *given* to the world." Christ "once *suffered*, so now every day He *offers* the fruit of His sufferings to us through the Gospel which He has given to the world as a sure and certain record of

---

54. Calvin, Matt 26:39, *Harmony of the Gospels*, vol. 3, 150–52. While describing the crucifixion, Calvin declares that "the hour was approaching in which our Lord Jesus would have to suffer for the redemption of mankind" (Calvin, *Deity of Christ and Other Sermons*, 55). "Christ offered Himself as a Victim for the salvation of the human race" (Calvin, *Harmony of the Gospels*, vol. 3, 125). Jesus Christ "suffered for the sins of the world" (Calvin, *Sermons on the Epistles to Timothy and Titus*, 612; English spelling updated).

55. Calvin, Isa 53:12, *Commentary on the Book of the Prophet Isaiah*, vol. 4, 131.

56. Calvin, *Sermons on Isaiah's Prophecy of the Death and Passion of Christ*, 74, 70.

57. Calvin, *Deity of Christ and Other Sermons*, 52. As Calvin explains more fully, "But here there is a special regard. It is that He must be the Redeemer of the world. He must be condemned, indeed, not for having preached the Gospel, but for us He must be oppressed, as it were, to the lowest depths and sustain our cause, since He was there, as it were, in the person of all cursed ones and of all transgressors, and of those who had deserved eternal death" (ibid., 95).

58. Calvin, *Deity of Christ and Other Sermons*, 155–56.

59. Calvin, Isa 42:6, *Commentary on the Book of the Prophet Isaiah*, vol. 3, 295; italics added. One notes the parallel use of "calls" and "gives," implying the correspondence of a general "call" with a general "provision."

His completed work of reconciliation."[60] The Spirit then uses the general call of the gospel and its universal promises in forming faith in the elect.[61] God therefore uses the general provision proclaimed in the gospel as a means in his sovereign and effectual calling of the elect, thereby preserving the universality of the provision and the particularity of election.[62]

VII

Seventh, is the fact that the provision of Christ is universally offered important to the elect themselves?[63] Calvin seems to affirm that this is the

---

60. Calvin, 2 Cor 5:19, *Second Epistle of Paul the Apostle to the Corinthians and the Epistles to Timothy, Titus and Philemon*, 79; italics added. Calvin explained, "But there is a special love for those to whom the gospel is preached: which is that God testifies unto them that he will make them partakers of the benefit that was purchased for them by the death and passion of his Son" (Calvin, *Sermons on Deuteronomy*, 167; English spelling updated).

61. Due to space constraints, the matter of those who die in infancy apart from conscious faith is not addressed here (cf. Crisp, *Deviant Calvinism*, 227n16).

62. In the view of Charles Bell, "It is quite clear that Calvin taught a doctrine of universal atonement. It is also clear that he taught a doctrine of predestination in which faith is limited to the elect. He could do so because he did not link the doctrines of election and atonement in a logical order of cause and effect" (Bell, *Calvin and Scottish Theology*, 17). Cf. Bell, "Calvin and the Extent of the Atonement," 120–21; Ferguson, "Nature of the Connection between Election and Atonement." John Gerstner speaks of the atonement as "unlimited in its sufficiency—in its offer" and "limited only in its specific design for those who believe," who are the elect (Gerstner, "Atonement and the Purpose of God," 51). Being argued here is that Calvin saw the unlimited offer as rooted in an unlimited provision (Christ as "given") in divine intention. Gerstner's further distinction still holds true, that Christ must work "*in* us" (through the Spirit) what he did "*for* us" on the cross (ibid., 63). Gerstner thus distinguishes offer and application. Here, a fuller view distinguishes the accomplishment of provision and the accomplishment of application.

63. Cf. Knox, *Doctrine of God*, 260–66. If there is both a divine intention of universal provision and a divine intention of particular, efficacious application, one might be inclined to speak of a "multiple intentions" view. If the two are logically interlocked somehow, one might speak of a "complex-intentioned" view (cf. Gatiss, *For Us and for Our Salvation*, 91). Those of a "limited atonement" bent are inclined to emphasize the "nugatory" nature of the intent to provide salvation for all (Nicole, "Case for Definite Atonement," 203). "In other words, why create the entire empty set of 'people who would be saved by the universal atonement *if* they believed, but who won't believe because God will not grant them faith'?" (Gatiss, *For Us and for Our Salvation*, 96). But if there is a manner of interweaving a divine intent of universal provision with a divine intent of efficacious application, the universal provision is not "nugatory" in such a "complex-intentioned" arrangement. For a discussion of other "empty atonement"

case. The Holy Spirit does not "create" faith in the elect *ex nihilo* as if it were some kind of a substance or material or object or property. Faith is a confident, relational trust in God's promises centered in the person and work of Christ. "For it is not enough that Jesus Christ suffered in His person and was made a sacrifice for us; but we must be assured of it by the Gospel; we must receive that testimony and doubt not that we have righteousness in Him, knowing that He has made satisfaction for our sins."[64] The underlying provision of Christ functions as an important, objective ground of the faith of believers. "It would have done us no good for Christ to have been given by the Father as the Author of salvation, if He had not been available to all without distinction.... We should know that salvation is openly displayed in Christ to all the human race, for in all reality He is called son of Noah and son of Adam."[65]

The Holy Spirit, in his particular call, points the elect to the general call of the universal promises revealed in the gospel. The elect do not receive an extra-biblical or special revelation of their inclusion in the secret, eternal decree. The Holy Spirit, in his efficacious work, points believers to Christ as proclaimed in the gospel.[66]

> But we should remember, as I have already said, that the secret love in which our heavenly Father embraced us to Himself is, since it flows from His eternal good pleasure, precedent to all other causes; but the grace which He wants to be testified to us and by which we are stirred to the hope of salvation, begins with the reconciliation provided through Christ.... And He has used a general term [i.e., whosoever], both to invite indiscriminately all to share in life and to cut off every excuse from unbelievers. Such is also the significance of the term "world" which He had used before. For although there is nothing in the world deserving of God's favour, He nevertheless shows He is favourable to the whole world when He calls all without exception to the faith of Christ, which is indeed an entry into life.[67]

---

arguments, see Thomas, *Extent of the Atonement*, 232–36.

64. Calvin, *Sermons on Isaiah's Prophecy*, 117.

65. Calvin, Matt 1:1–17; Luke 3:23–38, *Harmony of the Gospels*, vol. 1, 56.

66. See Lane, "Calvin's Doctrine of Assurance Revisited," 306–7.

67. Calvin, John 3:16–17, *Gospel according to St John 1–10*, 74–75. One notes that while the English translation of the previous quotation included "all without distinction," this latter quotation includes "all without exception."

In a sermon on Gal 2:20, Calvin notes how the apostle Paul shows how "every of us must apply to himself particularly" the universal redemption given in Christ ("who loved me and gave himself for me").[68] "But when we once know that the thing which was done for the redemption of the whole world, pertains to every of us severally: it behooves every of us to say also on his own behalf, The son of God has loved me so dearly, that he has given himself to death for me."[69] In his sermon on Psalm 119, Calvin affirms, "So likewise, when it is said in the holy scripture that this is a true and undoubted saying, that God hath sent his only begotten son, to save all miserable sinners: we must include it within this same rank I say, that every of us apply the same particularly to himself: when as we hear this general sentence, that God is merciful."[70] Calvin adds, "Since it is so, that the love and goodness of God is declared unto the world, in that his son Christ Jesus hath suffered death, I must appropriate the same to myself, that I may know that it is to me, that God hath spoken, that he would I should take possession of such a grace, and therein to rejoice me."[71]

This centering upon the promises proclaimed in the gospel comports well with Calvin's overall emphasis upon the revealed Word as the foundation of confident faith.[72]

> None need now wonder or worry how he can escape death, since we believe it was God's purpose that Christ should rescue us from it. The word world comes again so that no one at all may think he is excluded, if only he keeps to the road of faith. . . . And whenever our sins press hard on us, whenever Satan would drive us to despair, we must hold up this shield, that God does

---

68. Calvin, *Sermons on Galatians*, 299–300. Calvin insists that "every of us must apply to himself particularly, the virtue of the death and passion of our Lord Jesus Christ. Whereas it is said that the Son of God was crucified, we must not only think that the same was done for the Redemption of the world: but also every of us must on his own behalf join himself to our Lord Jesus Christ, and conclude, It is for me that he has suffered" (ibid.). For Calvin, communion is a means of applying Christ's work in faith (Calvin, *Institutes* IV.17.2; IV.17.5). See Wendel, *Calvin*, 318.

69. Calvin, *Sermons on Galatians*, 300.

70. Calvin, *Sermons on the Hundred and Nineteenth Psalm*, 133.

71. Calvin, *Sermons on the Hundred and Nineteenth Psalm*, 134. Calvin ties Rom 8:32 into this passage (see Ponter, "Review Essay (Part Two)," 262–63).

72. Calvin, *Institutes* III.21.2.

not want us to be overwhelmed in everlasting destruction, for He has ordained His Son to be the Saviour of the world.[73]

As a corollary, believers are to focus on Christ, the "mirror of our election," as he is revealed in the gospel.[74] Christ in the gospel is "a warrant for our salvation, so as we ought to think ourselves thoroughly assured of it."[75] Calvin pulls all this together in his comments upon John

---

73. Calvin, John 3:16-17, *Gospel according to St John 1-10*, 74-75.

74. Calvin, *Institutes*, III.24.5; Calvin, *Concerning the Eternal Predestination*, 127; Calvin, John 15:9; *Sermon* on 2 Tim 1:9-10. "Calvin's theological and pastoral acuteness made him aware that to look to Christ by faith is very different from looking at one's faith in Christ" (Thomas, "Calvin and English Calvinism," 115). "Seeing then that God gives us such a sure certificate of his will, see how he puts us out of doubt of our election, which we know not of, neither can perceive it, and it is as much, as if he should draw out a copy of his will, and give it to us" (Calvin, *Sermons on the Epistles to Timothy and Titus*, 253; English spelling updated). According to Calvin in his work *Concerning the Eternal Predestination*, Christ as the mirror of election "is more than a thousand testimonies to me" (see Shepherd, *Nature and Function of Faith*, 75).

75. Calvin, *Sermons on Galatians*; as quoted in Clifford, *Calvinus*, 33. Cf. Calvin, *Institutes*, III.24.4-6. "Furthermore," according to Bell, "it is clear that this doctrine of universal atonement is important for Calvin's teaching on faith and assurance" (Bell, *Calvin and Scottish Theology*, 17). Cf. Calvin, John 19:12. Helm recommends attaining certainty of one's election "by the nature of our response to the preaching of the Christian Gospel" (Helm, *Calvin and the Calvinists*, 26). Rainbow argues, "But Calvin had good news: God does in fact reveal to the believer the knowledge of his election" (Rainbow, *Will of God and the Cross*, 83). "If I know that Christ died for me (which knowledge is, in Calvinism, imparted by the testimony of the Spirit), then I know, without further probing or speculation, that I am elect" (ibid., 88). Yet Blocher explains Calvin's counsel to troubled consciences: "'Consciences that are fearful and thunderstruck by God's judgment can only find rest if there is a sacrifice and a washing to wipe away sins' (*Institutes* 2.16.5; cf. 17 and comfort for the consciences of God's servants); 'our consciences cannot apprehend the benefits [of God's favor] except through the intervention of Christ's sacrifice.' But this implies no *reduction* to subjective effects: it is objective satisfaction that appeases conscience" (Blocher, "Atonement in John Calvin's Theology," 302). One wonders, if the objective ground of a "limited redemption" is only epistemologically ascertained through subjective means (by an internal testimony or by looking at the fruit of one's sanctification), how is the assuring comfort objectively established for the sake of conscience? Calvin points toward the disposition and promise of God in God's revealed will of the gospel, while allowing a secondary and corroborative role in ascertaining signs of one's sanctification. "But we do not forbid him [the Christian] from undergirding and strengthening this faith by signs of the divine benevolence toward him" (Calvin, *Institute* III.14.18). In matters of assurance, Calvin spoke of faith as "a firm and certain knowledge of God's benevolence toward us, founded upon the truth of the freely given promise in Christ, both revealed to our minds and sealed upon our hearts through the Holy Spirit" (ibid., III.2.7). "This boldness arises only out of a sure confidence in divine benevolence and salvation"

3:16: "The whole substance of our salvation is not to be sought anywhere else than in Christ, and so we must see by what means Christ flows to us and why He was offered as our Saviour. Both points are clearly told us here—that faith in Christ quickens all and that Christ brought life because the heavenly Father does not wish the human race that He loves to perish."[76] Calvin adds, "God has most abundantly declared His love toward us and therefore whoever is still doubtful and unsatisfied by this testimony does Christ a serious injury, as if He had been some ordinary man who had died accidentally."[77]

(ibid., III.2.15). Yet Calvin also declared, "Surely, while we teach that faith ought to be certain and assured, we cannot imagine any certainty that is not tinged with doubt, or any assurance that is not assailed by some anxiety" (ibid., III.2.17). Therefore, "believers are in perpetual conflict with their own unbelief" so that their consciences do not remain in peaceful repose undisturbed by tumult (ibid., III.2.17). Believers do not always enjoy a peaceful state, since the natural instincts of their hearts are inclined toward unbelief (ibid., III.2.20; III.2.37). Moreover, "in the course of the present life it never goes so well with us that we are wholly cured of the disease and entirely filled and possessed by faith" (ibid., III.2.18). Nevertheless, faith is not content with this disease of doubt. "For, as faith is not content with a doubtful and changeable opinion, so is it not content with an obscure and confused conception; but requires full and fixed certainty, such as men are wont to have from things experienced and proved. For unbelief is so deeply rooted in our hearts, and we are so inclined to it, that not without hard struggle is each one able to persuade himself of what all confess with the mouth: namely, that God is faithful. Especially when it comes to reality itself, every man's wavering uncovers hidden weakness. And not without cause the Holy Spirit with such notable titles ascribes authority to the Word of God. He wishes to cure the disease" (ibid., III.2.15). Therefore, "He who, struggling with his own weakness, presses toward faith in his moments of anxiety, is already in large part victorious" (ibid., III.2.17). See Muller, "Calvin, Beza and the Later Reformed," 244–76. See also Helm, "Faith, Atonement, and Time," 412–16; Shepherd, *Nature and Function of Faith*, 24–28; Letham, "Faith and Assurance in Early Calvinism."

76. Calvin, John 3:16, *Gospel according to St John 1–10*, 73.

77. Calvin, John 3:16, *Gospel according to St John 1–10*, 74. In his commentary on Ezek 18:1–4, Calvin reiterates that God "is affected with fatherly love towards the whole human race since he created and formed it; . . . True indeed, we are abominable in God's sight, through being corrupted by original sin, as it is elsewhere said, (Ps. XIV.1, 2;) but inasmuch as we are men, we must be dear to God, and our salvation must be precious in his sight" (from Calvin, *Commentaries on the First Twenty Chapters of the Book of the Prophet Ezekiel*, vol. 2, 217).

VIII

Eighth, are there ramifications of Christ's all-sufficient, universal provision in the ministry of evangelism? Most assuredly.[78] Calvin insists, "If we wish to serve our Master, that is the way we must go about it. We must make every effort to draw everybody to the knowledge of the gospel. For when we see people going to hell who have been created in the image of God and redeemed by the blood of our Lord Jesus Christ, that must indeed stir us to do our duty and instruct them and treat them with all gentleness and kindness as we try to bear fruit this way."[79] Calvin adds, "It is, as I have already said, that, seeing that men are created in the image of God and that their souls have been redeemed by the blood of Jesus Christ, we must try in every way available to us to draw them to the knowledge of the gospel."[80] Calvin laments, "For it is no small matter to have the souls perish which were bought by the blood of Christ."[81] "For to give over a man at the first dash when he has done amiss, or when he is as it were in the highway to destruction: is a furthering of the destruction of the wretched soul that was redeemed by the bloodshed of our Lord Jesus Christ."[82] Elsewhere, Calvin decries the indifference of casually watching as "the poor souls whom our Lord Jesus Christ has bought so dearly that he did not spare himself to save them, perish and are given into Satan's possession."[83]

---

78. Cf. Beza's view that a "hypothetical" dimension is irrelevant (Thomas, *Extent of the Atonement*, 57; see also Archbald, "Comparative Study of John Calvin and Theodore Beza," 196–98). Richard Muller maintains, "It is superfluous to speak of a hypothetical extent of the efficacy of Christ's work beyond its actual application. As shown in the doctrine of election, salvation is not bestowed generally but on individuals" (Muller, *Christ and the Decree*, 35). Specifically, "it is superfluous to argue a hypothetical dimension to its efficacy, as distinct from its sufficiency, given that the efficacy, as far as Calvin was concerned, was assumed to be governed by divine election and that the referent of the argument for the universality of Christ's satisfaction was its sufficiency" (Muller, *Calvin and the Reformed Tradition*, 77n24).

79. Calvin, *Sermons on the Acts of the Apostles, Chapters 1–7*, 587.

80. Calvin, *Sermons on the Acts of the Apostles, Chapters 1–7*, 593.

81. Calvin, *Sermons on the Epistles to Timothy and Titus*, 817.

82. Calvin, *Sermons on Deuteronomy*, 731.

83. Calvin, *Sermons on Ephesians*, 525. He adds, "Yet we remain quite indifferent. Do we not in this show that we do not have so much as one drop of love in us?" Cf. Calvin, *Sermon on Eph 6:18–19, Sermons on Ephesians*, 684–85. "However, St. Paul speaks here expressly of the saints or faithful, but this does not imply that we should not pray generally for all men. For the wretched unbelievers and the ignorant have great need to be pleaded for with God; behold them on the way to perdition. If we saw

Similarly, Calvin's sermons on Ephesians exhort: "Also we ought to have good care of those that have been redeemed with the blood of our Lord Jesus Christ. If we see souls which have been so precious to God go to perdition, and we make nothing of it, that is to despise the blood of our Lord Jesus Christ."[84] Calvin's sermons on Micah explain, "Because to see souls created in the image of God move toward their own damnation is hardly a light matter, especially souls that were redeemed at such a cost by the blood of God's son."[85] Calvin can even state, "So we must beware, or souls redeemed by Christ may perish by our carelessness, for their salvation to some degree was put into our hands by God."[86] And he adds, "We

a beast at the point of perishing, we would have pity on it. And what shall we do when we see souls in peril, which are so precious before God, as he has shown in that he has ransomed them with the blood of his own Son? If we see then a poor soul going thus to perdition, ought we not to be moved with compassion and kindness, and should we not desire God to apply the remedy?" For other passages that speak of Christ's dying for those who perish or are perishing, see Ponter, "Brief History of Deviant Calvinism," 5–12. Some, but not all, relate to Christ's purchasing the church with his blood. This gives Rainbow warrant to believe that Calvin speaks only from a "judgment of charity" (Rainbow, *Will of God and the Cross*, 159–74). However, Calvin applies the same principle to apostates and those outside the church. See Calvin on 2 Pet 2:1; Jude 4. Ponter comments, "There is absolutely nothing within the statements to suggest that Calvin meant to indicate that 'these apostates, as now known, he *formerly assumed* had been redeemed. He knows that these men are apostates, and, still, he says that they had been redeemed by the blood of Christ. Rainbow's interpretation, therefore, is highly forced and unnatural" (Ponter, "Brief History of Deviant Calvinism," 16). Rainbow's argumentation on pages 170–74 seems to flounder on this point. Cf. the interpretive exertion in Archbald, "Comparative Study of John Calvin and Theodore Beza," 254, 318–19.

84. Calvin, *Sermons on Ephesians*, 521; cf. 684–85; Calvin, *Sermons on the Epistles to Timothy and Titus*, 735: "That is a terrible honesty, when we shall suffer silly souls, which were so dearly bought, to go to destruction" (English spelling updated); "when we see the souls that were bought with the blood of our Lord Jesus Christ, so led to ruin and destruction" (Calvin, *Sermons on Galatians*, 217).

85. Calvin, *Sermons on the Book of Micah*, 371; cf. Calvin, Sermon on Deut 22:2–4.

86. Calvin, Jas 5:20, *Harmony of the Gospels: Matthew, Mark and Luke, vol. 3, and The Epistles of James and Jude*, 318. The diluted translation of an earlier Eerdmans series remains curious: "We must therefore take heed lest souls perish through our sloth, whose salvation God puts in a manner in our hands" (Calvin, *Commentaries on the Catholic Epistles*, 361). Cf. Calvin on Acts 20:28: "For it follows from this, that unless they [pastors] are faithful in putting out their labour on the Church, not only are they made accountable for lost souls, but they are guilty of sacrilege, because they have profaned the sacred blood of the Son of God, and have made useless the redemption acquired by Him, as far as they are concerned. But it is a hideous and monstrous crime if, by our idleness, not only the death of Christ becomes worthless, but also the fruit of it is destroyed and perishes." Yet Calvin quickly adds, "But the Church is said to

should never gloat as many do who laugh and smirk over someone else's misfortune. Instead, we should mourn and say, 'How sad, that poor man has given offence to God.' It should distress us to see someone perishing who has been so dearly redeemed by Christ's precious blood; it should distress us to see God's righteousness and his glory diminished."[87]

The pastoral implications are patent:

> Thus, when in the present day the Church is afflicted by so many and so various calamities, and innumerable souls are perishing, which Christ redeemed with his own blood, we must be barbarous and savage if we are not touched with any grief. And especially the ministers of the word ought to be moved by this feeling of grief, because being appointed to keep watch and to look at a distance, they ought also to groan when they perceive the tokens of approaching ruin.[88]

Calvin insists, "If the faith of one single man is in danger of being overthrown, if there is at stake the ruin of a single soul redeemed by Christ's blood, the pastor should immediately gird himself to resist; how much less can he endure to see whole houses overthrown!"[89] "And surely it is an iron hardness not to feel pity when we see souls, redeemed by Christ's blood, going to ruin."[90]

"And again," adds Calvin, "hath not our Lord Jesus Christ redeemed men's souls? True it is that the *effect* of his [Christ's] death comes not to the whole world. Nevertheless, forasmuch as it is not in us to discern between the righteous and the sinners that go to destruction, but that Jesus Christ has suffered his death and passion as well for them as for us, therefore it behooves us to labor to bring every man to salvation, that the grace of our Lord Jesus Christ may be available to them."[91]

---

have been acquired by God so that we may know that he intends it to remain complete for Himself, because it is right that He have and hold those whom He has redeemed" (Calvin, *Acts of the Apostles 14-28*, 183-84).

87. Calvin, *Sermons on the Beatitudes*, 46. Calvin clearly was not as guarded in his wording as many later high orthodox Calvinists tended to be. See Daniel, "Hyper-Calvinism and John Gill," 789. Cf. Hodge, *Atonement*, 390: "It is true that at times Calvin uses general terms with respect to the design of Christ's death in a more unguarded manner than would *now* be done by one of his consistent disciples."

88. Calvin, Isa 22:4, *Commentary on the Book of the Prophet Isaiah*, vol. 2, 114.

89. Calvin, Titus 1:11, *Second Epistle of Paul the Apostle to the Corinthians and the Epistles to Timothy, Titus and Philemon*, 363.

90. Calvin, 1 John 5:16, *Gospel according to St John 11-21 and the First Epistle of John*, 310.

91. Calvin, *Sermons on Job*, 548; English spelling updated; italics added. To soften

And indeed, our Lord Jesus was offered to all the world.... Our Lord Jesus suffered for all and there is neither great nor small who is not inexcusable today, for we can obtain salvation in Him. Unbelievers who turn away from Him and who deprive themselves of Him by their malice are today doubly culpable. For how will they excuse their ingratitude in not receiving the blessing in which they could share by faith? And let us realize that if we come flocking to our Lord Jesus Christ, we shall not hinder one another and prevent Him being sufficient for each of us.... Let us not fear to come to Him in great numbers, and each one of us bring his neighbours, seeing that He is sufficient to save us all.[92]

IX

Ninth, do unbelievers despise the grace that is offered to them? Yes, affirms Calvin. He asserts that "the obstinacy of men rejects the grace which has been provided and which God willingly and bountifully offers."[93] He exclaims: "As for example, behold the Turks, which cast away the grace which was purchased for all the world by Jesus Christ: the Jews do the like: the Papists, although they say not so openly, they show it in effect. And all they are as well shut out, and banished from the redemption which is purchased for us, as if Jesus Christ had never come into this world.... And thus we see now, how men are not partakers of this benefit, which was purchased them by our Lord Jesus Christ."[94] This is because one who rejects the universal offer of the gospel despises the grace of the sufferings of Christ: "For those who reject the grace offered in Him

---

the meaning, Golding added an interpolation: "Jesus Christ has [to our knowledge] suffered his death and passion as well for them as for us." This interpolation, however, is unwarranted by the French original: "Iesus Christ a enduré mort et passion pour eux aussi bien que pour nous."

92. Calvin, *Sermons on Isaiah's Prophecy*, 141. Calvin himself supported the Reformed mission effort to the Bay of Guanabara, Brazil. See Gordon, "First Protestant Missionary Effort," 12–18; Barro, "Election, Predestination and the Mission of God," 194–95; Haykin and Robinson, "How Very Important This Corner Is."

93. Calvin, Hos 13:14, *Commentaries on the Twelve Minor Prophets*, vol. 1, 477.

94. Calvin, *Sermons on the Epistles to Timothy and Titus*, 177; English spelling updated. Calvin adds, "For we see how a great part of the world deprives itself of this witness, and we see how others cast it away, or at the least, profit so little by it, that Jesus Christ dwells not in them by faith, to make them partakers of all his benefits" (ibid., 178).

[Christ] deserve to find Him the judge and avenger of such unworthy and shocking contempt."[95] After citing the apostle Paul in this context, Calvin notes, "It is as if he [Paul] had said that the Gospel is especially and in the first place intended for believers, that it may be salvation for them; but that afterwards unbelievers will not escape unpunished when they despise the grace of Christ and would rather have Him as the author of death than of life."[96]

In Calvin's sermons on Deuteronomy, he pictures the Lord Jesus Christ declaring in the day of judgment:

> ... I delivered you from endless death by suffering most cruel death myself, and for the same cause I became a man, and submitted myself even to the curse of GOD my father, that you might be blessed by my grace and by my means: and behold the reward that you have yielded me for all this, is that you have (after a sort) torn me in pieces and made a jestingstock of me, and the death that I suffered for you has been made a mockery among you, the blood which is the washing and cleansing of your souls has been as good as trampled under your feet, and to be short, you have taken occasion to ban and blaspheme me, as though I had been some wretched and cursed creature.[97]

For Calvin, unbelievers are culpable of rejecting Christ's sufferings which were "for" them and offered in mercy and grace:

> God is said to have ordained from eternity those whom he wills to embrace in love, and those upon whom he wills to vent his wrath. Yet he announces salvation to all men indiscriminately. I maintain that these statements agree perfectly with each other. For by so promising he merely means that his mercy is extended to all, provided they seek after it and implore it. But only those whom he has illumined do this. And he illumines those whom he has predestined to salvation. These latter possess the sure and unbroken truth of the promises, so that one cannot speak of any disagreement between God's eternal election and the testimony of his grace that he offers to believers.[98]

---

95. Calvin, John 3:17, *Gospel according to St John 1–10*, 76.
96. Calvin, John 3:17, *Gospel according to St John 1–10*, 76.
97. Calvin, *Sermons on Deuteronomy*, 196.
98. Calvin, *Institutes*, III.24.17; italics added. Notice the strong predestinarian language in this passage.

"As a result," explains Calvin, "all those who do not repose in him voluntarily deprive themselves of all grace."[99] "Today also, God invites all men alike to salvation through the Gospel, but the world's ingratitude makes only a few enjoy the grace, which is set out equally for all."[100]

X

Tenth, in our finite comprehension of matters, may we distinguish between our understanding of a revealed will in the universal promises of the gospel and a secret will in God's eternal decree? Yes, concedes Calvin cautiously, if we understand that we thereby manifest our human, limited comprehension—as God's will is truly unified, being "one and undivided."[101]

Hearers of the gospel are to take heart from God's redemptive desires reflected in Christ's saving mission proclaimed in the gospel.[102] "Christ bears witness not only to his power but also to his goodness, so that He may attract men to Himself by the delightfulness of His grace. For He came to save, and not to condemn, the world (John 3:17)."[103] "By saying that He did not come to condemn the world, He points to the

---

99. Calvin, *Institutes*, II.16.1. The preceding sentence states, "Accordingly, the moment we turn away even slightly from him, our salvation, which rests firmly in him, gradually vanishes away."

100. Calvin, Luke 2:10, *Harmony of the Gospels*, vol. 1, 75. Calvin adds, "While the joy, then, has been confined to a small number, in respect to God, it is called universal. And though the angel is speaking only of the chosen people, yet now with the partition wall gone the same tidings are presented to the whole human race" (ibid.).

101 Calvin, Matt 23:37, *A Harmony of the Gospels*, vol. 3, 69–70. See Thomas, *Extent of the Atonement*, 23–26. Strehle maintains that "such a dichotomy in the divine will is to be considered as attributed to our finitude and does not impugn the true oneness of the divine will in itself" (Strehle, "Universal Grace and Amyraldianism," 346n6). David Ponter agrees that, for Calvin, "in terms of our perception and finitude, we perceive diversity within the will of God. Yet within God the will is wholly unified" (Ponter, "Brief History of Deviant Calvinism," 41). Cf. Foord, "God Wills All People to Be Saved." A medieval scholastic distinction already existed between God's *voluntas signi* and *voluntas beneplaciti* (see Thomas, *Extent of the Atonement*, 23, 53). "The concept of two wills is necessary because there are many things done by God's providence which are forbidden by God's law" (ibid., 24). See also Archbald, "Comparative Study of John Calvin and Theodore Beza," 163.

102. Cf. the differing tenor in Shultz, "God's Purposes in the Atonement for the Nonelect," 161–62.

103. Calvin, Acts 5:12, *Acts of the Apostles 1–13*, 138. Cf. Calvin's comments on John 5:34; 12:47.

true purpose of His coming. For what need was there for Christ to come to destroy us who were already ruined over and over again? Therefore we should not regard anything else in Christ than that God out of His infinite goodness wished to help and save us who were lost."[104] "Now let us see to what end the Gospel is preached, and after what manner. What else is contained in it [the Gospel], but that God intends to be reconciled to the world, as says St. Paul in his fifth of the second to the Corinthians [2 Corinthians 5]?"[105] "And it is not without cause that many understand Jesus Christ only as their Judge; for they were not willing to receive Him when God wished to give Him to them as Redeemer."[106] Such comments seem to go beyond a purely abstract sufficiency; they seem to require a theology capable of including a compassionate desire of God that He does not will to administer efficaciously.[107]

104. Calvin, John 3:16–17, *Gospel according to St John 1–10*, 75.

105. Calvin, *Sermons on Deuteronomy*, 77; English spelling updated. Calvin frequently echoed the sentiment of 2 Cor 5:20 that "God was in Christ, reconciling the world unto himself."

106. Calvin, *Deity of Christ and Other Sermons*, 241–42; cf. Calvin, *Sermon on Deut 5:11*.

107. Many stumble over an "inefficacious intentionality" or "velleity" in God (see Ponter, "Brief History of Deviant Calvinism," 3–5). Such reasoning is the unspoken axiom behind such statements as, "For Calvin, all for whom Christ died are saved, and not all men are saved, it follows that Christ did not die for all men" (Helm, *Calvin and the Calvinists*, 17). Rainbow agrees that "there could be no such thing in Calvin's theology as Christ dying for someone and that person not being saved" (Rainbow, *Will of God and the Cross*, 178). Luther clearly had room for such reasoning; cf. Luther's comments on God incarnate desiring the salvation of all in Matt 23:37. Theodore Beza, however, asserted, "Nothing more absurd can be said about God than that there will be something God has not willed, or that something he has willed will not be" (Thomas, *Extent of the Atonement*, 53). For Beza, the Lutheran view of a universal atonement was "intolerable," for then Christ would have died for those already damned, and thus failed (Thomas, *Extent of the Atonement*, 56). Employing language of "desire," Reformed theologian Rienk Kuiper affirmed that God "makes on the ground of the universally suitable and sufficient atonement a most sincere, *bona fide*, offer of eternal life, not only to the elect but to all men, urgently invites them to life everlasting, and expresses the ardent desire that every person to whom this offer and this invitation come accept the offer and comply with the invitation" (Kuiper, *For Whom Did Christ Die?* 86). John Murray agreed, "We found that God himself expresses an ardent desire for the fulfillment of certain things which he has not decreed in his inscrutable counsel to come to pass.... This will of God to repentance and salvation is universalized and reveals to us, therefore, that there is in God a benevolent loving-kindness towards the repentance and salvation of even those whom he has not decreed to save. This pleasure, will, desire is expressed in the universal call to repentance" (Murray, "Free Offer of the Gospel," 131–32). For a study combining the universal call with definite

> This is His wondrous love towards the human race, that He desires all men to be saved, and is prepared to bring even the perishing to safety.... It could be asked here, if God does not want any to perish, why do so many in fact perish? My reply is that no mention is made here of the secret decree of God by which the wicked are doomed to their own ruin, but only of His loving-kindness as it is made known to us in the Gospel. There God stretches out His hand to all alike but He only grasps those (in such a way as to lead to Himself) whom He has chosen before the foundation of the world.[108]

Although this may sound like a divine inconsistency, Calvin avers:

> So again with the promises which invite all men to salvation. They do not simply and positively declare what God has decreed in His secret counsel but what He is prepared to do for all who are brought to faith and repentance.... Now this is not contradictory of His secret counsel, by which He determined to convert none but His elect. He cannot rightly on this account be thought variable, because as lawgiver He illuminates all with the external doctrine of life. But in the other sense, He brings to life whom He will, as Father regenerating by the Spirit only His sons.[109]

In his commentary on Matt 23:37, Calvin attempts a further explanation:

> Seeing that in His Word He calls all alike to salvation, and this is the object of preaching, that all should take refuge in His faith and protection, it is right to say that He wishes all to gather to Him. Now the nature of the Word shows us that here there is no description of the secret counsel of God (*arcanum Dei consilium*)—just His wishes. Certainly those whom He wishes effectively to gather, He draws inwardly by His Spirit, and calls them not merely by man's outward voice. If anyone objects that it is absurd to split God's will (*duplicem in Deo voluntatem*

---

atonement, see Nicole, "Covenant, Universal Call and Definite Atonement," 403–11).

108. Calvin, 2 Pet 3:9, *The Epistle of Paul the Apostle to the Hebrews and the First and Second Epistles of St Peter*, 364. Cf. Jerome Bolsec's criticism of Calvin's theology: "He should explain how God can be said to be simple, seeing he says that there are two wills in God, and how there can be a union in him between two contraries, to will and not to will, to have pleasure and not to have pleasure, to ordain and to forbid the same thing" (from Thomas, *Extent of the Atonement*, 15). See Holtrop, *Bolsec Controversy on Predestination*.

109. Calvin, *Concerning the Eternal Predestination*, 106.

fingi), I answer that is exactly our belief, that His will is one and undivided: but because our minds cannot plumb the profound depths of His secret election (*ad profundam arcanae electionis abyssum*) to suit our infirmity, the will of God is set before us as double (*bifarium*).... I would briefly say that as soon as doctrine, which is the rallying-point of unity, is brought into the centre, it is God's will to gather all men together (*Deum velle omnes colligere*), so that those who do not come are without excuse.[110]

Calvin clarifies elsewhere: "Truth it is, that God changes not, neither has he two wills, neither does he use any counterfeit dealing, as though he meant one thing, but would not have it so. And yet does the Scripture speak unto us after two sorts touching the will of God.... God does exhort all men generally, thereby we may judge, that it is the will of God, that all men should be saved, as he says also by the Prophet Ezekiel, 'I will not the death of a sinner, but that he turn himself and live.'"[111]

---

110. Calvin, Matt 23:37, *A Harmony of the Gospels*, vol. 3, 69–70. Beza (and many high orthodox Reformed) tended to interpret Matt 23:37 as Jesus speaking as a man, but not as the God-man (Thomas, *Extent of the Atonement*, 54). Calvin, however, connects Jesus' desire (as the God-Man) to gather in the nations with the revealed will of God.

111. Calvin, *Sermons on the Epistles to Timothy and Titus*, 152–54; English spelling updated. Calvin affirmed, "We hold then, that God wills not the death of a sinner, since he calls all equally to repentance, and promises himself prepared to receive them if they only seriously repent. If any should object—then there is no election of God, by which he has predestinated a fixed number to salvation, the answer is at hand: the Prophet does not here speak of God's secret counsel, but only recalls miserable men from despair, that they may apprehend the hope of pardon, and repent and embrace the offered salvation. If any one again objects—this is making God act with duplicity, the answer is ready, that God always wishes the same thing, though by different ways, and in a manner inscrutable to us. Although, therefore, God's will is simple, yet great variety is involved in it, as far as our senses are concerned. Besides, it is not surprising that our eyes should be blinded by intense light, so that we cannot certainly judge how God wishes all to be saved, and yet has devoted all the reprobate to eternal *destruction*, and wishes them to perish. While we look now through a glass darkly, we should be content with the measure of our own intelligence" (Calvin, Ezek 18:23, *Commentaries on the First Twenty Chapters of the Book of the Prophet Ezekiel*, vol. 2, 247–48). "But even though his will is one and simple in him, it appears manifold to us because, on account of our mental incapacity, we do not grasp how in divers ways it wills and does not will something to take place." (Calvin, *Institutes* I.18.3). The Beveridge translation (Eerdmans, 1964) has "He makes no pretense of not willing what he wills, but while in himself the will is one and undivided, to us it appears manifold, because, from the feebleness of our intellect, we cannot comprehend how, though in a different manner, he wills and wills not the very same thing" (vol. 1, 202). See also Helm, "Calvin,

Therefore, preachers may boldly proclaim that God desires sinners to repent and believe.[112] "This slowness to wrath proves that God provides for the salvation of mankind, even when he is provoked by their sins. Though miserable men provoke God daily against themselves, he yet continues to have a regard for their salvation."[113]

XI

Eleventh, so then did Christ die for all people *or* for the elect? In view of the totality of Calvin's materials, he would seemingly answer, "Yes," with further explanations.[114] Christ died intentionally as a sufficient expiation and redemption for the sins of all humanity, and he died intentionally for the efficacious salvation of the elect in particular.[115] According to Calvin, "Christ was so ordained to be the Savior of the whole world, as that He might save those that were given unto Him by the Father out of the whole world, that He might be the eternal life of them of whom He is the Head."[116] Calvin affirms that Isaiah 53 teaches that "not only were the death and passion of our Lord Jesus Christ sufficient for the salvation of the world, but that God will make them efficacious and that we shall see the fruit of them and even feel and experience it."[117] Calvin discusses

---

Indefinite Language, and Definite Atonement," 112–13.

112. Calvin declares that "God desires nothing more earnestly" (see Kuiper, *For Whom Did Christ Die?* 94).

113. Calvin, Jonah 4:2, *Commentaries on the Twelve Minor Prophets*, vol. 3, 125.

114. Calvin can do so because the universal and limited designs do not ultimately contradict one another. Curt Daniel therefore refers to a "Dualist" position in Calvin.

115. "In short," asserts Alan Clifford, "Christ died for all *sufficiently* (pardon being *conditional*), though for the elect *absolutely* and *efficiently*" (Clifford, "Geneva Revisited," 323–24). "When Calvin speaks of the effectuality of Christ's death for believers, he speaks to the efficiency side of the traditional sufficiency-efficiency formula. However, this does not impinge upon the fact that Calvin also held that in another sense, Christ died for all men" (Ponter, "Brief History of Deviant Calvinism," 24).

116. Translation from Rouwendal, "Calvin's Forgotten Position," 332. Concerning this statement, Rouwendal claims, "Just one quotation seems to say, or at least imply, that Christ died only for the elect" (ibid.). Rouwendal's claim is curious, since Calvin's comments manifestly fit within the sufficiency-efficiency distinction Rouwendal himself describes throughout the article. On connections between election, redemption, Christ as head, and believers as members of his Body, see Kennedy, *Union with Christ and the Extent of the Atonement*; cf. Rainbow, *Will of God and the Cross*, 97.

117. Calvin, *Sermons on Isaiah's Prophecy*, 116. "Christ was so ordained to be the Savior of the whole world, as that He might save those that were given unto Him by the

the case of the pardoned thief on the cross specifically, "when our Lord made effective for [the thief] His death and passion which He suffered and endured for all mankind."[118]

Calvin drew implications from these tenets, including a distinction between the purchased ransom and the application of the ransom.[119] "And what shall we do when we see souls in peril, which are so precious before God, as he has shown in that he *has ransomed them with the blood of his own Son*? If we see then a poor soul going thus to perdition, ought we not to be moved with compassion and kindness, and should we not desire God *to apply the remedy*?"[120] As mentioned above, Calvin describes the penitent thief's conversion: "God called him so suddenly, when our Lord made effective for him His death and passion which He suffered and endured for all mankind."[121]

Since Christ died for all, the gospel promises are objectively true for all. Calvin makes clear that in rejecting the external call of the gospel, one also rejects this "redemption that was purchased" in the person of Christ.[122] Unbelievers "reject the mean that God had ordained: and their unthankfulness shall be so much the more grievously punished, because they have trodden under foot the blood of our Lord Jesus Christ, which was the ransom for their souls."[123] When unbelievers reject the gospel, they are "doubly culpable" for rejecting the provision and the offer, rooted in divine love.[124]

Father out of the whole world" (as quoted in Rouwendal, "Calvin's Forgotten Classical Position," 332).

118. Calvin, *Deity of Christ and Other Sermons*, 151.

119. See Daniel, "Hyper-Calvinism and John Gill," 790; Lovell, "Love of God in Time and Eternity," 42.

120. Calvin, *Sermons on Ephesians*, 684–85; italics added. Calvin appends, "We should pray generally for all men." Archbald recognizes that Calvin is speaking of "wretched unbelievers and the ignorant" in this context. See Archbald's attempted interpretations of Calvin's statements in his "Comparative Study of John Calvin and Theodore Beza," 316–19.

121. Calvin, *Deity of Christ and Other Sermons*, 151. See Daniel, "Hyper-Calvinism and John Gill," 802.

122. See the Deuteronomy materials above.

123. Calvin, *Sermons on Galatians*, 39.

124. "For a heavier judgment remains upon the wicked because they reject the testimony of God's love" (Calvin, *Institutes*, III.24.2). Cf. Shultz, "God's Purposes in the Atonement," 161–63. Here some would distinguish (more than Shultz) between purpose and result, in consideration of John 3:16–17.

Second Peter 2:1 describes false teachers who espoused "destructive heresies," "even denying the Lord who bought them" (NKJV).[125] Calvin's commentary on this verse explains: "Christ redeemed us to have us as a people separated from all the iniquities of the world, devoted to holiness and purity. Those who throw over the traces and plunge themselves into every kind of license are not unjustly said to deny Christ, by whom they were redeemed."[126] In a collection of sermons, Calvin referred to those "who, through God, have come to know the truth of the gospel, but who defile themselves with popish abominations which are completely opposed to the Christian religion, since in doing so they disown, so far as they can, the Son of God who has redeemed them."[127] In his comments on Jude 4 ("denying the only Lord God, and our Lord Jesus Christ"), Calvin applies the text to "those who have been redeemed by His blood, and now enslave themselves again to the devil, frustrating (as best they may) that incomparable boon."[128]

XII

Twelfth, if Christ suffered as a provision for all humanity (as understood through one intentional aspect), and the Spirit works efficaciously only in particular individuals (the elect), does this mean the Trinity is not unified in redemption?[129] Some believe the Trinity would indeed be wrenched in

---

125. The Greek word behind "Lord" is *despotēs*. "But also false prophets rose among the people, just as there will be false teachers among you, who will secretly bring in destructive heresies, even denying the Master who bought them, bringing upon themselves swift destruction" (2 Pet 2:1, ESV).

126. Calvin, 2 Pet 2:1, *The Epistle of Paul the Apostle to the Hebrews and the First and Second Epistles of St Peter*, 346. Calvin explicitly states that Judas was present still at the Last Supper when Jesus declared, "This is my body, which is given for you," etc. (see the citations in Daniel, "Hyper-Calvinism and John Gill," 823n104).

127. Calvin, *Faith Unfeigned*, 1–2.

128. Calvin, Jude 4, *Harmony of the Gospels: Matthew, Mark and Luke, vol. 3, and The Epistles of James and Jude*, 325.

129. The matter of Trinitarian agreement is a common "limited atonement" argument—all members of the Godhead agreed in the divine intention of Christ dying for the elect alone (Jeffery et al., *Pierced for Our Transgressions*, 273; Nicole, "Particular Redemption," 172; cf. Macleod, *Christ Crucified*, 126). Nicole argues that a universal provision within Calvin's theology would cause inner-Trinitarian contradictions (see Nicole, "John Calvin's View of the Extent of the Atonement," 197–225; see also Letham, "Triune God, Incarnation, and Definite Atonement," 437–60). "Multi-intentioned" theologians argue that all three Trinitarian members fully agreed with the

its working.[130] According to Paul Helm, a universal provision imperils the unity of the divine operations of the Trinity. "This is a serious weakness, for Calvin takes great pains to stress both the unity of the divine will, and its singularity, that it is one will."[131] Robert Peterson, following Robert Letham, believes that Trinitarian harmony is the most important argument for so-called "limited atonement."[132] But is a lack of Trinitarian unity necessitated by a view that unites a universal provision with a decreed, particular application? Calvin declares, "For it was God who appointed His Son to be the Reconciler [or Propitiation] and determined that the sins of the world should be expiated by His death."[133] Yet, a little earlier, Calvin affirms, "For however proud men may be, they are the possession of the devil, until they are regenerated by the Spirit of Christ. For in the word *world* is here embraced the whole human race."[134]

Calvin's understanding of the outworking of redemptive history encompassed the eternal decrees, the event of the cross, and the efficacious call in one's personal life.[135] Calvin may be interpreted as describing

---

multi-intentioned nature of the atonement (cf. Hammett, "Multiple-Intentions View of the Atonement," 173; Shultz, *Multi-Intentioned View of the Atonement*, 8; Schultz, "Biblical and Theological Defense of a Multi-Intentioned View," 226). Bruce Ware, a "multi-intentioned" theologian, has authored "*Cur Deus Trinus?*" 48–56. Ware concludes, "*Cur Deus Trinus?* Must God be triune for Christ to be a Savior? Indeed, the Trinity is necessary for the identity of Christ as Savior, and the Trinity is necessary also for the efficacy of his atoning death. The God of salvation, then, can be none other than the Triune God of the Bible" (ibid., 55). Ty Kieser insists that Ware's multi-intentions view cannot be correct, based upon his understanding that "all acts of the Trinity towards creation are without division" (*opera Trinitatis ad extra sunt indivisa*) (Kieser, "Multiple Intentions, Indivisible Operations, and Christ's Atoning Work").

130. Letham, "Triune God, Incarnation, and Definite Atonement," 442; Ferguson, "'Blessèd Assurance, Jesus Is Mine'?" 629.

131. Helm, "Calvin, Indefinite Language, and Definite Atonement," 100.

132. Peterson, *Salvation Accomplished by the Son*, 567–71. Peterson highlights Eph 1:3–14; John 17:2, 6, 9–10, 19, 24; 1 Pet 1:1–2 (ibid., 571).

133. Calvin, John 14:31, *Gospel according to St John 11–21 and the First Epistle of John*, 92. The "Propitiation" rendering comes from the Pringle translation (Calvin, *Commentary on the Gospel according to John*, vol. 2, 106).

134. Calvin, John 14:30, *Gospel according to St John 11–21 and the First Epistle of John*, 92.

135. As Trueman insists, "Salvation is as surely linked to history as it is to eternity" (Trueman, "Necessity of the Atonement," 222). Jonathan Gibson refers to "four key moments of God's saving work In Christ: redemption predestined, accomplished, applied, and consummated" (Gibson, "Glorious, Indivisible, Trinitarian Work of God in Christ," 342). James B. Torrance maintains, "As in the doctrine of the Trinity there

a unified work in eternity and history: the Father's choice of the elect in eternity past within his unified plan encompassing the redemptive work of Christ and the effectual work of the Spirit, the Son's sacrificial provision at Calvary as generally proclaimed in the gospel used in the Spirit's particular work, and the Holy Spirit's effectual formation of faith in the elect through the general promise of the gospel.[136] God's master plan included the objective provision of Christ's sufferings, the general proclamation of the gospel, and the Holy Spirit's subjective, individual application of Christ's work to the elect in particular.[137] Calvin explains: "Christ's proper work was to appease the wrath of God by atoning for the sins of the world, to redeem men from death and to procure righteousness

---

are three persons, but one God, so there are three 'moments' in the one work of grace and forgiveness" (Torrance, "Incarnation and 'Limited Atonement,'" 83–84). Thomas F. Torrance grounded his view of universal atonement in the ontological relationship between Christ and all humanity through the incarnation (see Habets, "Doctrine of Election in Evangelical Calvinism," 339). Like T. F. Torrance, Andrew Purves has sought to discuss "the extent of the atonement" in "the light of the incarnation" (Purves, *Exploring Christology and Atonement*, 39, 223, 234). Summoning John McLeod Campbell, Purves argues that atonement is not to be viewed instrumentally as Christ's work, as something external to his person. "We will not drive back, as it were, into the secret councils of God to find an answer to the question of God's intention. We will, rather, attend to Jesus Christ and seek out the requested answer from the one who is himself the atonement" (ibid., 37). Cf. Torrance, *Atonement*, 182; Van Dyk, *Desire of Divine Love*; Goodloe, *John McLeod Campbell*.

136. This does not contradict statements that Christ is "the Author of election" (see Calvin, *Institutes*, III.22.7). On the distinction between accomplished provision and effectual application, see Elliott, "Availability and Application of the Atonement," 66; Chafer, "For Whom Did Christ Die?" 317; Shultz, "God's Purposes in the Atonement," 151. According to Bruce Demarest, the question should be divided into "the divine intention concerning the *provision* of the cross, which is universal, and his intention concerning the *application* thereof, which is particular" (Demarest, *Cross and Salvation*, 193; cf. 189). Demarest continues, "We find biblical warrant for dividing the question into God's purpose regarding the *provision* of the Atonement and his purpose concerning the *application* thereof" (ibid., 193). A. H. Strong claimed, "Not the *atonement* therefore is limited, but the *application* of the atonement through the work of the Holy Spirit" (Strong, *Systematic Theology*, 421).

137. Lane, "Quest for the Historical Calvin," 112; Banman, "Union with the Incarnate Saviour," 45–47; Faber, "Saving Work of the Holy Spirit in Calvin," 1–11. In the case of Old Testament saints, "Christ's work is proleptically effectual for those who died before Christ" (Crisp, *Deviant Calvinism*, 227n17). The prophets, for example, trusted in a coming provision, and the application of salvation was predicated upon such faith. The retrospective application of salvation to Old Testament saints illustrates that "simultaneity is not necessity" (ibid., 278). See also Elliott, "Availability and Application of the Atonement."

and life. That of the Spirit is to make us partakers not only of Christ Himself, but of all His blessings."[138]

Furthermore, the three roles of the Trinitarian Members are interwoven in perfect unity.[139] In this Trinitarian plan, Christ died for all as offered in the gospel and for the effectual salvation of the elect, and the Spirit uses the proclamation of the gospel promises to form faith in the elect, whom the Father chose in eternity past, to be reached through the gospel pointing to the underlying provision.[140] All three Members are of one, eternal mind concerning this interweaving of election, provision, proclamation, and application.[141]

The Son offers himself as a sacrifice for the sins of the world, providing an objective basis for believers to cast upon as they are efficaciously drawn by the Spirit, in keeping with the Father's pretemporal ordination and decree concerning the elect.[142] Consider a Trinitarian prayer of Calvin:

---

138. Calvin, John 14:16, *Gospel according to St John 11–21 and the First Epistle of John*, 82. At the same time, the three Trinitarian members are unified in the single, divine plan executed through distinctive roles. It would be a mistake to imply that the Father's wrath was turned to love only upon the sacrifice of the Son, as the Father had already sent the Son in love (see Hay, "Heart of Wrath," 361–78); McCormack, "For Us and Our Salvation," 301–7; Calvin, *Institutes* II.16.2.

139. Lovell, "Love of God in Time and Eternity," 43.

140. In Calvin, the Father is the cause (*causa*), the Son is the substance (*materia*), and the Spirit is the effect (*effectus*) of our salvation (see Rainbow, *Will of God and the Cross*, 89); cf. Calvin, *Institutes* III.14.17, where the "instrumental cause" is faith and the "final cause" is divine justice and praise for God's goodness. Clifford further interrelates the Trinitarian works, as he affirms, "The Father reaches out to all while only grasping the elect; the Son redeems all sufficiently but only the elect effectually; the elect alone are regenerated by the Holy Spirit but others are still subject to His influence" (Clifford, "Calvin & Calvinism," 67). See also Clifford, *Amyraut Affirmed*, 51–52.

141. Blacketer contends, "Thus to claim, for example, that God the Father intends the salvation of the elect, while the Son intends the salvation of every individual, would be considered absurd, since there cannot be two contradictory wills in the godhead" (Blacketer, "Definite Atonement in Historical Perspective," 322). This argument misses the possibility that all three Members agree to a unified plan in which each Member fulfills distinctive roles, and they *all* jointly intend *both* the universal aspects *and* the particular aspects of the unified plan.

142. Calvin, *Deity of Christ and Other Sermons*, 87; cf. Calvin, Sermon on 1 Tim 6:13–16, *Sermons on the Epistles to Timothy and Titus*, 612: "If we will be partakers of all that was gotten us by the Son of God, we must have patience: after that he has shown that when Jesus Christ had suffered for the sins of the world, he went up into heaven, he added, 'that this was to arm us to patience.' For it is nothing, if the fruit of this redemption, which was purchased for us, does not show itself by faith: for otherwise,

> Moreover, we offer up our prayers unto Thee, O most Gracious God and most merciful Father, for all men in general, that as Thou art pleased to be acknowledged the Saviour of the whole human race by the redemption accomplished by Jesus Christ Thy Son, so those who are still strangers to the knowledge of him, and immersed in darkness, and held captive by ignorance and error, may, by Thy Holy Spirit shining upon them, and by Thy gospel sounding in their ears, be brought back to the right way of salvation, which consists in knowing Thee the true God and Jesus Christ whom Thou hast sent.[143]

This Trinitarian prayer weaves together the provision of the Son as "Saviour of the whole human race" (general) with the efficacious work of the Holy Spirit (particular). Even as Paul fervently prayed for the unsaved among his fellow Israelites in the context of his extended discussion on election (Rom 10:1; cf. 9:1–3), so Calvin entreated the Triune God for the lost of the whole human race.

We have highlighted a multitude of evidences for some notion of a *provision* of "universal redemption" in Calvin.[144] One is struck by the number of universal-sounding statements he made concerning the death of Christ, without at all discounting other affirmations that Christ died "for us" or "for our sake" or "for our sins."[145]

Before moving on, one other point should be emphasized. Statements that teach that Jesus died for the church—or believers, the flock, or the Body of Christ—do not necessarily prove that Jesus *only* intended

---

it will become a thing of naught, and for our parts utterly perish" (English spelling updated). Some would say that Christ's death is necessary to make salvation possible for the elect, Spirit-formed faith is necessary to make it actual, and the Father's election makes it certain (cf. Ware, "Extent of the Atonement").

143. Calvin, "Forms of Prayer for the Church," 102.

144. For more examples, see Ponter, "John Calvin (1509–1564) on Unlimited Expiation." While there are both "universalist" and "particularist" teachings in Calvin, Lane finds the "universalist" materials to be "found in wider contexts" and to be "the most compelling, being the very structure of the *Institutes*," and thus "the overwhelming emphasis in Calvin is that Christ died for all" (Lane, "Calvin versus Calvinism Revisited," 35). According to Thomas, "How is it that Calvin could teach limited and universal redemption in the same place? Only by appreciating that he viewed the atonement from two vantage points can this apparent confusion be understood. From the perspective of election, Christ died for 'all sorts' but not all individuals. From the perspective of the promise of the gospel, he died for all the world, even for those who do not participate in the purchased benefit" (Thomas, *Extent of the Atonement*, 33).

145. See also Kennedy, "Was Calvin a 'Calvinist'?" 196–99.

his atonement as a provision for the elect *alone*.¹⁴⁶ Nor do they logically necessitate a *single* intention in the atonement.¹⁴⁷ In the same way, the apostle Paul's statement that Jesus Christ "loved me and gave himself for me" does not prove that Christ died *only* for Paul alone.¹⁴⁸ If some passages in Calvin speak of Christ's dying for the elect and some speak of his dying for all (in some sense), the general and particular statements can be reconciled into one system that teaches both (in differing ways), but they cannot be reconciled without difficulty into one system that maintains *only* strict, limited redemption *alone*.¹⁴⁹

---

146. See Rainbow, *Will of God and the Cross*, 112–16; Archbald, "Comparative Study of John Calvin and Theodore Beza," 326–27. Calvin could repetitively emphasize that Christ died "for us," "for our sins," and "for our sake," as in his comments upon 1 Pet 2:24, where such phrases appear numerous times.

147. Dabney, *Lectures in Systematic Theology*, 521.

148. See Daniel, "Hyper-Calvinism and John Gill," 811–12.

149. Hammett, "Multiple-Intentions View of the Atonement," 159. See also Suhany, "John Calvin and the Extent of the Atonement Revisited," 4.

CHAPTER THREE

Evidences for "Limited Atonement"

THE MATERIALS FOUND IN the previous chapter have not convinced all interpreters of John Calvin that he espoused a provision of "universal redemption." Doubtless, Calvin often described Jesus Christ as redeeming the elect, his church, his people, and his sheep.[1] And facets of Calvin's theology (such as his doctrine of God's decreed will; his version of double predestination; and his espousal of eternal, unconditional election) definitely favor particularist themes.[2] But does the divine intention to apply

---

1. See Shultz, *Multi-Intentioned View of the Extent of the Atonement*, 25. Cf. Luke 22:19; 1 Cor 11:24; 15:3; Gal 2:20; 3:13; Eph 5:2; 1 Thess 5:10; Demarest, *Cross and Salvation*, 191. Moreover, Beza commented more explicitly on the limits and intentions of Christ's satisfaction during Calvin's lifetime (although still not fully elaborated), without any response from Calvin (Blacketer, "Blaming Beza," 123).

2. See Shepherd, *Nature and Function of Faith*, 69; McGowan, "Was Westminster Calvinist?" 52; Thomas, *Extent of the Atonement*, 34–35; Horton, "Traditional Reformed View," 112–13; Greenbury, "Calvin's Understanding of Predestination." Calvin spoke of divine permission as "babble" and "absurd talk," unlike a doctrine of the "permissive will" of God as a commonplace tenet in some versions of later Reformed theology (Calvin, *Institutes* I.18.1; see Trueman, "Calvin and Calvinism," 237). "While Calvin did not invent the notion of double predestination—it can be found in Augustine and Gottschalk, and was revived by Bradwardine—his advocacy of it in a variety of writings certainly popularized the idea in the Reformed tradition" (Sinnema, "Calvin and the Canons of Dordt," 90). Muller hypothesizes that Calvin initially added the doctrine of predestination to his *Institutes* in 1539 because he was laboring on his Romans commentary at the time (Muller, "Placement of Predestination in Reformed Theology," 195). Timothy George summarizes Calvin's doctrine of predestination in three words: *absolute, particular,* and *double* (George, *Theology of the Reformers*, 233). George also emphasizes the Christocentric, pastoral, and doxological nature of Calvin's doctrine of predestination. "Predestination, as Calvin understood it, is neither a church steeple from which to view the human landscape, nor a pillow to sleep on. It

Christ's death effectually to the elect alone (who are reached by God's own gracious, unconditional initiative) entail the fullness of God's intention in the death of Christ, in a singularly strict manner?

In several instances, Calvin uses terminology that lends itself to the narrower and more defined "limited atonement" perspective emphasized by many later theologians in the Reformed tradition.[3] These materials have encouraged various interpreters to argue that the later "limited atonement" tradition simply made more explicit what was implicitly Calvin's own view or at least his bent of inclination.[4] Scholars who portray Calvin as a proponent of strictly "limited atonement" accentuate three of the reformer's passages in particular.[5]

First evidence for "limited atonement"

First, a text that is commonly discussed appears in Calvin's 1561 "Reply to Heshusius," a Lutheran.[6] Regarding this text, Frederick Leahy (a proponent of "limited redemption" himself) asserts, "Students of Calvin have found only one passage which could be regarded as explicitly denying an unlimited atonement."[7] William Cunningham called the passage in

---

is rather a stronghold in times of temptation and trials and a confession of praise to God's grace and to His glory" (ibid., 234). On Calvin's predestinarian understanding of reprobation, see also Klooster, *Calvin's Doctrine of Predestination*, 55–88.

3. Garcia, *Life in Christ*, 192.

4. See Gatiss, *For Us and for Our Salvation*, 75.

5. For example, see Leahy, "Calvin and the Extent of the Atonement," 59–62; Murray, "Calvin on the Extent of the Atonement," 21–22; Blacketer, "Definite Atonement in Historical Perspective," 314–15; Cunningham, *Reformers and the Theology of the Reformation*, 400; Reymond, "Consistent Supralapsarian Perspective on Election," 162n14; Gatiss, *For Us and for Our Salvation*, 71; cf. Bell, "Calvin and the Extent of the Atonement," 118–20. Ponter focuses the argumentation: either "these three instances must be read in the light of the larger body of evidence" or "these three instances regulate and determine the meaning and intent of all that Calvin says regarding the extent of the atonement" (Ponter, "Review Essay (Part Two)," 269). Ponter opts for the former. Rainbow adds a fourth passage: Calvin's comments on John 12:32 (Rainbow, *Will of God and the Cross*, 65, 177). Yet Calvin interprets this verse as a reference to the efficacious gathering of the elect without drawing an implication concerning the extent of the provision of the atonement. Daniel notes Calvin's comments on 1 Pet 2:22 yet disagrees with a strict "limited" view of the material (see Daniel, "Hyper-Calvinism and John Gill," 815–16).

6. Available as Calvin, "Clear Explanation of Sound Doctrine concerning the True Partaking."

7. Leahy, "Calvin and the Extent of the Atonement," 61.

Calvin's "Reply to Heshusius" "a very explicit denial of the universality of the atonement," but one that "stands alone—so far as we know—in Calvin's writings."[8] Hans Boersma highlights this same text as an unambiguous example of strictly "particular atonement."[9] In his "Reply to Heshusius," Calvin wrote, "The first thing to be explained is how Christ is present with unbelievers, to be the spiritual food of their souls, and in short the life and salvation of the world. As he [Heshusius] adheres so doggedly to the words [in 1 Cor 11], I should like to know how the wicked can eat the flesh of Christ which was not crucified for them, and how they can drink the blood which was not shed to expiate their sins?"[10]

The context is Calvin's opposition to the "monstrous dogma" of an orally consumed, real presence of Christ in the Eucharistic elements, received by both believers *and* unbelievers.[11] Rouwendal notes, "Calvin's intention was to make clear that Christ is not corporally present. In the immediate context of the quoted sentence, he uses the argument that if Christ were present corporally, the ungodly would eat his flesh and drink his blood, which Calvin deemed impossible."[12] Heshusius adhered to the "barbarous eating" of an oral consumption of Jesus' body and blood. In response, Calvin queried how "the flesh of Christ is eaten by unbelievers, and yet is not vivifying."[13] Calvin explained elsewhere,

> Wherefore the supper is a certain attestation, which is addressed to the bad as well as the good, in order to offer Christ to all indiscriminately; but this is not to say that all receive him when he is offered to them. And in fact it were grossly absurd to hold

---

8. Cunningham, *Reformers and the Theology of the Reformation*, 396.

9. Boersma, "Calvin and the Extent of the Atonement," 333.

10. Calvin, *Theological Treatises*, 285; cf. 270, 286; the Latin is available in Strehle, "Universal Grace and Amyraldianism," 354n62.

11. Cf. Bell, "Calvin and the Extent of the Atonement," 119-20: "It is readily seen that throughout this debate, Calvin is *not* discussing the atonement, but rather, the necessity of the presence of the Spirit and faith for the efficacy of the sacrament. He definitely is *not* making a statement on the extent of the atonement" (cf. Bell, *Calvin and Scottish Theology*, 16-17). This context compels Henri Blocher to "confess a small measure of uncertainty" in using the text as an argument for limited redemption, though he is still inclined to do so (see Blocher, "Atonement in John Calvin's Theology," 280).

12. Rouwendal, "Calvin's Forgotten Classical Position," 331.

13. Calvin, *Theological Treatises*, 273; cf. 263, 267, 277. "Christ cannot be separated from his Spirit" and "as the living bread and the victim immolated on the cross, cannot enter a human body devoid of his Spirit" (ibid., 285).

that Jesus Christ is received by those who are entire strangers to him, and that the wicked eat his body and drink his blood while destitute of his Spirit.... Their offence then is that they rejected Christ when he was presented to them.[14]

Curt Daniel reasons, "What Calvin is denying is that these [Lord's Supper] verses are interpreted literally and that the wicked eat Christ. He is not denying that the flesh of Christ was crucified for the wicked."[15]

In such a polemical context, Calvin emphasized the reception of Christ by the believer alone—in faith—and therefore drew his argument from the efficacious, vivifying application of the atonement to the believing recipient.[16] Only a few paragraphs earlier, Calvin himself declared that when the ungodly at the Lord's Table "impiously reject what is liberally offered to them, they are deservedly condemned for profane and brutish contempt, inasmuch as they set at nought that victim by which the sins of the world were expiated and men reconciled to God."[17]

Elsewhere, Calvin's own theology of the Lord's Supper further spoke of the universal provision of Christ's sacrifice.[18] Calvin interpreted Jesus' words as affirming, "The bread which I will give is my flesh which I will give for the life of the world ... as the flesh was offered once *on the cross*

---

14. Calvin, "Confession of Faith in Name of the Reformed Churches of France," 158. Cf. "given" vs. "received" in Calvin, *Theological Treatises*, 283.

15. Daniel, "Hyper-Calvinism and John Gill," 820. For an alternative interpretation by Alan Clifford, see Daniel, "Hyper-Calvinism and John Gill," 819n98.

16. Rouwendal, "Calvin's Forgotten Classical Position," 331.

17. Calvin, Theological Treatises, 284. "Indeed he is certainly offered in common to all, unbelievers as well as believers" (ibid., 316). See also Daniel, "Hyper-Calvinism and John Gill," 819n97.

18. Cf. Calvin on Mark 14:24: "The word *many* does not mean a part of the world only, but the whole human race: he contrasts *many* with *one*, as if to say that he would not be the Redeemer of one man, but would meet death to deliver many of their cursed guilt.... So when we come to the holy table not only should the general idea come to our mind that the world is redeemed by the blood of Christ, but also each should reckon to himself that his own sins are covered" (from Calvin, *Harmony of the Gospels*, vol. 3, 139; cf. Calvin's comments on Luke 22:19: "There is no benefit in the crucified flesh itself except for those who eat it by faith" [ibid., 138]). See also Calvin, Matt 20:28, *Harmony of the Gospels*, vol. 2, 277, interpreting the phrase "and to give his life a ransom for many": "'Many' is used, not for a definite number, but for a large number, in that He sets Himself over against all others. And this is its meaning also in Rom. 5.15, where Paul is not talking of a part of mankind but of the whole human race." Cf. Kennedy, "Was Calvin a 'Calvinist'?" 202; Kennedy, *Union with Christ and the Extent of the Atonement*, 32–33 and 66n41 on Calvin's understanding of "definite" in this passage.

for the salvation of the world."[19] Calvin explained, "Also when we minister the Lord's Supper, we rehearse what was said by our Lord Jesus Christ: This is my body which is delivered for you: this is my blood which is shed for the salvation of the world."[20] "We are ordered to eat the body which was crucified for us; in other words, to become partakers of the sacrifice by which the sins of the world were expiated."[21] "He addresses the disciples by name and encourages the faithful as individuals to apply the pouring-out of His blood to their benefit. So when we come to the holy table not only should the general idea come to our mind that the world is redeemed by the blood of Christ, but also each should reckon to himself that his own sins are covered."[22] When such evidence is compared with the "Reply to Heshusius," it underscores how Calvin's opposition was targeting Heshusius' (Lutheran) view of communion, not all senses of a universal dimension in Christ's cross death as offered.[23]

Second evidence for "limited atonement"

As a *second* evidence for a strictly "limited atonement" in Calvin, some scholars point to his commentary on 1 John 2:2.[24] For example, Robert Peterson asserts that it is "significant" that the *Institutes* are "silent" on the question of the extent of the atonement.[25] "However," Peterson

19. Calvin, "Last Admonition to Joachim Westphal," 425; italics added.
20. Calvin, *Sermons on Deuteronomy*, 1208; English spelling updated.
21. Calvin, "Last Admonition to Joachim Westphal," 481.
22. Calvin, Mark 14:24, *Harmony of the Gospels*, vol. 3, 139. All of these points (and more) have been made by others. See Daniel, "Hyper-Calvinism and John Gill," 817–23; Ponter, "John Calvin and Tileman Heshusius"; Kennedy, *Union with Christ and the Extent of the Atonement*, 53–56; Costley, "Understanding Calvin's Argument against Heshusius"; Costley notes that Calvin did not speak of the "non-elect," but the "ungodly" or "wicked." Calvin was referring to unbelievers (some of whom might later become believers in God's outworked plan, thereby manifesting their divine election).
23. Williams, *Heart of Piety*, 132–35; Allen, "Calvin and the Extent of the Atonement," 7–9. On differences between the Lutheran and Reformed views of the Lord's Supper, see Denlinger, "'Men of Gallio's Naughty Faith?'" 57–83.
24. Blacketer, "Blaming Beza," 135.
25. Peterson, "Calvin on Christ's Saving Work," 246. "The *Institutes* seem to offer little help in determining Calvin's view. . . . Above all, why does Calvin not even mention the extent of the atonement when he summarizes his views on the person and work of the mediator in the *Institutes*? . . . In his preface to the reader in the 1559 *Institutes*, Calvin gives his own methodological statement that one should interpret his commentaries doctrinally on the basis of the *Institutes*" (Peterson, *Calvin and the Atonement*, 117–20). Calvin himself affirmed that the pattern of his theology was

adds, "appeal can be made to Calvin's commentaries to argue for limited atonement."[26] Peterson then appends a footnote that cites Calvin's commentary upon 1 John 2:2 as an example. Concerning this verse ("He is the propitiation for our sins, and not for ours only but also for the sins of the whole world" [ESV]), Calvin wrote,

> He put this in for amplification, that believers might be convinced that the expiation made by Christ extends to all who by faith embrace the Gospel. But here the question may be asked as to how the sins of the whole world have been expiated. I pass over the dreams of the fanatics, who make this a reason to extend salvation to all the reprobate and even to Satan himself. Such a monstrous idea is not worth refuting. Those who want to avoid this absurdity have said that Christ suffered sufficiently for the whole world but effectively only for the elect. This solution has commonly prevailed in the schools. Although I allow the truth of this, I deny that it fits this passage. For John's purpose was only to make this blessing common to the whole Church. Therefore, under the word "all" he does not include the reprobate, but refers to all who would believe and those who were scattered through various regions of the earth. For, as is meet, the grace of Christ is really made clear when it is declared to be the only salvation of the world.[27]

Calvin applied the verse to "the expiation made by Christ" that "extends [*extendi*] to all who by faith embrace the Gospel," as his polemical sights were set upon the "monstrous idea" and "absurdity" of universalists who "admit into salvation" [*in salutem admittunt*] "all the reprobate and even Satan himself."[28] As Trueman quips, "Calvin clearly rejects

---

found in the *Institutes* rather than in his more occasional sermons, commentaries, and treatises (*Institutes*, preface ["John Calvin to the Reader"], 4–5). Why does Calvin not explicitly emphasize the extent of the atonement in the *Institutes*? Perhaps because he accepted some form of the "medieval synthesis" on the matter as a "given," and therefore scholarship must continue to investigate the continuities and discontinuities between Calvin and the Middle Ages (and his own contemporaries). See the materials being collected by David Ponter at "Calvin on Unlimited Expiation." Cf. Archbald, "Comparative Study of John Calvin and Theodore Beza," 9–68.

26. Peterson, "Calvin on Christ's Saving Work," 246.

27. Calvin, 1 John 2:2, *Gospel according to St John 11–21 and the First Epistle of John*, 244. See also Calvin, John 10:11.

28. Cf. the doctrine of *apokatastasis* found in Origen's writings. Calvin maintained an important distinction: "The benefit of redemption is offered to the ungodly, but not to the devils" (Calvin, Col 1:20, *Epistles of Paul the Apostle to the Galatians, Ephesians,*

the universalist interpretation of this verse."29 Calvin attacked this same "universalistic" interpretation of 1 John 2:2 in his *Concerning the Eternal Predestination of God*.30 Georgius argued that if Christ expiated the sins of the whole world, then reprobates also would be effectually saved—or the only other option is to say the reprobates are not a part of the world.31 Calvin's tactic was to accept 1 John 2:2 as relating to the effectual application of Christ's expiation, which "extends" only to "the whole Church."32 At the same time, Calvin affirmed, "It is incontestable that Christ came for the expiation of the sins of the whole world."33

Here one is reminded of Calvin's commentary upon Rom 5:18: "Paul makes grace common to all men, not because it in fact *extends* [*extendatur*] to all, but because it is offered to all."34 Calvin went on to acknowledge that "Although Christ suffered for the sins of the whole world, and is offered by the goodness of God without distinction to all men, yet not all receive him."35 As Nigel Westhead notes, "The co-ordinate and co-extensiveness of offering and suffering are clear in Calvin's comments on Romans 5:18. '... Christ *suffered for* the sins of the world, and is *offered* by the goodness of God without distinction to all men' . . . ."36 Neverthe-

---

Philippians and Colossians, 313).

29. Trueman, "Definite Atonement View," 38.

30. Calvin, *Concerning the Eternal Predestination*, 149.

31. Calvin opposed the use of 1 John 2:2 as found in Pighius and Georgius. See Ponter, "Review Essay (Part Two)," 266–67.

32. Ponter, "Review Essay (Part Two)," 266. "Hence, we conclude that, though reconciliation is offered to all through Him, yet the benefit is peculiar to the elect, that they may be gathered into the society of life. However, while I say it is offered to all, I do not mean that this embassy, by which on Paul's testimony (II Cor 5:18) God reconciles the world to Himself, reaches to all, but that it is not sealed indiscriminately on the hearts of all to whom it comes so as to be effectual" (Calvin, *Concerning the Eternal Predestination*, 149).

33. Calvin, *Concerning the Eternal Predestination*, 149.

34. Calvin, Rom 5:18, *Epistles of Paul the Apostle to the Romans and to the Thessalonians*, 117–18; italics added. In a published French sermon on Deuteronomy, Calvin employs "extends" in a general manner, declaring that "the first degree of love" (in which "Jesus Christ offers himself generally to all men without exception to be their redeemer") "extends" [*s'estend*] to all, represented by Jesus' arms "extended" [*estendus*] to all, both great and small (see Calvin, *Sermons on Deuteronomy*, 167).

35. Calvin, Rom 5:18, *Epistles of Paul the Apostle to the Romans and to the Thessalonians*, 118. See also Daniel, "Hyper-Calvinism and John Gill," 803.

36. Nigel Westhead as found in Clifford, *Calvinus*, 56. Roger Nicole conceded that Calvin's commentary upon Rom 5:18 "comes perhaps the closest to providing support for Amyraut's thesis" (see Clifford, "Calvin & Calvinism," 38). Nicole argued that the

less, the grace does not (efficaciously) "*extend*" to all. Elsewhere Calvin insisted, "the virtue and benefits of Christ are *extended* unto, and belong to, none but the children of God."[37]

Taking this evidence of salvation "extending" efficaciously only to the elect back into our examination of 1 John 2, Calvin's specific point was *not* to deny that Christ suffered for all or was offered to all. Rather, Calvin insisted that Christ's expiation did not efficaciously "extend" to all, but only to "all who by faith embrace the Gospel."[38] Calvin was willing to allow the "classical" maxim, "Christ suffered sufficiently for the whole world, but efficiently only for the elect."[39] Nevertheless, at this contextual juncture, he was battling opponents of a "universalist" stripe (who asserted that all would be saved in the end), who read *propitiatio* as efficacious reconciliation.[40] Calvin granted that 1 John 2:2 spoke of the *efficacious* work of salvation, and he was (understandably) unwilling to apply that efficacious work to the reprobate and Satan himself. He therefore interpreted "the whole world" in 1 John 2:2 as "the whole Church." In this step, Calvin paralleled Augustine's interpretation.[41] Moreover, Calvin took the opportunity to emphasize the exclusivity of salvation in Christ: "For, as is

---

passage "may well refer simply to the relevance of the sacrifice of Christ to a universal offer, without actually asserting a substitutionary suffering for all mankind" (Nicole, "Moyse Amyraut," 83n38). A nineteenth-century translator of the passages recorded in a footnote, "It appears from this sentence that Calvin held general redemption" (see Bell, *Calvin and Scottish Theology*, 34n30). Contrast Helm, *Calvin and the Calvinists*, 44. See Beach, "Calvin's Treatment of the Offer of the Gospel," 63.

37. Calvin, *Treatise on the Eternal Predestination of God*. English translation from Cole, *Calvin's Calvinism*, 208.

38. Cf. Calvin, John 17:9. Contrast the tenor of this reading with Gatiss, *For Us and for Our Salvation*, 71.

39. Nettles, "John Calvin's Understanding of the Death of Christ," 299. Contrast Kendall, *Calvin and English Calvinism*, 16n2. At the same time, Calvin seemed to believe that the classical formula did not do justice to the full divine plan in that it did not explicitly recognize God's sovereign application of salvation (see Shultz, *Multi-Intentioned View of the Extent of the Atonement*, 25).

40. See Daniel, "Hyper-Calvinism and John Gill," 804n68.

41. See Augustine's "First Homily" of his "Homilies on 1 John," in *Augustine: Later Works*, 265–66; cf. Blacketer, "Definite Atonement in Historical Perspective," 309–10; Thomas, *Extent of the Atonement*, 32. Blacketer could have added Fulgentius of Ruspe to his discussion on page 310. See Gumerlock, *Fulgentius of Ruspe on the Saving Will of God*.

meet, the grace of Christ is really made clear when it is declared to be the only salvation of the world."[42]

To reiterate, Calvin allowed the scholastic formula to stand as true.[43] But he did not believe this maxim was the interpretive key to 1 John 2:2. Within his polemic (as Calvin's argumentative sights were set upon "universalists" who used 1 John 2:2 to espouse the ultimate salvation of the reprobates and even Satan), Calvin granted that the text spoke of the *efficientia* of salvation. But he replied that 1 John 2 describes Christ's "efficient" expiation for "the whole Church," including those "scattered through various parts of the world." In such an interpretation, the text was irrelevant to the question of "sufficiency." Calvin therefore parts company from so-called "four-point Calvinists" who interpret 1 John 2:2 as an all-sufficient provision of expiation for the "whole world." On the other hand, in various other passages, Calvin could speak of the expiation of the sins of the world without any further comment or explanation.[44]

Interestingly, Calvin's interpretation of "world" in 1 John 2:2 is in tension with his own approach to the meaning of *world* in John 17:21 ("that the world may believe that thou hast sent me"). Calvin commented on this verse, "Some explain *the world* as the elect who were then still dispersed. But since the word 'world' all through this chapter means the reprobate, I am more inclined to take a different view. It happens that immediately afterwards He separates the same world which He now mentions from all His people."[45] In the context of John 17, Calvin accentuated the fact that Christ intercedes only for disciples and not for the world (John 17:9).[46] Throughout the Johannine literature, the "world" stands

---

42. Calvin, 1 John 2:2, *Gospel according to St John 11-21 and the First Epistle of John*, 244. Elsewhere, Calvin affirms, "And there was not any sacrifice sufficient to make atonement [reconciliation] between God and the world, but only our Lord Jesus Christ's offering up of himself" (Calvin, *Sermons on Deuteronomy*, 660; English spelling updated).

43. See R. Scott Clark's overview of the doctrines of election and predestination in the Middle Ages (Clark, "Election and Predestination," 90-96); cf. Rainbow, *Will of God and the Cross*.

44. See Ponter, "John Calvin (1509-1564) on Unlimited Expiation."

45. Calvin, John 17:21, *Gospel according to St John 11-21 and the First Epistle of John*, 148.

46. See Muller, *Christ and the Decree*, 34-35: "The Gospel appeal is universal but Christ's intercession, like the divine election, is personal, individual, particular." Even in his comments upon John 17:9, however, Calvin adds, "And Christ Himself afterwards prayed for all indiscriminately." He saw this as instructive for believers: "We ought to pray that this and that and every man may be saved and so embrace the

in opposition to God's values and people. In his comments upon John 16:33, Calvin explained, "Under the name *world*, Christ here embraces everything that is opposed to the salvation of the godly and especially all the corruptions which Satan uses to lay snares for us."[47] Finally, it should be noted that both Girolamo Zanchi and Jacob Kimedoncius espoused a "limited" reading of 1 John 2:2, and yet they are acknowledged by Richard Muller as teaching a form of universal redemption.[48]

Third evidence for "limited atonement"

The *third* set of materials scholars often cite as evidence for a strictly "limited atonement" in Calvin can be found in his explanations of 1 Tim 2:4.[49] While interpreting this verse (in which God "desires all people to be saved and to come to the knowledge of the truth" [NKJV]), Calvin contended that "no one unless deprived of sense and judgement can believe that salvation is ordained in the secret counsel of God equally for all."[50] This, of course, would entail universalism in ultimate salvation. As

---

whole human race, because we cannot yet distinguish the elect from the reprobate" (Calvin, John 17:9, *Gospel according to St John 11-21 and the First Epistle of John*, 140). Contra Nettles, Ponter insists that "there is no evidence in Calvin that the intercession delimits the scope of the expiation or that both are restricted to the same group" (Ponter, "Review Essay (Part Two)," 269; cf. 261). Ponter adds: "All that can be shown, and which is entirely correct, is that, for Calvin the intercession is grounded upon the expiation, such that no expiation, then no intercession is possible. There is no evidence for the inverse, that if there is an expiation for a person, then there will be an effectual high-priestly intercession for that same person" (ibid.). Ponter provides a "historically instructive" parallel from Musculus: "Moreover it is the office of a Mediator not only to pray but also to offer. And he offered himself upon the Cross for all men. For (as says Paul) 'Christ died for all men'" (as found in ibid., 261). Contra John Owen's understanding of "the inseparability of oblation and intercession" (see Tay, *Priesthood of Christ*, 18).

47. Calvin, John 16:33, *Gospel according to St John 11-21 and the First Epistle of John*, 133.

48. I thank Tony Byrne for this insight. See Muller, "Review of *English Hypothetical Universalism*," 149-50; Muller, "Revising the Predestination Paradigm."

49. For a classification of five explanations of "God wills all people to be saved" in the medieval era, see Foord, "God Wills All People to Be Saved—Or Does He?" 190.

50. Calvin, *Concerning the Eternal Predestination*, 109. Calvin discusses this Scriptural text in eight places, six of which can be found at http://calvinandcalvinism.com/?p=128. "Calvin's basic understanding of 1 Timothy 2:4 appears to remain stable throughout these writings" (Foord, "God Wills All People to Be Saved," 197). For the delineation of the eight passages, see the listing in ibid.: *De aeterna Dei praedestinatione*

in his comments upon 1 John 2:2, Calvin warned against using this text to defend such heretical universalism.[51] Calvin responded, "Who does not see that the reference [to "all men" in 1 Tim 2:4] is to orders of men rather than individual men? Nor indeed does the distinction lack substantial ground: what is meant is not individuals of nations but nations of individuals."[52] Calvin added, "At any rate, the context makes it clear that no other will is intended than that which appears in the external preaching of the Gospel. Thus Paul means that God wills the salvation of all whom He mercifully invites by the preaching of Christ."[53]

Thus Calvin interprets "all men" in 1 Tim 2:4 as a reference to "orders" or "classes" of humans (a common "five-point Calvinist" view today).[54] But then he correlates the passage to the *external preaching* of the gospel rather than the "secret counsel of God." This view is confirmed by his commentary on 1 Tim 2:3–5:

> For although it is true that we must not try to decide what is God's will by prying into His secret counsel, when He has made it plain to us by external signs, yet that does not mean that God has not determined secretly within Himself what He wishes to do with every single man. But I pass from that point which is not relevant to the present context, for the apostle's meaning here is simply that no nation of the earth and no rank of society is excluded from salvation, since God wills to offer the Gospel to all without exception. Since the preaching of the Gospel brings life, he rightly concludes that God regards all men as being equally worthy to share in salvation. But he is speaking of

---

8.2 (1552), *Commentarii in priorem epistolam ad Timotheum* (1556, second revised edition), *Commentarii in priorem epistolam Pauli ad Corinthios* I.27 (1556, second revised edition), *De Occulta Dei Providentia* Article I (1558), *Institutio Christianae Religionis* III.24.16 (1559), *Commentarii in Acta Apostolorum* 17.11 (1560), *Ioannis Calvini Praelectiones in librum prophetiarum Danielis* 7.27 (1560), *Sermons sur les épitres à Timothee et à Tite*, Sermon 13 (1561).

51. As in Origen's *apokatastasis* (cf. John Wyclif's opposition to Origen's doctrine in Foord, "God Wills All People to Be Saved," 190). Calvin insists that the doctrine of salvation is not "effectually available to all" (Calvin, *Institutes* III.22.10).

52. Calvin, *Concerning the Eternal Predestination*, 109.

53. Calvin, *Concerning the Eternal Predestination*, 109. "Thus, this verse is not to be understood as teaching anything about God's actual intention to save certain individuals. Rather, it should be understood only to be dealing with the universal offer of salvation" (Kennedy, *Union with Christ and the Extent of the Atonement*, 44).

54. "That is, a distinction must be made between the world as comprised of classes of individuals, and the world as comprised of individuals of a class" (Helm, "Calvin, Indefinite Language, and Definite Atonement," 117).

classes and not of individuals and his only concern is to include princes and foreign nations in this number.... For as there is one God, the Creator and Father of all, so, he declares, there is one Mediator, through whom access to God is opened to us, and this Mediator is not given only to one nation, or to a few men of a particular class, but to all, for the benefit of the sacrifice, by which He has expiated for our sins, applies to all. Since at that time a great part of the world had alienated itself from God, he explicitly mentions the Mediator through whom those who were far off now draw nigh. The universal term "all" must always be referred to classes of men but never to individuals. It is as if he had said, "Not only Jews, but also Greeks, not only people of humble rank but also princes have been redeemed by the death of Christ." Since therefore He intends the benefit of His death to be common to all, those who hold a view that would exclude any from the hope of salvation do Him an injury.[55]

Thus Calvin consistently interpreted "all men" in 1 Tim 2:4 as all "classes of men" rather than "individuals." But he added that the passage does not concern God's "secret counsel" concerning individuals (which pertains to the elect alone) but to the *preached* offer of the gospel "to all without exception."[56] An article by Martin Foord claims that Calvin may have meant "all kinds of people" in the sense of "*all* from all kinds,"

---

55. Calvin, 1 Tim 2:4-5, *Second Epistle of Paul the Apostle to the Corinthians and the Epistles to Timothy, Titus and Philemon*, 208-10. On Christ as mediator, see Baylor, "'With Him in Heavenly Realms,'" 152-75; Thompson, "Calvin on the Mediator," 106-35; Allen, "Perfect Priest," 120-34.

56. Calvin asserts that the apostle is not speaking of specific individuals (such as Peter or John) as they relate to God's secret, eternal decree (Calvin, *Sermons on the Epistles to Timothy and Titus*, 149). Rather, in Calvin's interpretation, 1 Timothy 2 addresses the external proclamation of the gospel (as the revealed will of God). Therefore, in his comments upon 1 Timothy 2, when Paul emphasized God's revealed will for "all classes" and "all orders," he may actually have meant by this *not* to exclude particular individuals. In his *Sermon* on 1 Timothy 2, Calvin expressly states, "For Jesus Christ is not a Saviour of three or four, but he offers himself to all" (ibid., 159). Cf. Calvin, Isa 53:12. To paraphrase Kennedy, Calvin is using the word "individuals" (*singuli*) for a fixed number of individuals (Kennedy, *Union with Christ and the Extent of the Atonement*, 46). And (according to Calvin) Paul is not addressing the topic of such particular "individuals" within God's "secret will"; therefore, "all" is used for "all" of all classes, orders, and peoples, in the "revealed will" of gospel proclamation (see Ponter, "Review Essay (Part Two)," 256-60). In the same manner, according to 1 Tim 2:1, we are to pray for "all" (Calvin, *Sermons on the Epistles to Timothy and Titus*, 160; see Costley, "Answering Roger Nicole on 1 Timothy 2:5"). More precisely, the objective provision is for all, but not every individual hears a gospel presentation.

rather than in the ("Owenist") sense of "some from all kinds."[57] In Foord's understanding, when Calvin maintains that 1 Tim 2:4 does *not* speak of "every particular individual," he is referring to "*God's hidden will concerning particular individuals.*"[58] That is, Calvin asserts that the text does not speak of God's hidden plan for individuals but his *revealed will* (the proclamation of the gospel).[59] According to Calvin's commentary on the passage, "But he [Paul] is speaking of classes and not of individuals and his only concern is to include princes and foreign nations in this number. *God's will that they also should share the teaching of the Gospel* is clear from the passages already quoted and from others like them."[60] Again, Calvin commented, "For although it is true that we must not try to decide

---

57. Foord, "God Wills All People to Be Saved," 198–99; following the observations of David Ponter (ibid., 199n121); cf. Ponter, "Review Essay (Part Two)," 256–60, 269. By tracing the medieval discussions and by citing relevant materials in Calvin, Foord concludes that "'All' is a reference firstly to orders (or kinds) of people, but that doesn't necessarily entail some from all kinds. Rather Calvin means *all* from all kinds." For counterargument, see Muller, *Calvin and the Reformed Tradition*, 85n55; Blacketer, "Blaming Beza," 139n91. Putting together Calvin's comments on 1 Timothy in *Concerning the Eternal Predestination* and his *Commentaries*, Calvin argues that God wills to offer the gospel to "all without exception" (*Concerning the Eternal Predestination*, 109), but God does not will "all without distinction" to be saved in His hidden eternal counsel (1 Tim 2:4). Such evidence may point to Calvin's understanding of the Mediator being for all humans of every kind in the revealed will of 1 Tim 2:4 and 5. Peter Vermigli put forward three understandings of the passage, declaring that "all these interpretations are quite probable and also fitting": first, the text speaks "of all states and kinds of men, that is, that God will have some of all kinds of men to be saved"; second, "God will have all men to be saved, for as many as are saved, they are saved by his will"; third, the text refers "to the signified will or antecedent will, that all men are invited since preaching is set forth to all indifferently." Vermigli added his own, fourth option: the "all men" is "understood only of the saints," to "the godly who are elected" (Ponter, "Peter Martyr Vermigli"). Concerning the third option, Vermigli stated, "Thus if we relate this to the will of God, we will easily grant that he will have all men to be saved. They will not have it to be understood of the hidden and effective will which they call the consequent will. In this way one may understand such speed as 'God illumines every man who comes into this world' and 'Come unto me all who are weary and heavy laden' (John 1:9; Matt. 11:21), for all are provoked by the oracles of God and all are inwardly moved by some spur." Cf. also Kimedoncius, who interpreted "all men" in 1 Tim 2:4 as a reference to some of all kinds, but seems to have been a proponent of "universal redemption." See Muller, "Review of *English Hypothetical Universalism*," 149–50; Muller, "Revising the Predestination Paradigm."

58. Foord, "God Wills All People to Be Saved," 199; italics original.

59. Ponter, "Review Essay (Part Two)," 258.

60. Calvin, 1 Tim 2:4–5, *Second Epistle of Paul the Apostle to the Corinthians and the Epistles to Timothy, Titus and Philemon*, 209.

what is God's will by prying into His secret counsel, when He has made it plain to us by external signs, yet that does not mean that God has not determined secretly within Himself what He wishes to do with every single man."[61] Of course, not all scholars have concurred with Foord's reading.[62]

In his prayer that he ordinarily made at the ending of his sermons, Calvin declared, "Let us fall down before the face of our good God . . . That it may please Him to grant this grace, not only to us, but also to all people and nations of the earth, bringing back all poor ignorant souls from the miserable bondage of error and darkness, to the right way of salvation."[63] The context of 1 Tim 2:1–7 concerns prayers for the salvation of unbelievers ("all men in general"), and Calvin roots this summons to prayer in the *imago Dei* shared by all humans, thus distributing "all men" to include all bearers of the image of God.[64] "Yet notwithstanding, (as we have here exhorted) let us not leave off, to pray for all men in general: For S. Paul shows us, that God will have all men be saved, that is to say all people and all nations . . . [lest] we forget that God has made us all in his image and likeness, that we are his workmanship, that he may stretch forth his goodness over them which are at this day far from him, as we have a good proof of it."[65] This understanding of 1 Timothy 2, with its context of praying for unbelievers, fits Paul's sentiments in Rom 10:1–4, where he prays for the salvation of his fellow Israelites who did not believe.[66] It also fits Calvin's own Trinitarian prayer for the lost:

---

61. Calvin, 1 Tim 2:4–5, *Second Epistle of Paul the Apostle to the Corinthians and the Epistles to Timothy, Titus and Philemon*, 208.

62. See Blacketer, "Blaming Beza," 139n91; Muller, *Calvin and the Reformed Tradition*, 85n55.

63. Calvin, *Sermons on Job*, 751; English updated. Cf. the same material in Calvin, "Prayer Which John Calvin Ordinarily Made at the Ending of His Sermons," 730.

64. "It is, as I have already said, that, seeing that men are created in the image of God and that their souls have been redeemed by the blood of Jesus Christ, we must try in every way available to us to draw them to the knowledge of the gospel" (Calvin, *Sermons on the Acts of the Apostles, Chapters 1–7*, 593). See also Ponter, "Review Essay (Part Two)," 258.

65. Calvin, *Sermons on the Epistles to Timothy and Titus*, 160. One may not feasibly pray for every individual universally but for all kinds and stations and nations of people.

66. "Brethren, my heart's desire and prayer to God for Israel is that they may be saved. For I bear them witness that they have a zeal for God, but not according to knowledge" (Rom 10:1–2, NKJV; cf. Rom 9:1–5).

Moreover, we offer up our prayers unto Thee, O most Gracious God and most merciful Father, for all men in general, that as Thou art pleased to be acknowledged the Saviour of the whole human race by the redemption accomplished by Jesus Christ Thy Son, so those who are still strangers to the knowledge of him, and immersed in darkness, and held captive by ignorance and error, may, by Thy Holy Spirit shining upon them, and by Thy gospel sounding in their ears, be brought back to the right way of salvation, which consists in knowing Thee the true God and Jesus Christ whom Thou hast sent.[67]

In any case, as we have seen, Calvin purposely did not correlate 1 Tim 2:4 with God's *efficacious* work of salvation, but with the *external* call of preaching and teaching. As Calvin insisted, Paul "is showing that God has at heart the salvation of all men, for He calls all men to acknowledge His truth."[68] Moreover, according to Calvin, "the context makes it clear that no other will of God is intended than that which appears in the external preaching of the Gospel. Thus Paul means that God wills the salvation of all whom He mercifully invites by preaching to Christ."[69] Calvin affirmed that the revealed will of the "Gospel" being preached to all classes and orders was indeed "good news."[70] Individuals will not find their particular names listed out in gospel proclamation, but their warrant remains in "the external preaching of the Gospel," since "God wills the salvation of all whom He mercifully invites by preaching to Christ."[71] Therefore, Calvin did not associate the verse with God's hidden decree but rather with the proclamation of the gospel (the will of God as found in the Word preached).[72]

---

67. Calvin, "Forms of Prayer for the Church," 102.

68. Calvin, 1 Tim 2:4–5, *Second Epistle of Paul the Apostle to the Corinthians and the Epistles to Timothy, Titus and Philemon*, 208.

69. Calvin, *Concerning the Eternal Predestination*, 109. "This verse does not mean to teach that all will be saved, rather, this verse deals with God's revealed will only. Calvin's only intent in this passage is to make clear that the Scriptures do not teach that all will be saved" (Kennedy, *Union with Christ and the Extent of the Atonement*, 47).

70. Rainbow, *Will of God and the Cross*, 142; Foord, "God Wills All People to Be Saved," 199.

71. Calvin, *Concerning the Eternal Predestination*, 109 cf. Calvin, *Sermons on Isaiah's Prophecy*, 137–52. See Daniel, "Hyper-Calvinism and John Gill," 797–99.

72. Calvin distinguishes between particular individuals as found in the hidden will of God and the general summons to people of all nations and estates as found in the Word preached (Calvin, *Sermons on the Epistles to Timothy and Titus*, 154). "However, the critical point to grasp is this: Calvin's use of 'individuals' (and 'every particular

Calvin's sermon on 1 Timothy 2 echoes these same ideas, dancing between the revealed will of God, the gospel offer, salvation, election, and the efficacious call. "As Saint Paul speaks now of all nations, so speaks he also of all estates, as if he should say, that God will save kings and magistrates, as well as the least and baser sort. And we must not restrain his fatherly goodness either to ourselves only, or to some certain number of people. And why so? For he shows that he will be favorable to all."[73] As a corollary, Calvin speaks of "all classes" of people as a positive way of motivating a generalized preaching of the gospel (and prayer), not with the intention of limiting the gospel proclamation.[74]

Calvin applied the generality of God's revealed will to both prayer and evangelism, reflecting the biblical context of 1 Tim 2:1–6. "But Saint Paul commands us to pray for all the world."[75] "Let us not leave off to pray for all men in general: for Saint Paul shows us that God will have all men to be saved, that is to say of all people and nations."[76] We cannot pray for every person of the world individually, but we can pray for them in general, including all kinds and stations and nations. God shows us his revealed will "as his word is preached unto us. And what will is that? That is, whereby he calls and exhorts us all to repentance. . . . In that God does exhort all men generally, thereby we may judge that it is the will of God that all men should be saved."[77] Thus, "God would have all the world to

---

man') refers to *God's hidden will concerning particular individuals.* Thus, when he says that Paul is not speaking of 'individuals,' Calvin means 1 Tim. 2:4 speaks of *God's revealed will*" (Foord, "God Wills All People to Be Saved"). In this manner, Calvin differed from the Augustinian interpretation of 1 Tim 2:4, which tied the "all kinds" or "all classes" into the hidden will of God in His eternal decree (see Ponter, "Brief History of Deviant Calvinism," 18). For a comparison of Calvin's interpretation with various medieval authors, see Foord, "God Wills All People to Be Saved."

73. Calvin, *Sermons on the Epistles to Timothy and Titus*, 150; English spelling updated.

74. "Are the Apostles sent to publish the truth of God to all people, and to all estates? It follows then that God presents himself to all the world, and that the promise belongs both to great and small, as well as to the Gentiles now, as to the Jews before" (Calvin, *Sermons on the Epistles to Timothy and Titus*, 150; English updated). Cf. also ibid., 176–77.

75. Calvin, *Sermons on the Epistles to Timothy and Titus*, 149; English spelling updated.

76. Calvin, *Sermons on the Epistles to Timothy and Titus*, 160; English spelling updated.

77. Calvin, *Sermons on the Epistles to Timothy and Titus*, 154; English updated.

be saved to the end that as much as lies in us, we should also seek their salvation."[78]

Calvin's sermon adds, "And thus we see now, how men are *not partakers* of this benefit, *which was purchased* them by our Lord Jesus Christ. And why so? For they receive not the witness."[79]

> For it is faith that puts us in possession of this salvation: although we find it not but in the person of our Lord Jesus Christ, and we must needs come thither, yet if we have not this key of faith, Jesus Christ shall be (as it were) strange to us, and all that he has suffered, shall not profit us one whit, as in deed it belongs not to us. This is a very profitable doctrine: for there is no man but confesses, that it is the greatest benefit that man can desire in this world, to be partaker of that salvation which Jesus Christ has brought us, but there are very few that take the right way. For we see how the Gospel is despised, we see that all men are deaf, or else stop their ears against this voice, which God will have to be published throughout all the world.[80]

In sum, Calvin's materials on 1 Timothy opposed any "universalism" that taught all humanity would be saved in the end.[81] Calvin's sermonic material also supported a general offer of the gospel and emphasized the importance of prayer and evangelism.[82] He used the opportunity to re-

---

78. Calvin, *Sermons on the Epistles to Timothy and Titus*, 148; English spelling updated. See Muller, "'To Grant this Grace to All People and Nations,'" 225.

79. Calvin, *Sermons on the Epistles to Timothy and Titus*, 177; English spelling updated; italics added.

80. Calvin, *Sermons on the Epistles to Timothy and Titus*, 178; English spelling updated.

81. See also Calvin, *Institutes* III.22.10, where Calvin states that the doctrine of salvation "is falsely debased when presented as effectually profitable to all." Evangelism is founded upon the divine summons of the gospel offer, even though God has not decreed that the gospel should be effectually profitable to all. "That God would have all the world to be saved: to the end that as much as lies in us, we should also seek their salvation" (Calvin, *Sermons on the Epistles to Timothy and Titus*, 148; English updated).

82. "Therefore Saint Paul's meaning is not that God will save every particular man, but he says that the promises which were given to one only people [the Jews], are now stretched out through all the world" (Calvin, *Sermons on the Epistles to Timothy and Titus*, 149; English spelling updated). Thus, "forasmuch as God will have his grace to be known of all the world, and has commanded his Gospel to be preached to all creatures, we must as much as lies in us, procure the salvation of all them which are at this day strangers from the faith, and seem utterly to be despised of the goodness of God, that we may bring them to it" (ibid., 159; English spelling updated).

state the bondage of sin upon unbelievers and the necessity of the Spirit's supernatural work.[83] Calvin's homilies instructed regarding election, faith, and the culpability of unbelief. Moreover, his sermonic material (in acquiescing to human finite understanding) distinguished the "secret" will of God and the "revealed" will of God.[84]

Yet Calvin's overall theology did not posit a *duplex* will in the sense of an equivocal willing in God, even though one could speak of a double (*duplex*) manifestation of God's willing—two ways of executing a united will.[85] God always wills the same, but through different modes—*Deum semper idem velle, sed diversis modis*.[86] It is not entirely clear how Calvin understood "this one will of God in relation to its different or diverse modes."[87] Yet the will of God is "one and simple, albeit with distinctions that can be observed in its revelation."[88] Commenting upon Ezek 18:23, Calvin remarks that "God puts on a twofold character (*Deum duplicem personam induere*)."[89] In the revealed promise of the general call of the gospel (the promise of salvation on fulfillment of the condition of faith),

---

83. "And can we come to him of the motion of our own nature? Alas no: for we are wholly against him, and there is not one iota of affection in us, but it is his utter enemy, as St. Paul says, and we do daily rebel against him" (Calvin, *Sermons on the Epistles to Timothy and Titus*, 159; English spelling updated). "But we are all of us so contrary and such enemies to God.... So then, how can it be that we may be partakers of that salvation which is offered unto us in the Gospel, unless God draw us to it by his Holy Spirit?" (ibid., 151; English spelling updated).

84. "Truth it is, that God changes not, neither has he two wills, neither does he use any counterfeit dealing, as though he meant one thing, but would not have it so. And yet does the Scripture speak unto us after two sorts touching the will of God.... It is because of our grossness and rudeness: for we know, that if God will come down to us, and give us any understanding of things, he must change his own hue" (Calvin, *Sermons on the Epistles to Timothy and Titus*, 152; English spelling updated). Just as our eyes cannot bear to look directly at the sun, so our minds cannot "comprehend that infinite majesty which is in God" (ibid., 156; English spelling updated). "So then these beasts, which would destroy God's election, must not abuse this place, nor say, that we make a double will in God: for therein they do impudently and villainously misreport us. But we say as every man sees, that is to wit, that as far as we can perceive, God would have all men to be saved, whenever and how oft ever he appoints his Gospel to be preached unto us" (ibid., 156; English spelling updated).

85. Muller, "Tale of Two Wills?" 218–19.

86. Muller, "Tale of Two Wills?" 219. Calvin denied that *Deum hoc modo fieri duplicem* (ibid., 223).

87. Muller, "Tale of Two Wills?" 218.

88. Muller, "Tale of Two Wills?" 224.

89. As quoted in Muller, "Tale of Two Wills?" 220. Calvin commented on Ezek 18:23 at least three times (ibid., 217). See also his comments on Matt 23:37.

God broadcasts a "paternal benevolence."[90] This is a preceptive will or *voluntas signi*, not an eternal decree parallel to the determination to save the elect. This differentiation parallels traditional distinctions between the *voluntas arcana* or *voluntas beneplaciti* on the one hand and the *voluntas revelata* or the *voluntas signi* on the other hand—that is, when accommodated to humans, God's will appears twofold.[91] Muller argues, "These kinds of willing are distinct, but they cannot, without grave error, be set against one another or identified as contraries."[92]

With such distinctions in hand, Foord re-examined Calvin's interpretation of 1 Tim 2:4, in comparison and contrast with his predecessors.[93] While Augustine and Peter Martyr Vermigli interpreted the text of 1 Tim 2:4 as a reference to God's *voluntas beneplaciti* and all kinds of people and not all individuals, Calvin applied it to God's *voluntas signi*. That is, Calvin consistently interpreted the phrase "Who will have all men to be saved" as a reference to God's revealed will (*voluntas signi*) in the external preaching of the gospel.[94] He explicitly maintained that the text does not speak of God's secret counsel, "neither that he means to lead us to this everlasting election and choice which was before the beginning of the world, but only shows us what God's will and pleasure is, so far forth as we may know it."[95]

---

90. This sentence and the two that follow are paraphrased from the lengthy discussion found in Muller, "Tale of Two Wills?" 220–23.

91. Foord, "God Wills All People to Be Saved," 196. On the *voluntas signi*, see Lynch, "Richard Hooker," 281. Unlike the later Amyraut, Calvin does not explicitly differentiate between a *voluntas antecedens et hypothetica* (an antecedent and hypothetical will) and a *voluntas consequens et absoluta* (a consequent and absolute will). See Muller, "Tale of Two Wills?" 222. Therefore, Amyraut was not a "precise follower of Calvin," yet one could nevertheless trace a trajectory from Calvin "toward a more specific conclusion than he himself had proposed" (Muller, "Tale of Two Wills?" 224–25). On Calvin's practice of "accommodation" while speaking of divine matters, see Wright, "Calvin's Accommodating God," 3–19; Wright, "Calvin's 'Accommodation' Revisited," 19–38; Battles, "God Was Accommodating Himself," 19–38.

92. Muller, "Davenant and Du Moulin," 148.

93. Foord, "God Wills All People to Be Saved."

94. "It follows then, if through the will of God the Gospel be preached to all the world, there is a token that salvation is common to all. And thus Saint Paul proves, that God's will is that all men should be saved" (Calvin, *Sermons on the Epistles to Timothy and Titus*, 150; English spelling updated). Foord lists eight discussions of 1 Tim 2:4, as found in Calvin (Foord, "God Wills All People to Be Saved," 197).

95. Calvin, *Sermons on the Epistles to Timothy and Titus*, 152; English spelling updated.

In this explicit context of his "revealed will," God invites all classes, orders, and peoples to be saved.[96] "In that God does exhort all men generally, thereby we may judge, that it is the will of God, that all men should be saved, as he says also by the Prophet Ezekiel [18:23; 33:11]."[97] "For he offers his gospel says he, to all, which is the mean to draw us to salvation."[98] "For we see how he calls all them to salvation, to whom his word is preached."[99] Yet, because of our sinfulness, we do not come. "Therefore, God must go further to bring us to salvation, he must not only appoint men and send men to teach us faithfully, . . . he must touch us to the quick, he must draw us unto him, and must make his work not to be unprofitable unto us, and cause it to take root in our hearts."[100] In sum, Calvin seemingly does not exactly follow the Augustinian reading of 1 Tim 2:4 nor does he slavishly copy a specific medieval reading, but he sought his own solution by placing the focused framework in God's "revealed will" (*voluntas signi*) rather than his "will of pleasure" (*voluntas beneplaciti*).[101]

As a result, some facets found within Calvin's interpretations of 1 John 2:2 and 1 Tim 2:4 may parallel the interpretations of many so-called five-point Calvinists. Other details within his interpretations do not, however. In his comments on 1 John 2:2, Calvin allowed the maxim "Christ died sufficiently for the whole world, but efficiently for the elect alone" to stand. Of course, throughout history, this maxim has been used in divergent ways by various theologians.[102] More curiously, Calvin ap-

---

96. Calvin connects God's desire for all to be saved with the next phrase in 1 Timothy 4 as the means to the end ("and to come unto the knowledge of the truth" [NKJV]) (Calvin, *Sermons on the Epistles to Timothy and Titus*, 150, 159). "Thus the Scripture holds us in this simplicity, that if we desire to have salvation, we must hold the mean which is appointed for us, and which God sets before us, that is to say, we must receive his word with obedience of faith" (ibid., 159; English spelling updated).

97. Calvin, *Sermons on the Epistles to Timothy and Titus*, 154; English spelling updated.

98. Calvin, *Sermons on the Epistles to Timothy and Titus*, 156; English spelling updated.

99. Calvin, *Sermons on the Epistles to Timothy and Titus*, 158; English spelling updated.

100. Calvin, *Sermons on the Epistles to Timothy and Titus*, 156; English spelling updated.

101. Foord, "God Wills All People to Be Saved," 201–3. Though see Blacketer, "Blaming Beza," 139n91.

102. See Godfrey, "Reformed Thought on the Extent of the Atonement," 133–71.

plied 1 Tim 2:4 to "all orders" or "all classes" of humans, *even though* he argued that the text is not about God's elective decree but rather about the proclaimed gospel. But if Calvin viewed 1 Tim 2:4 as a reference to "the preached Word," why did he feel compelled to interpret the "all men" as "classes of humans" rather than "individuals"?[103] Is there another way of considering that phenomena in Calvin?

Employing some of Foord's initial insights, one might take them in a slightly different direction. According to Foord, if 1 Tim 2:4 is a reference to God's revealed will in the preaching and teaching of the gospel, "it would make little sense to limit the word 'all.'"[104] Perhaps, however, following the implications of Calvin's argument concerning the "revealed will" in the proclamation of the gospel, Calvin understood that *not* every *individual* actually hears the gospel proclaimed, although the gospel is *now* preached to every nation and class ("kind of people").[105] Confirmation of this interpretation can be found in Calvin's other comments on 1 Tim 2:4: He notes that *formerly* in the Old Testament, God "lit the light of life for the Jews alone" and "allowed the Gentiles to wander for many

---

103. "It is indeed a strange fact that Calvin sometimes interpreted 'many' as 'all,' and sometimes he interpreted 'all' as 'many'" (Rouwendal, "Calvin's Forgotten Classical Position," 332). Thomas concurs that "Calvin bewilderingly takes 'all' to mean 'some' in some places dealing with the atonement, and 'some' to mean 'all' in others where the context is similar" (Thomas, "Calvin and English Calvinism," 118; cf. Doyle, "Context of Moral Decision Making in the Writings of John Calvin," 276). See Calvin's comments on Mark 14:24 above. In John 6:45, Calvin notes that "all" must be "limited to the elect" ("and they shall be all taught of God"). Cf. Calvin, Matt 20:28, *Harmony of the Gospels*, vol. 2, 277, where he explicitly reiterates that "many" refers to "all," not a part of humanity but "the whole human race." "Yet I approve of the ordinary reading, that he alone bore the punishment of many, because on him was laid the guilt of the whole world. It is evident from other passages, and especially from the fifth chapter of the Epistle to the Romans, that 'many' sometimes denotes 'all'" (Calvin, *Commentary on the Book of the Prophet Isaiah*, vol. 4, 131). "*To bear the sins* means to free those who have sinned from their guilt by his satisfaction. He says many meaning all, as in Rom. 5.15. It is of course certain that not all enjoy the fruits of Christ's death, but this happens because their unbelief hinders them" (Calvin, Heb 9:28, *Epistle of Paul the Apostle to the Hebrews and the First and Second Epistles of St Peter*, 131). In his comments on Heb 5:9, Calvin explains, "At the same time he has inserted the universal term 'to all' to show that no one is excluded from this salvation who proves to be attentive and obedient to the Gospel of Christ" (ibid., 67). See Kennedy, *Union with Christ and the Extent of the Atonement*, 32–35; Kennedy, "Hermeneutical Discontinuity between Calvin and Later Calvinism," 301–7.

104. Foord, "God Wills All People to Be Saved," 200.

105. An arguable point historically, considering Calvin's specific sixteenth-century context at the inception of the Age of Discovery, but see Rev 5:9–10 and 7:9–10.

ages in darkness (Acts 14:16)." Even in the New Testament, the Spirit sovereignly prohibited Paul from preaching in specific territories (Acts 16:6–7).[106] "And so the Lord sends his Gospel where it pleases him, and yet is not his grace poured out upon Judea only or upon one corner of that land, but upon all the world both here and there, although there be not the like order in every place."[107] Therefore, although the gospel is to be proclaimed to all in general and is now sent to every nation and class, Calvin realistically understood that not every individual will actually hear a gospel presentation much less be efficaciously drawn by the Spirit.[108]

Calvin affirms that "the *preaching* of the gospel brings life," yet he adds that the apostle "is speaking of classes and not of individuals and his only concern is to include princes and foreign nations in this number."[109] In this understanding, therefore, Calvin maintains that all individuals are *not* elected in God's "secret counsel," but he seems further to maintain that all individuals are *not* necessarily even recipients of the externally preached Word of the general call of the gospel. Neither of these statements, however, explicitly addresses a third question, whether Christ's death was a provision for all individuals. This point may sound strangely exacting, until one considers an interpretive key that appears in Calvin's sermons on Deuteronomy:

> It is true that St John says generally, that [God] loved the world. And why? For Jesus Christ offers himself generally to all men without exception to be their redeemer. It is said afterward in the covenant, that God loved the world when he sent his only son: but he loved us, us (I say) which have been taught by his Gospel, because he gathered us to him. And the faithful that are enlightened by the holy Ghost, have yet a third use of God's love, in that he reveals himself more familiarly to them, and seals up his fatherly adoption by his holy Spirit, and engraves it upon

---

106. Calvin, *Concerning the Eternal Predestination*, 108; cf. Calvin, *Sermons on the Epistles to Timothy and Titus*, 152, 157. See also Calvin's preface to Olivetan's French New Testament; Titus 2:11. Cf. some Lutheran attempts to posit a universal gospel proclamation to all humans before Christ (Kuiper, *For Whom Did Christ Die?* 84).

107. Calvin, *Sermons on the Epistles to Timothy and Titus*, 157; English spelling updated.

108. Put differently, Calvin recognized the tension highlighted by Strange, "Slain for the World?" 585–605.

109. Calvin, 1 Tim 2:4–5, *Second Epistle of Paul the Apostle to the Corinthians and the Epistles to Timothy, Titus and Philemon*, 209.

their hearts.... Thus we see three degrees of the love that God has shown us in our Lord Jesus Christ. The first is in respect of the redemption that was purchased in the person of him that gave himself to death for us, and became accursed to reconcile us to God his Father. That is the first degree of love, which extends to all men, inasmuch as Jesus Christ reaches out his arms to call and allure all men both great and small, and to win them to him. But there is a special love for those to whom the gospel is preached: which is that God testifies to them that he will make them partakers of the benefit that was purchased for them by the death and passion of his Son. And forasmuch as we be of that number, therefore we are double bound already to our God: here are two bonds which hold us as it were [closely] tied to him. Now let us come to the third bond, which depends upon the third love that God shows us: which is that he not only causes the gospel to be preached to us, but also makes us to feel the power thereof, so as we know him to be our Father and Saviour, not doubting but that our sins are forgiven us for our Lord Jesus Christ's sake, who brings us the gift of the Holy Spirit, to reform us after his own image.[110]

God has diachronically worked out his eternal plan of salvation in human history, and Calvin distinguishes three specific historical moments in this passage: First, the purchased redemption of Christ (in which he offers himself to all men and summons them). Second, the preaching of the gospel (which is a general call to humanity, though the proclamation has not in fact reached all at all times).[111] Third, God's efficacious forma-

---

110. Calvin, *Sermons on Deuteronomy*, 167; English updated. In personal correspondence, Alan Clifford has highlighted further materials from Calvin's *Sermons on Deuteronomy*. According to Calvin, God calls "the world to salvation" (181.a.50), and behind such a general call is the fact that "Jesus Christ went out of the City Jerusalem, bearing the reproach and curse of the whole world upon him" (30.a.40; English spelling updated). "Let us mark then that here is no exception, and that God's intent is to bring all the world to his lure" (667.a.40; English spelling updated). Such texts concern the revealed will of gospel proclamation (and its accompanying provision) rather than the decree of predestination.

111. At other times, Calvin could move toward conflating the first and second points: "Some object that God would be contrary to himself if he should universally invite all men to him but admit only a few as elect. Thus, in their view, the universality of the promises removes the distinction of special grace.... I have elsewhere explained how Scripture reconciles the two notions that all are called to repentance and faith by outward preaching, yet that the spirit of repentance and faith is not given to all" (Calvin, *Institutes* III.22.10). According to Richard Muller, "the promise of grace was assumed to be limited to the actual preaching of the gospel" by John Davenant

tion of faith in the elect, "as he not only causes the gospel to be preached to us, but also makes us to feel the power thereof." Moreover, one might picture Calvin's three "degrees of love" as three concentric circles. In love, Christ purchased redemption for "all humans," of which only a smaller circle are historical hearers of the "second degree of love" of the general proclamation, of which an even smaller circle are recipients of "the third love" of the Spirit's efficacious work.[112]

Furthermore, the three "degrees of love" can be distinguished in time.[113] This passage may provide insights into a diachronic, complex structure behind Calvin's views of election, redemption, general call, and efficacious call. In eternity past, God chose the elect. In a historical event, Jesus suffered for all humanity (and for the efficacious salvation of the elect). In history, the universal provision of Christ's suffering is proclaimed through the general call of the gospel, although not everyone hears a gospel presentation (thus distinguishing between an objective availability of the promises and a personal hearing of them).[114] God fur-

---

and Samuel Ward (members of the British delegation to Dort), thus differing from the Amyraldian notion of universal grace (Muller, "Davenant and Du Moulin," 136). Davenant quoted Prosper of Aquitane: "They live without grace, and are not partakers of Christian grace, to whom Christ was never preached" (in ibid., 142). Davenant argued that the necessary condition of "the object having been proposed to the sinner, in which he may believe" cannot be fulfilled "unless God wills to send them preachers of the gospel" (in ibid., 143). Muller thus refers to "historical and geographical limitations placed on the extent of salvation by the absence of the preaching of the gospel from some times and places" (ibid., 158). He concludes that "since there is no calling to repentance and salvation outside of the church's preaching of the gospel and since the preaching of the gospel has not gone out to all people in the world, there is no universal calling sufficient to save all people" (ibid., 143). By contrast, Amyraut maintained that the grace of salvation is available to all, even if some live in locations where the gospel or even Christ are not known (ibid., 153–54). In such contexts, those with an "indistinct faith" could be saved by general revelation. Both Zwingli and Bullinger discussed the possible salvation of "heathens," in differing manners (Stephens, "Bullinger and Zwingli," 283–300).

112. Beza described the external call of the gospel as *indefinite* rather than *universal*, as many will never hear the gospel (Blacketer, "Blaming Beza," 137). Cf. the approach of Zemek, *Biblical Theology of the Doctrines of Sovereign Grace*, 271–72; Kuiper, *For Whom Did Christ Die?* 68.

113. There is a danger in collapsing the outworking of succession in history. See Blocher, "Jesus Christ *the* Man," 581.

114. This is one reason why one's perspective cannot be based upon human views of "fairness." In both Calvinistic and Arminian views (traditionally, at least), not all human beings receive equal opportunity to hear the gospel. Attempts to establish "egalitarian" fairness have sometimes led to the espousing of postmortem opportunities to

ther works through the general call by the particular, efficacious work of the Spirit among only some of those who do hear (the elect). The first and third notions of love are found in Calvin's "Fourth Sermon on the Passion of our Lord," where they are positioned distinctly in time: "For as [God] declared His love toward mankind when He spared not His Only Son but delivered Him to death for sinners, also He declares a love which He bears especially toward us when by His Holy Spirit He touches us by the knowledge of our sins and He makes us wail and draws us to Himself with repentance."[115]

This may be a reading of Calvin's comments on 1 Timothy 2 worthy of consideration. What seems patent is that Calvin explicitly affirmed that 1 Tim 2:4 concerned God's revealed Word through the specific prism of the preaching and teaching of the gospel (and as reflected in evangelism and the prayer of saints), not his efficacious will. If so, Calvin's exegesis of texts was "not a slavish rendition of any one divine or school of thought," and he felt free to veer from classic Augustinian readings, while seeking to resolve tensions "with a reasonable solution."[116]

Such intricacies of thought and personal formulation allowed Calvin to combine a form of so-called "universal redemption" (in the sense of a universal provision) with "unconditional election." And when the few, key texts summoned as evidences for a strict "limited atonement" in Calvin (such as his comments on 1 John 2 and 1 Timothy 2) are interpreted within Calvin's wider, intricate theology, they manifest the complexity

---

hear the gospel. See Pinnock, *Wideness in God's Mercy*; Fackre, "Divine Perseverance," 71–95. Furthermore, the fact that there is no biblical plan of redemption for angels illustrates that God did not "have to" save anyone—he freely chose to do so (Orrick, *Mere Calvinism*, 91).

115. Calvin, *Deity of Christ and Other Sermons*, 108. According to Stephen Strehle, Calvin "argues that it is not the atonement which produces limitation, nor the preaching of the gospel, but the God who works faith in his elected few and applies the benefits of Christ's work to them alone." (Strehle, "Universal Grace and Amyraldianism," 354n62). Yet—within Calvin's wider theology—this "third degree of love" also corresponds to God's eternal, unconditional election of those same individuals prior to all human history. As Helm notes, "At some point in Calvin's system, and in the system of any Calvinist, the scope of election and of the application of redemption must coincide" (Helm, "Calvin, English Calvinism and the Logic of Development," 182).

116. Foord, "God Wills All People to Be Saved," 201–3. As Anthony Lane has reminded me in personal correspondence, if we accept Calvin and his methodology of biblical exegesis at face value, he genuinely sought to get to the meaning of each individual passage, not just to impose a theological system. This led to "sometimes surprising exegesis." See, for example, Calvin's peculiar approaches to the materials in Acts 10 and James 2 that have ramifications for a theology of justification.

of his thought but cannot serve to overturn the evidence of his many references to Christ's universal provision of redemption. His interpretations of 1 John 2 and 1 Timothy 2 do not place him among so-called "four-point Calvinist" interpretations of those texts today, nor does his language reflecting some form of universal provision mirror strict "five-point Calvinists." One's assessment of Calvin's complex theology must be characterized by neither naive anachronism nor reductionist simplification. Yet a basic framework emerges in Calvin's materials.

Nevertheless, Calvin never developed a full, systematic approach to these reflections in his extant corpus, unlike the later yet differing systematic approaches represented by the likes of Moïse Amyraut and John Owen.[117] In various facets of what would have been a full systemization, "Calvin did not provide a clear solution and projected his arguments toward a more specified conclusion than he himself had proposed."[118] Later theologians in these trajectories expounded specified conclusions not explicitly developed in Calvin. Calvin's exegesis therefore offers "little useful ammunition" to later definitively-particularistic views, nor was Amyraut "a precise follower of Calvin."[119]

---

117. On John Owen's theology of atonement, see Tay, *Priesthood of Christ*. For a critique of Owen's argumentation, see Chambers, "Critical Examination of John Owen's Argument."

118. Muller, "Tale of Two Wills?" 224–25.

119. Muller, "Tale of Two Wills?" 224.

Chapter Four

Calvin and Reformed Diversity

ADMITTEDLY THIS QUESTION OF historical theology is complex, perhaps the Gordian knot of Calvin studies. On balance, however, it seems to the present writer that Calvin did *at times* posit a view of Christ's death for all *in some sense* of universal provision along with his resolute stance on particular election. It further seems that Calvin maintained God's sovereign use of the general call (proclaiming the provision) in his particular and efficacious application of salvation to the elect (who were elected in his eternal decree).[1]

One can understand how the *overall* tenor of Calvin's system may lend itself to the so-called "limited atonement" interpretation of the "first approach" discussed in the first chapter of this study.[2] "It was hardly possible," claims G. Michael Thomas, "that any number of warnings against investigating the secret will of God could hold back Calvin's successors, in seeking to understand a doctrine so prominent in his theology, from that dangerous but fascinating exercise. In the scope thus given for speculation and logical deduction, a theology more consistently particularistic than

---

1. In other contexts, Calvin's recognition that Scripture does not directly address every question is indicated by his use of *quodammodo* ("in some way or other") (Thompson, "Calvin on the Mediator," 121).

2. For example, "the parity of relation which his account seemed to establish between God and the two diverse decrees of election and reprobation" (Reid, "Editor's Introduction," 40; cf. 33-38); cf. Thomas, "Calvin and English Calvinism," 121-23. Amyraut preferred to speak of "preterition" rather than "predamnation" (see Strehle, "Universal Grace and Amyraldianism," 350n33). For a distinction between preterition and predamnation, see Ponter, "Calvin and the Decree," 3-4. Ponter explains that one may describe an asymmetrical causation between election unto glorification and reprobation unto damnation. Cf. Archbald, "Comparative Study of John Calvin and Theodore Beza," 126-33.

Calvin's was almost bound to emerge."[3] However, numerous materials remain in Calvin's own corpus that do not nicely or easily fit within most constructions of a strict "limited atonement" view, at least as commonly understood.[4] When interpreters carry their *a priori* systems, structure, and terminology into Calvin, they may miss inductively discovering Calvin's own views (in varying degrees).[5] Sometimes an inferential, deductive approach may skew one's understanding of Calvin.[6]

Along with interpreters of the "third approach" (see Chapter One), I recognize that some "tensions" and "ambiguities" do exist within Calvin.[7] One could argue that Calvin purposefully retained those tensions, however, because he believed that the attempt to relieve them would do disservice to the multifaceted scriptural evidence.[8] Therefore, Calvin's

3. Thomas, *Extent of the Atonement*, 34–35.

4. This current essay could not interact with the multitude of similar examples. I encourage readers to peruse the collection of David Ponter in "Calvin on Unlimited Expiation." In email correspondence, Curt Daniel has informed me that he has "collected well over a hundred citations from Calvin on the subject" (cf. Daniel, "Hyper-Calvinism and John Gill," 778, 781, 787–90). Contrast Helm, *Calvin and Calvinism*, 39n20: "In Calvin research the same few references in Calvin which appear to teach general atonement are appealed to time and again."

5. Ponter, "Review Essay (Part One)," 139. Cf. Raymond Blacketer's framing of "the extent of the atonement" in false dilemmas, without a nuanced discussion of more complex possibilities: "Did God the Father, in sending His Son into the world to make atonement for sinners, intend to make salvation available to every individual person, or was his purpose that his Son's death should provide satisfaction for the sins of the elect alone? Did Christ go to the cross in order to make salvation possible for whoever might believe, or did he have in mind those whom the Father had foreknown, elected and given to him" (Blacketer, "Definite Atonement in Historical Perspective," 304). Nicole also put forward a rigid dichotomy: "The choice, therefore, is not between universal atonement and definite atonement as properly representative of Calvin's theology, but rather between universal salvation and definite atonement" (Nicole, "John Calvin's View of the Extent of the Atonement," 218).

6. Consider statements that Calvin was committed to limited atonement even though he did not commit himself to limited atonement (cf. Helm, *Calvin and the Calvinists*, 18). One senses that interpreters acknowledge the paucity of evidence in the latter half of the statement but may still read their own views into Calvin's mind in the first half, simply because (in their view) it *must* have been so.

7. See Bouwsma, "Quest for the Historical Calvin," 47–57; Armstrong, "*Duplex cognitio Dei*," 135–53. According to Shultz, "He [Calvin] held to universality in regards to the universal gospel offer and particularity in regards to election. Depending upon the context of his remarks, he stressed either the particularity or the universality of the atonement. He never fully resolved this tension" (Shultz, *Multi-Intentioned View of the Extent of the Atonement*, 26).

8. "Calvin's 'strong biblicism' does lead him to make statements that are only

theology may not answer all questions to the full satisfaction of modern theologians. I agree with those many scholars (including those affiliated more with versions of the "third approach") who caution against anachronistically forcing Calvin to answer issues or precise questions that he did not intend to address.[9] Certainly, "He was every inch a sixteenth-century man."[10] There is a danger in importing categories that were sharpened in a much later period ("they would not have been recognized by many in the sixteenth century"), especially since the issues may not have been the focus of controversy at the time.[11] Specifically, the use of "atonement" in the entire discussion is somewhat problematic, since Calvin preferred to use terms like *expiation, satisfaction, reconciliation,* and *redemption*.[12]

'apparent' contradictions" (Bell, "Calvin and the Extent of the Atonement," 118). "It is clear that Calvin preferred to stand piously submissive to the revelation of God, often explicitly imitating the expressions of Scripture, avoiding any explorations into divine mysteries" (Strehle, "Universal Grace and Amyraldianism," 356).

9. Besides those quoted above, see also Helm, *Calvin: A Guide for the Perplexed*, 145: "But in fact Calvin's views on these matters [controversies about the intended effect of the death of Christ] were undeveloped by comparison with what came after, simply because he was not faced with the later issues and forced to come to a view on them. So it is anachronistic to attempt to measure Calvin's various statements about the atonement against what came later. The most we can ask is whether Calvin's views are consistent with what came later." Cf. Donald Macleod: ". . . surely some allowance must be made for the fact that Calvin, precisely because he died almost fifty years before the Arminian controversy, never addressed the precise question posed by the Remonstrants in 1610. . . . In this particular debate precise formulation of the question is everything, and it is unfair to adduce the material authority of Calvin on an issue he never faced" (Macleod, "*Amyraldus redivivus*," 211). According to Carl Trueman, ". . . the choice of Calvin, a sixteenth-century theologian, as the criterion for judging seventeenth-century theology, is, historically speaking, an entirely arbitrary move. Even in the sixteenth century, Calvin was at best first among equals; his theology did not represent the entire Reformed tradition and was not the only model available to subsequent theologians" (Trueman, *Claims of Truth*, 10–11).

10. Thompson, "Calvin on the Mediator," 107.

11. Thompson, "Calvin on the Cross of Christ," 125.

12. See Rainbow, *Will of God and the Cross*, 1; Daniel, "Hyper-Calvinism and John Gill," 787n15, 787n19; Muller, "John Calvin and Later Calvinism," 147; Muller, *After Calvin*, 14. Muller notes, "In a strict sense, 'atonement' is not Calvin's word: Calvin uses *expiatio, satisfactio,* and *reconciliatio* as well as the more general term *redemptio* (particularly in *Institutes*, II.16.4–6). The two former terms refer to the work of Christ as it relates to the problem of sin and guilt, *expiatio* indicating specifically the propitiation or propitiatory sacrifice (i.e., the 'atonement') and *satisfactio* indicating the reparation or amends made for the wrong against divine justice. Here Calvin insists on the fullness of Christ's work, the complete expiation or satisfaction for sin—which is to say an unlimited 'atonement.' On the other hand, the benefits of Christ's death,

Calvin's employment of "satisfaction" possesses "an imprecise sense that expresses various themes of the atonement."[13] Nevertheless, Calvin (as we have seen) makes various statements concerning a universal expiation and redemption, while still insisting upon a firm view of unconditional election and efficacious, particular grace.[14]

Along with P. L. Rouwendal, I acknowledge that Calvin allowed the "classic" statement of Christ's atonement to stand.[15] Calvin did not deny the maxim "Christ's sufferings were sufficient for all but efficient

---

the *reconciliatio* or actual *redemptio*, the restoration and purchase of individuals, is restricted to the elect, to those upon whom Christ bestows his benefits; and thus if the term 'atonement' is loosely construed to mean 'reconciliation' or 'redemption,' Calvin arguably teaches 'limited atonement'" (Muller, *Christ and the Decree*, 34; Muller, *Calvin and the Reformed Tradition*, 76). Muller rightly notes the problematic term "atonement." Yet this study has discussed examples of "redemption" and "reconciliation" being used in an "unlimited" sense (see multiple examples in Ponter, "John Calvin (1509–1564) on Unlimited Expiation"). Cf. Clifford, "Calvin & Calvinism," 50: "Calvin clearly uses *all* these terms to express 'benefits' available to all but only 'actually' enjoyed by the elect. Surprisingly, Muller fails to document his claims." On the other hand, Calvin's commentary upon 1 John 2:2 interprets "expiation" in a "limited" sense in that specific text. It cannot be as simple as reserving some terms for a "limited" sense and others for an "unlimited" sense. "While Muller is right to detect both universal and particular aspects in Calvin's teaching on the atonement, it is not possible to categorize Calvin's use of words in this respect, and he over-simplifies when he concludes that 'this distinction well fits what is loosely called 'limited atonement' not only in Calvin's thought but in later Reformed theology" (Thomas, *Extent of the Atonement*, 30).

13. Sinnema, "Calvin and the Canons of Dordt," 87–103.

14. In email correspondence, David Ponter has noted, "Many just claim that because these later distinctions and nuances on the extent of the atonement were not 'debated' until post-Calvin, somehow Calvin could not have had a position on it. Yet, affirming a doctrine is not the same as debating or proving it by way of a sustained polemic. The lack of the latter in no way implies the lack of the former."

15. A fourth approach might be that Calvin changed his mind over time (cf. Curt Daniel's summary in Kendall, *Calvin and English Calvinism*, 232n4). "In the 19th century some scholars thought that Calvin started out holding to limited expiation and redemption, but later came to embrace an unlimited expiation and redemption position. In the 21st century, sometimes this is reversed at the popular level. Many think that Calvin first embraced the unlimited position and, then, later came to embrace particular or limited atonement" (Ponter, "Calvin on Unlimited Expiation"). According to Ponter, Calvin's overall collection of materials throughout his ministry proves "both of these claims to be unacceptable" (ibid.). Contrast the claim that Calvin mollified his doctrine "with mature reflection and advancing years," in Strong, *Systematic Theology*, 778, For a critique of Strong's (mis)quotation of Calvin, see Daniel, "Hyper-Calvinism and John Gill," 803n67.

for the elect alone."[16] But he admitted his reticence in using it as a simplistic hermeneutical solution.[17] Of course, the ambiguity of the term *sufficient* allows various interpretations of the classic maxim (sufficient in intrinsic, abstract, infinite value? or sufficient in extrinsic, divine intent of provision?).[18] The issue of multiple meanings associated with "suffi-

16. Contra T. F. Torrance, as critiqued by Donald Macleod and Robert Letham. See Torrance, *Scottish Theology*, 107; Letham, "Triune God, Incarnation, and Definite Atonement," 453. This classic, Lombardian formula exhibits a level of ambiguity, since "an intrinsic sufficiency does not entail an extrinsic sufficiency" (Crisp, *Deviant Calvinism*, 217; cf. Allen, *Extent of the Atonement*, 88–89, 92, 94; Allen, "Calvin on the Extent of the Atonement," 2, 12–13, 16). A bare infinite merit (intrinsic sufficiency) does not necessarily entail a divine intention to provide redemption for the non-elect (Crisp, *Deviant Calvinism*, 218, 221). Gomarus suggested that no one in the seventeenth-century debates would deny that Christ's death was of "infinite power" sufficient for the salvation of a thousand worlds (Muller, "Davenant and Du Moulin," 141). Beza declared that Christ's offering was intrinsically enough "to make satisfaction for an infinite number of worlds, if there were multiple worlds, and if all the inhabitants of these worlds were given faith in Christ, let alone for every individual person of one world, without exception, if God willed to have mercy on them all" (as quoted in Blacketer, "Blaming Beza," 136). Beza described the Lombardian formula as true "very roughly and ambiguously, as well as barbarously" (see Rouwendal, "Calvin's Forgotten Classical Position," 319–20).

17. Calvin, 1 John 2:2, *Gospel according to St John 11–21 and the First Epistle of John*, 244.

18. Clifford, *Atonement and Justification*, 4; Crisp, *Deviant Calvinism*, 177. According to Berkhof, Christ's death being "sufficient for the salvation of all men" is "admitted by all." The question concerns "the design of the atonement" (Berkhof, *Systematic Theology*, 393–94). Coming from a differing theological perspective, Oliver Crisp concurs that the question concerns "the actual intent or extent of Christ's work—that is, to what God wills" (Crisp, *Deviant Calvinism*, 218). "Those who defend the DA [Definite-Atonement] understand the sufficiency of Christ's work for fallen humanity only in the sense of an intrinsic sufficiency, whereas advocates of UA [Universal-Atonement] think of it as being both intrinsically and extrinsically sufficient" (ibid.). Furthermore, hypothetical universalism "is simply the extrapolation of one obvious way of understanding the distinction" (ibid., 177). For example, John Davenant contrasted between a "mere sufficiency" (*nuda sufficientia*) and an "ordained sufficiency" (*sufficientia ordinata*) (Davenant, *Dissertation* II.37–38, 378, 401–3, 409, 412; see Moore, "Extent of the Atonement," 138; Macleod, "Definite Atonement and the Divine Decree," 426; Compton, "John Davenant's *Dissertation on the Death of Christ*," 173n58; Lynch, "Richard Hooker," 282). The Scriptures, according to Davenant, "speak of the death of Christ so as to refer to its universal efficacy not to the mere dignity of the sacrifice offered, but to the act and intention of the offering" (Davenant, *Dissertation* II.410–11; as quoted in Moore, "Extent of the Atonement," 138–39). John Owen, highlighting the intrinsic sufficiency of Christ's death, told gospel preachers that they may "justifiably call upon every man to believe" since "there is enough in the death of Christ to save every one that shall do so" (Owen, *Works of John Owen*, vol. 10, 298).

ciency" was already recognized in the early modern era.[19] "Although the phrase may defuse tensions in many situations, it blurs distinctions and, therefore, is unhelpful to use for defining a position."[20] "To make this point another way," writes Richard Muller, "if 'atonement' is taken to mean the value or sufficiency of Christ's death, only a very few theologians involved in the early modern debates taught limited atonement—and if atonement is taken to mean the actual salvation accomplished in particular persons, then no one involved in those debates taught unlimited atonement (except perhaps the much-reviled Samuel Huber [a universalist])."[21]

Calvin did not merely leave matters there, however. Calvin's corpus reveals that more can be said than a mere repetition of the "classic" proposition. More research and study is needed, including more work that traces continuities back into the Middle Ages (with figures like Peter Lombard and Thomas Aquinas) and also places Calvin in his contemporary context among other reformers such as Bucer, Bullinger, Cranmer, de Valdés, Gualther, Hooper, Kimedoncius, Musculus, Trelcatius, Vermigli, Zanchi, and Zwingli.[22] One can, indeed, ascertain facets of a theologi-

---

If the issue of divine intent does not enter into "sufficient for all but efficient for the elect," then the latter half of the formula becomes a mere tautology (the elect, are, by definition, those for whom Christ's work has become effective). By parallel, if divine intention does not enter into the first half of the formula, then "sufficient for all" becomes a mere statement of bare intrinsic value, admitted by all. I thank Anthony Lane for this insight, in personal correspondence.

19. Gootjes, "John Cameron," 184–85.
20. Naselli, "John Owen's Argument for Definite Atonement," 74.
21. Muller, "Was Calvin a Calvinist?" 61. If "limited atonement" means that Christ's satisfaction is efficient only for the elect, then *all* forms of seventeenth-century hypothetical universalism (including Amyraldianism) could be construed as alternative forms of limited atonement (ibid., 61n21). The case of Samuel Huber was actually rather complicated. See Hardt, "Justification and Easter."
22. Ponter, "Review Essay (Part One)," 141–43; Foord, "God Wills All People to Be Saved," 179. Some research of this type has been done, coming from divergent perspectives, by Ponter, "Calvin and Calvinism" and Hogg, "'Sufficient for All, Efficient for Some." Cf. Denlinger, "Scottish Hypothetical Universalism," 93, 98; Thomas, *Extent of the Atonement*, 248–51; Shultz, *Multi-Intentioned View of the Extent of the Atonement*, 29. On Thomas Aquinas, see Gatiss, "Grace Tasted Death for All," 217–36. Ponter insists that the wider context of Reformation theology in Calvin's own day argues for Calvin himself espousing universal vicarious satisfaction (Ponter, "Review Essay (Part Two)," 270; cf. 255, 266). Ponter affirms that "Calvin's language mirrors the language of his contemporaries, which lends weight to the argument that Calvin's theology of satisfaction was continuous with them as well.... The point then is this: Why are we to imagine that the same language for Calvin apparently meant something completely different? What evidence is there within the data of the various texts that he himself

cal framework indicated by Calvin's disparate statements. This complex perspective (which can be expressed diachronically through God's eternal decree, Jesus' sacrifice in history, the proclamation of the gospel, and the personal application of salvation through the Spirit) included the espousal of *both* unconditional election *and* a universal "provision" *in some sense*. Furthermore, Calvin considered it *pastorally important* to preserve both of these positions, which distinguishes his approach from many strict "limited atonement" views as commonly understood today.

In this manner, my final assessment of the evidence may fit with some facets of the "second approach." Calvin apparently espoused *a form* of "universal redemption" along with his particularist view of "unconditional election." However, unlike some variants of the "second approach," one must also acknowledge that Calvin did not develop the "Amyraldian" system as found in the 1600s, including its developed explication of "conditional universal atonement" *within its own covenantal structure and ordering of the decrees.*[23] Interpreters should be careful so as not to make Calvin sound (anachronistically) "Amyraldian," since the details of Calvin's underlying structure were not developed into such a full, Amyraldian covenantal scheme or ordering of the decrees.[24] As Brian Arm-

---

adopted a different understanding of the critical terms like 'world' or 'redeemed souls perishing'?" (Ponter, "Review Essay (Part One)," 158; cf. 141, 157).

23. "Yet it is also clear that in terms of terminology, there is a shift away from Calvin by all sides. All sides are now trying to explain Scripture in the light of new concepts and categories. *Covenant* was a powerful category that came to dominate the Reformed landscape. This is especially true for Amyraut, following Cameron" (Ponter, "Brief History of Deviant Calvinism," 48). Many dispensational theologians who use the label "Amyraldian" do not acknowledge the covenantal structure behind Amyraut's espousal of "unconditional election" and "universal atonement." On the covenantal thought of Amyraut's predecessors at Saumur, see Muller, "Divine Covenants, Absolute and Conditional," 36–37. On the continuity between Amyraldianism and the Reformed symbols, see Muller, *Post-Reformation Reformed Dogmatics*, vol. 1, 76–81. For good introductions to the Amyraldian controversy, see Armstrong, *Calvinism and the Amyraut Heresy*; Laplanche, *Orthodoxie et predication*; van Stam, *Controversy over the Theology of Saumur*. For the French Reformed context in the period preceding Amyraut's career, see Armstrong, "Semper Reformanda," 119–40.

24. Systematic federalism is absent from Calvin's theology, although covenantal theology is there incipiently. See Helm, "Calvin and the Covenant"; Torrance, "Concept of Federal Theology," 15–40; Torrance, "Strengths and Weaknesses of the Westminster Theology," 48–50; Lillback, *Binding of God*. Ponter argues that Amyraut "clearly tried to integrate that Scriptural Universalism which he found in Calvin and the Bible with the theological schema of Federalism. It's as if Calvinism, now wedded to Federalism, is a system of thought struggling to adjust itself and find the most correct expression. But this struggle is painful, haphazard, irregular, and bumpy. What is more, Amyraut

strong notes, "The more one reads the treatises of Amyraut the more he realizes that the peculiar covenant theology he expounds is the key to the whole theological program at Saumur."[25] This statement needs to be nuanced, even as Muller has moderated the supposedly "central" role of covenantal theology in the teaching of John Cameron (Amyraut's teacher and mentor).[26] Nevertheless, Amyraut's emphasis upon covenantal theology did weave throughout his teaching.

Moreover, Amyraut's views cannot be interpreted apart from the significant role of Cameron, who served as a link between Calvin and Amyraut.[27] Amyraut himself praised Cameron as the greatest influence upon his theology after the Holy Scriptures.[28] Amyraut asserted that his theological system looked beyond Cameron back to Calvin.[29] Moreover, Amyraut is the first preacher known to have quoted Calvin in the pulpit, although he was reproached by Pierre Du Moulin for his practice

---

shows us the mine-field of complexity here" (Ponter, "Brief History of Deviant Calvinism," 38). See also Wenkel, "John Bunyan's Theory of Atonement"; Wenkel, "John Bunyan's Soteriology," 351–52.

25. Armstrong, *Calvinism and the Amyraut Heresy*, 140. Concerning Amyraut and the other Saumur theologians, Armstrong argues, "Unquestionably the predominant design of this covenant scheme was to restore what these men firmly believed to be the teaching of Scripture, Calvin, and the Dort Canons concerning the matter of predestination" (Armstrong, *Calvinism and the Amyraut Heresy*, 142). For a comparison of the Genevan and Saumurian theologians, see Grohman, "Genevan Reactions to the Saumur Doctrine"; Gootjes, "Calvin and Saumur," 203–14.

26. Muller, "Divine Covenants, Absolute and Conditional," 29. Cf. Shultz, *Multi-Intentioned View of the Extent of the Atonement*, 37. For an introduction to Cameron's theology, see Bonet-Maury, "Jean Cameron," 77–117; Bonet-Maury, "John Cameron," 325–45.

27. "Practically every insight which Amyraut revealed he owed, as he acknowledged, to Cameron" (Armstrong, *Calvinism and the Amyraut Heresy*, 265). Pierre Bayle claimed, "Never was a scholar filled with a greater Veneration for his Master, than Mr. Amyraut was for Cameron. It is said he imitated him even to the Tone of his Voice and a certain Motion of his Head" (as quoted in Rex, *Essays on Pierre Bayle*, 99–100). Cf. Gootjes, "John Cameron," 169–96.

28. Djaballah, "Controversy on Universal Grace," 168–69.

29. Armstrong, *Calvinism and the Amyraut Heresy*, 265. At the conclusion of his monograph, Armstrong declares, "On the basis of all that I have learned I would maintain that his claim is substantially correct" (ibid., 269). See, however, the differences collected in Thomas, *Extent of the Atonement*, 213–17. Thomas draws a much sharper distinction between Calvin and Amyraut. One should note that Cameron denied the imputation of Christ's active obedience in justification (Gootjes, "Scotland and Saumur," 178). This view represented the Academy of Saumur (see Williams, *Heart of Piety*, 186n891).

of doing so.³⁰ Nonetheless, Amyraut's developed interpretation of Calvin came to fruition within the covenantal structure of Cameron's theology.³¹ Like Cameron, Amyraut posited a three-fold scheme of the covenant of nature, the covenant of law, and the covenant of grace.³² In Amyraut's

30. Djaballah, "Controversy on Universal Grace," 170–71.

31. Concerning Cameron's covenantal theology, Muller notes, "It was preceded by the efforts of thinkers like Ursinus, Olevianus, Fenner, Perkins, Polamus, and Rollock, but still belongs to the formative phase of covenant thought" (Muller, "Divine Covenants, Absolute and Conditional," 27). Cameron's treatise on the covenants "ought not to be identified as a full-scale covenant theology, such as would appear later in the works of Johannes Cocceius, Franz Burman, Francis Roberts, and Herman Witsius" (ibid., 29). And the importance of covenant to Cameron's theology should not be exaggerated (Muller, "Davenant and Du Moulin," 129). For a brief survey of the development of covenant theology within the Reformed/Calvinist movement, see Helm, *Calvin: A Guide for the Perplexed*, 138–42; Nicole, "Covenant, Universal Call and Definite Atonement," 404.

32. Armstrong claims, "Like Cameron, Amyraut developed his whole program on the foundation of a threefold covenant teaching" (Armstrong, *Calvinism and the Amyraut Heresy*, 265). Muller responds, "Such statements breathe too much of the air of the central dogma theory to stand scrutiny; and Cameron himself left no clear index to a center or foundation of his theology. As for the theological program at Saumur, it was far too variegated and *locus* oriented to be founded on any single doctrine" (Muller, "Divine Covenants, Absolute and Conditional," 29). Cameron spoke of at least five covenants, two absolute and three conditional/hypothetical (the three mentioned above)—see ibid., 28. "Arguably, it is this discussion of absolute covenants prior to the hypothetical that is the most striking aspect of Cameron's exposition, and one of its least appreciated elements" (ibid., 30). Cameron maintained that "'this distinction of the Covenant' into absolute and hypothetical covenants 'depends on the distinction of the love of God' into antecedent and consequent" (ibid., 33–34; cf. Thomas Aquinas, *Summa Theologiae* 1, quest. 19, art. 6, obj. 1). According to Cameron, using a fourfold structure, "The first decree has to do with the restoration of the image of God in the creature, but so as to be consistent with God's justice; the second with the sending of the Son who saves each and every one who believes in Him . . . ; the third with rendering men capable of believing; the fourth is to save those who believe. The first two degrees are general, the last two are particular" (as quoted in Armstrong, *Calvinism and the Amyraut Heresy*, 58). "This pattern has major implications for understanding the Salmurian soteriology. It indicates a covenantal or federal continuity with Reformed predestinarianism that has been left unexamined in discussions of hypothetical universalism. . . . It offers an element of the Salmurian theology that presses it away from rather than toward Arminianism; . . . it demonstrates the point, recognized even by seventeenth-century opponents of Amyraldianism like Francis Turretin, namely, that views of Cameron and his Salmurian successors were not heresy and, like it or not, were consciously framed to stand within the confessionalism of the Canons of Dort. In the specific case of Cameron's covenantal thought, it ought to be understood not as a protest against various developments in Reformed theology but rather as an integral part of the rather fluid and variegated history of early Reformed covenantal thought'"

own words, "First, that which was contracted in the earthly paradise and ought to be called *natural*; secondly, the one which God transacted in a special way with Israel and is called *legal*; and thirdly, that which is called *gracious* and is set forth in the gospel."[33] According to Amyraut, the eternal covenant of grace was bifurcated into a universal, conditional covenant and a particular, unconditional covenant.[34] On the other hand, "Calvin nowhere raises the issue of different covenant relationships or of

---

(Muller, "Divine Covenants, Absolute and Conditional," 36–37; cf. Trueman, "Election," 116–17). Scholarship seems to be moving toward an acknowledgement that at least some forms of hypothetical universalism were acceptable within the Canons of Dort (Gatiss, "Synod of Dort and Definite Atonement," 143–63) and perhaps even within the Westminster Standards—the latter being more disputed (Denlinger, "Scottish Hypothetical Universalism," 97). Richard Muller, however, affirms, "The Westminster Confession was in fact written with this diversity in view, encompassing confessionally the variant Reformed views on the nature of the limitation of Christ's satisfaction to the elect, just as it was written to be inclusive of the infra- and supralapsarian views on predestination" (Muller, *Post-Reformation Reformed Dogmatics*, vol. 1, 76–77). For a full discussion, see Gatiss, "'Shades of Opinion within a Generic Calvinism,'" 101–18; Gatiss, "Deceptive Clarity?" 194–95.

33. Amyraut, thesis 2, "De tribus foederibus divinis," *Theses Salmurienses* 1.212; English translation in Armstrong, *Calvinism and the Amyraut Heresy*, 144.

34. Bruce Demarest explains, "The Saumur school postulated a threefold covenant, viewed as three successive steps in God's saving program: (1) the covenant of nature established between God and Adam involved obedience to the divine law disclosed in the natural order; (2) the covenant of law between God and Israel focused on adherence to the written law of Moses; and (3) the covenant of grace established between God and all humankind requires faith in Christ's finished work. In Amyraldianism the covenant of grace was further divided into a conditional covenant of universal grace and an unconditional covenant of particular grace. For actualization the former required fulfillment of the condition of faith. The latter, grounded in God's good pleasure, does not call for the condition of faith; rather, it creates faith in the elect" (Demarest, "Amyraldianism," 48). Demarest adds, "Amyraut also developed a system of covenant theology alternative to the two-fold covenant of grace schema propounded by much of Reformed orthodoxy" (ibid., 53). However, as Muller explains, "Examination of Cameron's predecessors yields strong evidence that the understanding of covenant found in Cameron's *De triplici Dei cum homine foedere theses* cannot be interpreted as a departure from a 'two covenant' model for several reasons. In the first place, the fairly standard modern distinction between 'one covenant' and 'two covenant' models does not adequately describe the covenantal thought of the sixteenth and seventeenth centuries. Accordingly, second, one does not find a strict two covenant approach in the thought of Cameron's predecessors. And third, Cameron's multi-layered definitions of covenant actually reflect a development in Reformed thought resting positively on the initial covenantal theorizings of such writers as Musculus, Ursinus, Olevianus, Perkins, Polanus, and Rollock" (Muller, "Divine Covenants, Absolute and Conditional," 17).

two different mercies of God, deployed, as Amyraut indicates, in relation to differing covenants."[35]

Within this covenantal system, Amyraut emphasized a Trinitarian approach to redemptive history that allowed him to "bypass" the "limited atonement" of his high orthodox Calvinist peers.[36] According to G. Michael Thomas, Amyraut's theology "breaks new ground in relating the progressive revelation of the Trinity to the three covenants identified by the Saumur school. The covenants of nature and law pertain chiefly to the Father as creator, judge and law-giver. The covenant of grace relates to the Son, who is its mediator, and the application of the covenant of grace belongs to the Spirit. This co-ordination of the Trinity with covenantal salvation history underlines the importance of the covenant motif to Amyraut's theology, and highlights its historical orientation."[37]

Therefore, according to Armstrong, ". . . Amyraut places an unusually strong emphasis upon the work of the Holy Spirit. This is because he believes that the Holy Spirit is the member of the Godhead who works efficaciously."[38] Unlike some later theologians who have used the term "Amyraldian" of themselves, Amyraut believed that regeneration precedes faith.[39] Yet Amyraut tied this regeneration of the will specifically to an illumination of the understanding in a manner that most high orthodox Calvinists rejected. According to Amyraut (borrowing from Cameron), the Holy Spirit moves the will by illuminating the understanding.[40] Arm-

35. Muller, "Tale of Two Wills?" 218.

36. Armstrong, *Calvinism and the Amyraut Heresy*, 221.

37. Thomas, *Extent of the Atonement*, 197; cf. Nicole, "Covenant, Universal Call and Definite Atonement," 404.

38. Armstrong, *Calvinism and the Amyraut Heresy*, 148.

39. See Snoeberger, "Logical Priority of Regeneration to Saving Faith," 50n7. Recent historical scholarship has demonstrated the lack of a singular structuring of the *ordo salutis* among Reformed theologians in early modernity (Fesko, *Beyond Calvin*, 29). "There are certainly shared general patterns but there are also many differences in the details" (ibid.).

40. Armstrong, *Calvinism and the Amyraut Heresy*, 249–52. "So when Cameron talks of conversion he speaks of the Holy Spirit's action as one, though including two aspects, illumination and regeneration. And he customarily speaks of that action as occurring in the intellect, since he understands the will to be necessarily involved in any action on the intellect" (ibid., 64). "Moreover, he stated that in spite of his insistence on the role of secondary causes (i.e., the gospel object that is proposed to the intellect), he still did hold God to be the one who operates—through the intellect—on the will" (Gootjes, "Scotland and Saumur," 180). Contrast the views of Claude Pajon in ibid., 181–89; Gootjes, "L'héritage de John Cameron," 51–70. Gootjes classifies Amyraut and

strong asserts: "To explain this work of the Spirit, Amyraut used almost exclusively the concept of *illuminatio*."[41] Amyraut emphasized a double process, including an external preaching and hearing of the gospel and an internal illumination (or *entendement* worked by the Holy Spirit in the heart).[42]

In a related maneuver (again preceded by Cameron), Amyraut distinguished between the concepts of "natural ability" and "moral ability."[43] "The distinction itself is a very simple one, namely that man *can* respond to grace because he has been endowed with understanding and will, but that he *will not* respond because he is sinful."[44] This precise distinction of terms goes beyond Calvin's own explicit explanations, although the groundwork is there.[45] Furthermore, Amyraut was accused of allowing the possibility of salvation among the unevangelized by means of general revelation.[46] In principle, this would open up two possible ways of

---

the majority of French theologians who followed his Saumurian theology as "moderate" Cameronians, in contrast to the "radical" Cameronians represented by Testard, Pajon, and their disciples (Gootjes, "Scotland and Saumur," 189). Discussions of the intellect and the will filled the period. Calvin taught, "The understanding is, as it were, the leader and governor of the soul; . . . the will is always mindful of the bidding of the understanding, and in its own desires awaits the judgment of the understanding" (Calvin, *Institutes* I.15.7). For an explanation on how John Owen changed his views concerning the intellect and volition *within God* concerning the necessity of the atonement, see Trueman, "Necessity of the Atonement." "This is hardly surprising, as the debate as a whole can be seen as another example of the periodic battles between intellectualists and voluntarists that had started in the Middle Ages" (ibid., 221).

41. Armstrong, *Calvinism and the Amyraut Heresy*, 249. For a summary of Cameron's similar understanding of *illuminatio*, see Strehle, "Universal Grace and Amyraldianism," 347-48. Cf. Calvin, *Institutes*, III.14.21; III.18.1; III.24.17; Calvin, *On the Eternal Predestination*, 127; etc.

42. Djaballah, "Controversy on Universal Grace," 186-87.

43. Amyraut maintained that human inability involved "malice of heart" rather than physical, mental, or constitutional incapacity (Quick, *Synodicon in Gallia Reformata*, vol. 2, 356-57). Amyraut also distinguished between "objective" grace (or "sufficient external" grace) and "subjective" grace (or "efficient internal" grace) (see Thomas, *Extent of the Atonement*, 203). Cf. the objective and subjective dimensions of reconciliation in 2 Cor 5:16-21.

44. Armstrong, *Calvinism and the Amyraut Heresy*, 216. Cf. the distinction between "natural ability" and "moral ability" in Edwardsean theology (see Guelzo, *Edwards on the Will*). See also the distinction between "natural ability" and "moral ability" in the theologies of Joseph Bellamy, Thomas Manton, and Stephen Charnock (as pointed out to me by Reid Ferguson and Tony Byrne).

45. Cf. Calvin's discussion of issues in *Institutes* II.2.12-27.

46. Huldrych Zwingli, Philip Doddridge, and others held similar views. The

salvation: through the testimony of the Scriptures and through natural revelation.⁴⁷ John Quick's *Synodicon in Gallia Reformata*, however, asserts that Amyraut denied that this had actually ever happened.⁴⁸ In any case, many contemporary self-professed "Amyraldians" do not accept the *whole* theological package of Amyraut.⁴⁹

In his *Brief Treatise on Predestination*, Amyraut proclaimed that "Jesus Christ died for all men equally."⁵⁰ Nevertheless, this was only one pole

---

Helvetic Consensus Formula of 1675 opposed the notion. On Doddridge's general theology, see Strivens, *Philip Doddridge*.

47. Djaballah, "Controversy on Universal Grace," 181.

48. "Monsieur *Testard* and *Amyraud* declared further, that although the Doctrines obvious to us in the Works of Creation and Providence, do teach and preach Repentance, and invite us to seek the Lord, who would be found of us; yet nevertheless, by reason of the horrible Blindness of our Nature, and its universal Corruption, no Man was ever this way converted; yea, and it is utterly impossible that any one should be converted but by the hearing of the Word of God, which is the Seed of our Regeneration, and the Instrument of the Holy Ghost, whose Efficacy and Virtue only is able to illuminate our Understandings, and to change the Hearts and Affections of the Children of Men" (Quick, *Synodicon in Gallia Reformata*, vol. 2, 356). Questions remain concerning the caricatures of Amyraut by his opponents. See Proctor, "Theology of Moïse Amyraut," 279–89; van Stam, *Controversy over the Theology of Saumur*.

49. Consider the case of self-proclaimed "Amyraldian Dispensationalists." Especially due to opposition, Amyraut himself came to avoid certain terms and phrases, although his theology remained "essentially unchanged" (Strehle, "Universal Grace and Amyraldianism," 353). The Alençon Synod forbade the use of "conditional predestination," Christ dying for all humans "equally," and other terminology (Thomas, *Extent of the Atonement*, 190, 202). The synod further declared that all parties should avoid the language of "conditional and revocable decrees," using rather the terminology of a "revealed will of God" (see Muller, "Davenant and Du Moulin," 152). The Alençon Synod cautiously exonerated Amyraut and Testard (Djaballah, "Controversy on Grace," 167). Du Moulin and Rivet (opponents of Amyraut) were not criticized in any manner (ibid., 194).

50. "Jesus-Christ mourant Egalement pour Tous" (see Strehle, "Universal Grace and Amyraldianism," 353). When Amyraut insisted that "Christ died for all men equally," he spoke of the sufficiency side of the "classic" formula. This has been documented in Proctor, "Theology of Moïse Amyraut," 376n78. The original impetus for Amyraut's treatise was an apologetically oriented conversation over dinner at the Bishop of Chartres' residence. A nobleman present was "filled with horror by the doctrine of predestination as taught in our [Reformed] churches," and regarded it as "contrary to the nature of God and His gospel to say that He created the greatest part of mankind with the express purpose of damning them." Amyraut's explanations of predestination seemed helpful, and so he developed them and put them into writing (see Armstrong, *Calvinism and the Amyraut Heresy*, 81). Within this context, Amyraut's treatise emphasized the "universal" aspect of his view of the atonement, although he also held to unconditional election and God's particular, efficacious work in the elect.

of his overall view of the atonement. Amyraut also insisted that Jesus died especially for the efficacious salvation of the elect, who had been unconditionally chosen by God.[51] Although Amyraut's theology went beyond Calvin in various ways, many of the "raw materials" were already there in Calvin (especially the two-fold will of God *as perceived by humans yet truly undivided in God*; and the believer's focus upon Christ as revealed in the gospel rather than the eternal decree).[52] Yet Calvin seems to have emphasized more of the singularity of God's will (*simplex voluntas*) manifest in a duplex or diverse manner (*Deum semper idem velle, sed diversis modis*), while Amyraut tended to emphasize the phenomena of two wills (in our perception, though ultimately unified) corresponding to

---

51. Cf. Calvin's wide structure of God's *universal* love in Christ narrowed *especially* to believers: "For as He declared His love toward mankind when He spared not His Only Son but delivered Him to death for sinners, also He declares a love which He bears especially toward us when by His Holy Spirit He touches us by the knowledge of our sins and He makes us wail and draws us to Himself with repentance" (Calvin, *Deity of Christ and Other Sermons*, 108). Cf. the clarity of God's love for humanity in Calvin on John 3:16. According to Davenant, "Therefore the intention of Christ in offering himself regarded the elect in a special manner" (Davenant, *Dissertation* II:380, as quoted in Macleod, "Definite Atonement and the Divine Decree," 425). First Timothy 4:10 narrows a general salvation to a particular application: "God who is the Saviour of all men, specially of those that believe" (cf. Daniel, *Biblical Calvinism*, 6-7). Rainbow claims that Calvin interpreted "Saviour" in this verse as applicable to God's "common benevolence" or "preservation" (see Rainbow, *Will of God and the Cross*, 147). In this manner, Calvin echoed the Augustinian interpretation of the verse. See also Kuiper, *For Whom Did Christ Die?* 81; Shepherd, *Nature and Function of Faith*, 85.

52. For Amyraut's discussion of God's twofold will (in our perception), see Thomas, *Extent of the Atonement*, 166-67. "The two will distinction, adopted from the medieval scholastics, was taken for granted in Reformed theology" (Thomas, *Extent of the Atonement*, 166). The "two wills motif" had "a long and distinguished pedigree" (ibid., 220). Cf. Macleod, "*Amyraldus redivivus*," 212; Macleod, "Definite Atonement and the Divine Decree," 424-25. In his "heresy" trial during the Synod of Alençon, Amyraut affirmed that the divine decree could be considered "as diverse"; yet "The will of this most supreme and incomprehensible Lord, being but one only eternal act in him; so that could we but conceive of things as they be in him from all eternity, we should comprehend these [conditional and absolute] decrees of God by one only act of our understanding, as in truth they be but one only act of his eternal and unchangeable will" (Quick, *Synodicon in Gallia Reformata*, vol. 2, 355). For a modern example of distinguishing between God's "decretive will" and his "revealed will" by a proponent of "limited atonement," see John Hendryx, "Is it God's Desire for All Men to Be Saved?" Like many other theologians, Steve Jeffery, Michael Ovey, and Andrew Sach distinguish between God's "moral will" and his "sovereign will." "God does want all to be saved in the moral sense. That is to say, it is an offence to him when someone fails to repent and turn in faith to his Son. But God does not want all to be saved in the sovereign sense" (Jeffery et al., *Pierced for Our Transgressions*, 270n65).

two divine mercies.[53] Amyraut also reached behind Calvin to employ the traditional "classic" formula that "Christ died sufficiently for all but efficiently for the elect."[54] Calvin did not deny the formula, as demonstrated in his exegesis of 1 John 2:2, but he seemed reticent sometimes to employ it as an exegetical solution.[55] Amyraut appealed to Calvin's exegesis of John 3:16 on numerous occasions, yet he differed from Calvin in his interpretation of 1 Tim 2:4.[56]

Therefore, labels such as "the 'Calvin-Amyraut' outlook" mask the historical complexities of difference and development.[57] One should not uncritically set forth Amyraut, Cameron, and the like as "the true Calvinians."[58] Calvin never *fully* explained *how* Christ's dying "for" all was related to the secret decree of God in eternity past.[59] Calvin simply stated it as so: ". . . Christ was foreordained before the foundation of the

---

53. Muller, "Tale of Two Wills?" 218–25; Harding, "Atonement Theory Revisited," 62–63. Contrast Armstrong, *Calvinism and the Amyraut Heresy*, 188. Even Amyraut recognized that ultimately God's will is unified (Quick, *Synodicon in Gallia Reformata*, vol. 2, 355). John Piper speaks of "two wills" in God, one an expression of his sovereign control and the other an expression of his moral standards—God's "will of decree" and his "will of command," or God's "sovereign will" and his "moral will" (Piper, "Are There Two Wills in God?" 121–22; Piper, *Does God Desire All to Be Saved?* 23–24). Piper also distinguishes between God's desire (what God would like to see happen") and his decree ("what he actually does will to happen") (ibid.). Cf. the examination of Berkhof, Grudem, and Piper in Gardoski, "Will of God and the Death of Christ," 68–109.

54. Armstrong, *Calvinism and the Amyraut Heresy*, 92.

55. Calvin, 1 John 2:2, *Gospel according to St John 11–21 and the First Epistle of John*, 244. "Arguably, Calvin's language maintains the broad sense of the traditional sufficiency-efficiency distinction concerning Christ's work, a distinction held both by Amyraut and by his opponents" (Muller, "Tale of Two Wills?" 221).

56. Harding, "Atonement Theory Revisited," 66–68.

57. Clifford, "Calvin & Calvinism," 37. Clifford describes the views of the *Heidelberg Catechism*, the *Canons of Dort*, and even Augustine as "proto-Amyraldian" (ibid., 14). Nevertheless, he acknowledges that Cameron's views developed from the less systematized materials in Calvin (ibid., 16). See Proctor, "Theology of Moïse Amyraut," For works that place Amyraldianism in the wider post-Reformation perspective, see Prestwich, *International Calvinism*; Muller, *Post-Reformation Reformed Dogmatics*, vol. 1.

58. Muller, "Diversity in the Reformed Tradition," 13.

59. Armstrong refers to "Amyraut's constant insistence that this universal offer in the atonement was in fact the expression of the eternal will of God, even for those to whom the gospel message never comes" (Armstrong, *Calvinism and the Amyraut Heresy*, 211). His bifurcation of the eternal decree into the conditional decree of universal provision and the unconditional decree of election allowed him to focus upon the former.

world to wash away the sins of the world by His sacrifice. Without a doubt this means that the expiation of sin executed by Christ was ordained by the eternal decrees of God."[60] According to Calvin, the sacrifice of Christ "was ordained by the eternal decree of God, to expiate the sins of the world."[61] For Calvin, the center that tied the disparate tenets together was Christ himself: "Election and the work of expiation and reconciliation are conjoined because both are founded in Christ."[62] Yet unlike Amyraut, Calvin never overtly posited a hypothetical or conditional decree of salvation.[63] Unlike Amyraut, Calvin never explicitly contrasted a *voluntas antecedens et hypothetica* (an antecedent and hypothetical will) and a *voluntas consequens et absoluta* (a consequent and absolute will).[64] Again, Calvin did not develop a conditional, covenantal framework similar to the hypothetical universalism of John Davenant; nor, on the other hand, did he develop the *pactum salutis* within a covenantal structure in the manner of John Owen.[65]

60. Calvin, *Concerning the Eternal Predestination*, 71. Cf. Calvin, John 14:30–31, *Gospel according to St John 11–21 and the First Epistle of John*, 91–92.

61. Calvin, Matt 26:24, *Harmony of the Gospels*, vol. 3, 129–30. Cf. Calvin, 1 Pet 1:20, *The Epistle of Paul the Apostle to the Hebrews and the First and Second Epistles of St Peter*, 249–50.

62. Muller, *Christ and the Decree*, 34.

63. Muller, "Was Calvin a Calvinist?" 61.

64. Muller, "Tale of Two Wills?" 222–23. Previous theologians, including John of Damascus and Thomas Aquinas, had distinguished between an "antecedent will" and "consequent will" (Foord, "God Wills All People to Be Saved," 184–85). According to Foord, "The *via antiqua* divines all understood that the distinction between God's antecedent and consequent will was a further distinction in God's *voluntas beneplaciti* (Foord, "God Wills All People to Be Saved," 185). According to Muller, Calvin draws on the traditional *voluntas beneplaciti / signi* distinction rather than a *voluntas antecedens / consequens* distinction (Muller, "Tale of Two Wills?" 223).

65. Muller, "Toward the *Pactum Salutis*," 11–65; Muller, "Davenant and Du Moulin," 138; Moore, "Extent of the Atonement," 143. For a summary of Davenant's argumentation, see Compton, "John Davenant's Dissertation on the Death of Christ," 167–81; van Asselt, "Christ's Atonement," 61; Kang, "John Davenant," 1–24. Davenant's hypothetical universalism did not exactly match the Cameronian and Amyraldian forms (Moore, Extent of the Atonement, 143n89). The "burden of Owen's response to Baxter" lay in his understanding of the *pactum salutis* (covenant of redemption) (Tay, *Priesthood of Christ*, 53; Trueman, "Atonement and the Covenant of Redemption," 212). "This point is extremely important: for Owen, abstract discussions of universal sufficiency are just that: abstract and irrelevant. It is not a question of whether the death of the Son of God could be sufficient for all; it is a question of what that death was intended to accomplish. That intention was determined by God in the establishment of the covenant of redemption" (ibid. 215). The covenant of redemption can then

For that matter, Calvin never systematically listed an "order" to the decrees at all.[66] Amyraut himself recognized this:

> ... I am well aware that Calvin has said many things relating to the "impulsive" causes of the decrees of God, but as to their order I do not see that he has ever said a word. Why God has created man for hope of perpetual blessedness, he states that the only reason for this is His goodness. Why, man having fallen into sin and condemnation, God willed to send His son into the world to redeem men by His death, Calvin states that the only reason for this is an admirable love of God for mankind. Why He has elected some and passed by others in imparting the grace of faith, Calvin states that the only reason for this is the mercy and severity of God. Why God has preferred one individual to another in the distribution of this grace, Calvin does not recognize any other reason than solely the perfectly free will of God. Why He has willed to save believers and to condemn unbelievers unto eternal punishment, Calvin has thought that the reason for the latter must be taken from the justice of God whereas the reason for the former must be taken from His mercy. . . . But what has been the order according to which God has arranged all these things in His eternal wisdom, when it is a question of His having proposed of thinking or willing what comes first or last, Calvin has never explained this nor has he the least interest in doing so.[67]

By contrast, according to John Quick's *Synodicon in Gallia Reformata*, the Amyraldian party (in an accommodation to human perception)

---

be interwoven with an Owenian double payment argument, such that "the effects of Christ's death are determined by the covenant of redemption" (ibid., 219, 220). On Calvin's role in the development of subsequent covenant theology, see Lillback, *Binding of God*. Contrast Rolston, "Responsible Man in Reformed Theology," 129–56. On the doctrinal development of covenant in the period, see Trueman, "From Calvin to Gillespie on Covenant," 378–97.

66. See Archbald, "Comparative Study of John Calvin and Theodore Beza," 134–38. Calvin can state that the elect were drawn from a "corrupt mass" (Calvin, *Institutes*, III.23.3; see also III.22.7; cf., however, Calvin, *Concerning the Eternal Predestination*, 90–91; *Institutes*, III.21.5). On so-called "non-speculative" forms of purported "hypothetical universalism" prior to Amyraut, see Moore, *English Hypothetical Universalism*; cf. Rouwendal, "Calvin's Forgotten Classical Position," 322 (and his inclusion of insights from Richard Muller). Authors sometimes use "non-speculative" to refer to forms of so-called "hypothetical universalism" that do not postulate a "speculative" ordering of the decrees, etc. As in many related issues, the terms are debated.

67. Armstrong, *Calvinism and the Amyraut Heresy*, 163–64.

spoke of the "logical" order (but not the "chronological" order) of the decrees:

> As to making distinct decrees in the council of God, the first of which is to save all men, through Jesus Christ, if they shall believe in him, the second to give faith unto some particular persons, Amyraut, along with Testard, declared, that they did this upon no other account than of accommodating it unto that manner and order which the spirit of man observes in his reasonings for the succour of his own infirmity; they otherwise believing, that though they considered this decree as diverse, yet it was formed in God in one and the self-same moment, without any succession of thought or order of priority and posteriority.[68]

This setting of Calvin's positions into a more federalist system with some lapsarian structure is a development beyond Calvin.[69] Stephen Strehle queries, "One must ask, therefore, whether such lapsarian schemata do not in the end undermine Amyraut's stated devotion to Calvin."[70] Strehle also highlights Amyraut's "rationalistic explanations of the doctrines of irresistible grace and natural revelation."[71]

68. Quick, *Synodicon in Gallia Reformata*, vol. 2, 355; English spelling updated. One might refer to a "speculative" turn, simply because the Scriptures do not reveal an exact "order to the decrees" (logical or otherwise). Of course, there are many matters not fully explicated in Scripture that systematic theologians have nevertheless arranged in an orderly fashion. For a critical evaluation of lapsarian schemes in general, see Dabney, *Lectures in Systematic Theology*, 233: "In my opinion this is a question which never ought to have been raised.... God's decree has no succession; and to Him no successive order of parts; because it is a contemporaneous unit, comprehended altogether, by one infinite intuition."

69. See Ponter, "Brief History of Deviant Calvinism," 35. On the other hand, full systematic presentations of "the Amyraldian" order of the decrees, as found in B. B. Warfield and Robert L. Reymond go beyond the explicit, primary source evidence in Amyraut's own writings (see Warfield, *Plan of Salvation*, 31, 92–96; Reymond, *New Systematic Theology of the Christian Faith*, 475–79). For an order of the decrees in Jacob Arminius, see *The Works of Jacob Arminius*, vol. 2, trans. James Nichols and William Nichols (Grand Rapids: Baker, 1991), 718–19; cf. Muller, *God, Creation, and Providence*, 162–63. For the *ordo decretorum* in Cameron, see Thomas, *Extent of the Atonement*, 165; Gootjes, "John Cameron," 186.

70. Strehle, "Universal Grace and Amyraldianism," 355.

71. Strehle, "Universal Grace and Amyraldianism," 350. On older claims of the introduction of rationalism into Reformed theology, see Weber, *Reformation, Orthodoxie, und Rationalismus*; Bizer, *Frühorthodoxie und Rationalismus*; Hall, "Calvin and the Calvinists," 19–37. For the recent scholarly recognition that Reformed Scholasticism was highly exegetical and not only rationalistic, see Wenger, "New Perspective on Calvin," 315.

Calvin believed he was being faithful to Scripture with its disparate materials, and so he remained satisfied to leave such "incomprehensible" matters to *the mind of God*. Calvin cautioned,

> The election of God will be a fatal labyrinth for anyone who does not follow the clear road of faith. Thus, so that we may be confident of remission of sins, so that our consciences may rest in full confidence of eternal life, so that we may boldly call God our Father, under no circumstances must we begin by asking what God decreed concerning us before the world began. Rather we must begin by seeking what through His paternal love He has revealed to us in Christ and what Christ himself daily proclaims to us through the Gospel.[72]

Calvin's general approach may be seen as relatively non-speculative in comparison with the developed Amyraldian and high Calvinist models. Anthony Lane claims, "Calvin's position, acceptance of the paradoxical duality in God's will, is less logically tidy and less scholastically appealing, but truer both to Scripture and to human experience."[73] Lane concludes,

---

72. Calvin, *Concerning the Eternal Predestination* (CO 8:307); as quoted in Armstrong, *Calvinism and the Amyraut Heresy*, 163. According to Basil Hall, Calvin did not systematize any "lapsarian" order of decrees, and "he would have regarded discussion of it as being impertinently precise in setting out God's purposes" (Hall, "Calvin against the Calvinists," 27).

73. Lane, "Quest for the Historical Calvin," 110. Lane maintains that "Calvin was *happier* than them [the later high orthodox Calvinists] to allow paradox and tension in his theology and not to attempt to tie together all loose ends, but this does not mean that he renounced logic or had no interest in consistency" (ibid., 98). Nicole responds, "This is very true, but should be tempered by the principle that we should beware also of pressing him into an illogical mold!" (Nicole, "John Calvin's View of the Extent of the Atonement," 210). W. Stanford Reid acknowledges, "Although some might accuse Calvin of being a rationalist, the fact of the matter is that he was logical in his thinking, seeking to avoid false deductions and analogies. Yet at the same time, he was quite prepared to acknowledge that he did not have all the answers, since he was dealing with the mystery of God Himself. He was, therefore, always willing to draw a line and say, 'Thus far and no farther.' In this he showed a mixture of systematic logic and a sense of mystery into which he would not delve. . . . In formulating a doctrine such as election, for example, though it is based on the sovereignty of God, and one may be tempted to include many logical implications of the doctrine, he held that it is improper, in fact sinful, to go beyond what the Bible has to say on the matter. Even though this limitation leaves certain paradoxes in the Christian faith, they are to be accepted, he said, and ideas that seem irreconcilable should be held in tension, since the sovereign God has spoken through His prophets and apostles" (Reid, "Transmission of Calvinism in the Sixteenth Century," 43). William Placher agrees that Calvin

> Calvin was above all a biblical theologian.... His constant involvement with the biblical text, together with his aversion to speculation beyond what is revealed, kept him from abandoning some of the genuine biblical tensions and paradoxes.... Calvin was prepared to recognize both God's universal love for all mankind and his desire for all to repent and his purpose that some only should be saved. To the feeble human mind these are irreconcilable. The mark of the true disciple of Calvin is his willingness to accept biblical paradox and not to seek to reconcile it in the direction of one pole or the other.[74]

For this reason, Calvin rigorously defended the existence of the hidden decree of God, yet turned the reader's focus to the revealed Word of God (rather than to the inner workings of the secret decree), as demonstrated in his commentary on Ezekiel: "But we must remark that God puts on a twofold character: for he here wishes to be taken at his word. As I have already said, the Prophet [Ezekiel] does not here dispute with subtlety about [God's] incomprehensible plans, but wishes to keep our attention close to God's word."[75]

Amyraut, in his own way, also desired to keep our "attention close to God's Word," especially the conditional promises universally given to all. According to Armstrong, Amyraut accentuated God's "conditional will" more emphatically than Calvin had, but only because of the absence of this doctrine among the high orthodox Calvinists. "[Amyraut] frankly admitted that his almost exclusive emphasis on the conditional will of God is different from that of Calvin, but insisted that Calvin, too, taught this conditional will."[76] Muller goes further, insisting that Calvin never spoke of two such wills in God but only two *seeming* wills within the

---

"was willing to leave questions unanswered, 'necessary consequences' underived, and apparent inconsistencies suspended in tension" (Placher, *Domestication of Transcendence*, 53). For two opposing views on logic and the extent of the atonement, see Helm, "Logic of Limited Atonement," 47–54; and Bauder, "Limited Atonement." See Byrne, "Paradox and Mystery." A related issue is the rise of Ramist methodology in the sixteenth century. See Moltmann, "Zur Bedeutung des Petrus Ramus," 295–318; Strohm, "Theologie und Zeitgeist," 352–71.

74. Lane, "Quest for the Historical Calvin," 113.

75. Calvin, Ezek 48:23, *Commentaries on the First Twenty Chapters of the Book of the Prophet Ezekiel*, vol. 2, 248. Brian Armstrong points to Calvin's comments upon Ezek 18:23 as the source of Amyraut's distinction between "the revealed, conditional will" of God and "the hidden, absolute will" of God (Armstrong, *Calvinism and the Amyraut Heresy*, 186–87).

76. Armstrong, *Calvinism and the Amyraut Heresy*, 269; cf. 221.

truly single, unified will of God.⁷⁷ Amyraut also went beyond Calvin by distinguishing between a conditional predestination unto salvation and an absolute predestination unto faith.⁷⁸ And he set forth an explicitly structured order of the decrees.⁷⁹

Armstrong summarizes the resultant Amyraldian focal points as follows:

> By emphasizing the incomprehensibility of God's electing decree, [Amyraut] radically shifts the ground of discussion from speculation regarding God's pretemporal counsel to contemplation of the order of events as they have occurred in history.... By juxtaposing the conditional and absolute wills of God and emphasizing the conditional will, he likewise focuses the attention upon the mercy of God as revealed in Christ, in Christ as the cause of our election. In all of this he thinks he has faithfully represented Scripture and restored the true emphasis of Calvin.⁸⁰

Armstrong concludes, "At all times, Amyraut enjoined, we are to focus our attention upon Christ and contemplate God's merciful nature as revealed to us in Christ."⁸¹ Much of this tactic seemed to position Amyraut near the Lutheran approach to unconditional election, *gratia universalis*, Christ *ex nobis*, and the "extent of the atonement."⁸² "[Amy-

---

77. "If anyone object that it is absurd to split God's will (*duplicem in Deo voluntatem fingi*), I answer that this is exactly our belief, that His will is one and undivided: but because our minds cannot plumb the profound depths of His secret election (*ad profundam arcanae electionis abyssum*) to suit our infirmity, the will of God is set before us as double (*bifarium*)" (Calvin, Matt 23:37, *Harmony of the Gospels*, vol. 3, 69). Cf. Quick, *Synodicon in Gallia Reformata*, vol. 2, 355. As Timothy Williams explains Calvin's view, the believer "must leave to God the reconciliation of the secret and the revealed aspects of the single will of God" (Williams, *Heart of Piety*, 166).

78. Djaballah, "Controversy on Universal Grace," 188-89.

79. Djaballah, "Controversy on Universal Grace," 191. Djaballah also claims that "The bifurcation of God's will (revealed and secret) is the key to understanding Amyraut's doctrine of predestination and the atonement" (ibid., 190; Macleod, "Definite Atonement and Divine Decree," 428). But ultimately, Amyraut considered the "absolute" and "conditional" decrees of God to be "but one only act of his eternal and unchangeable will" (see John Quick, *Synodicon in Gallia Reformata*, vol. 2, 355).

80. Armstrong, *Calvinism and the Amyraut Heresy*, 221.

81. Armstrong, *Calvinism and the Amyraut Heresy*, 268.

82. Armstrong, *Calvinism and the Amyraut Heresy*, 213; Harding, "Atonement Theory Revisited," 64. It has often been claimed that Amyraut compromised with Arminianism (cf. Courthial, "Golden Age of Calvinism in France," 75-76). This charge was already leveled by Pierre du Moulin (Thomas, *Extent of the Atonement*, 210).

raut] replaced predestination by making the doctrine of justification his central teaching.... This in turn served to direct his attention to the law-gospel antithesis, which had almost completely disappeared from orthodox theology."[83] Armstrong notes,

> But although Amyraut has resort to Calvin as the source of his parceling the *foedus gratiae* into two heads, the use that he makes of this bifurcation is quite peculiar to Amyraldian theology. For while using it to emphasize the hidden and revealed nature of God's will, the absolute, incomprehensible and the conditional, accommodated work of God in grace, he shifts his emphasis decidedly to the latter as the proper object of religious contemplation. That is, while there can be but little doubt that Amyraut regarded this bifurcation as native to early Reformed theology—to Calvin in particular—his own use of it tends to sound a great deal like Luther.[84]

Nevertheless, Philip Schaff claimed that Amyraut's theology was "an approach, not so much to Arminianism, which he decidedly rejected, as to Lutheranism, which likewise teaches a universal atonement and a limited election" (Schaff, *Creeds of Christendom*, vol. 1, 481). Thomas contends that Amyraut's "many works give evidence of concern to resist union with Roman Catholicism and promote union with the Lutherans, to stress the importance of the Protestant doctrine of justification" (Thomas, *Extent of the Atonement*, 187). Amyraut defended Reformed-Lutheran intercommunion but considered union with Roman Catholics to be impossible (ibid., 212). See also the Reformed statements of the Confession of Thorn that purposely paralleled Lutheran views (ibid., 213). "To Amyraut, [the Colloquy of] Thorn was proof that universal atonement was not at variance with Reformed theology at its best, and a model for Reformed-Lutheran co-operation" (ibid., 213). For an explanation of the confessional Lutheran view of the extent of the atonement, see the Saxon Visitation Articles of 1592; Scaer, "Nature and Extent of the Atonement," 179–87.

83. Armstrong, *Calvinism and the Amyraut Heresy*, 268—arguably an overstatement. Armstrong uses "orthodox" of the post-Calvin congealing of Reformed theology. Against this reading, Muller retorts, "Thus, if one anachronistically draws a rather strict and narrow line of development from Calvin to Turretin and denominates only what fits in this particular Genevan trajectory as 'orthodoxy,' then various Reformed views, developed entirely within the confessional understanding of the sixteenth- and seventeenth-century Reformed, can be cordoned off and identified as opponents of the Reformed Orthodox" (Muller, *Post-Reformation Reformed Dogmatics*, vol. 1, 79). On confessional identity in the era, see Backus, *Historical Method and Confessional Identity*.

84. Armstrong, *Calvinism and the Amyraut Heresy*, 200. One might argue that our understanding of Calvin on "the extent of the atonement" places him closer to Luther than is often recognized. Calvin himself signed his name to the *Variata* form of the Augsburg Confession of Faith, which declared that Christ "truly suffered, was crucified, dead, and buried, that he might reconcile the Father unto us, and might be a sacrifice, not only for original guilt, but also for all actual sins of men" (Article III). See Billings,

In any case, Amyraut's particular version of uniting "unconditional election" with "unlimited redemption" was only one form of doing so among many approaches during the Reformation and the generations that followed. Lee Gatiss muses, "Perhaps this has been overlooked because our view of seventeenth century hypothetical universalism has been too monochrome and 'Amyraldian,' not sufficiently sensitive to the variation which existed at the time."[85] Muller has insisted that John Davenant (the English hypothetical universalist) was suspicious of the theology of John Cameron (the French hypothetical universalist from Saumur).[86] And Michael Lynch maintains that Andre Rivet, a French opponent of Amyraut, did not disapprove of Davenant's doctrine, while Herman Hildebrand (a Reformed minister from Bremen) heartily approved of the views of English hypothetical universalists like Davenant and Joseph Hall.[87]

Gatiss has documented that British espousers of "universal redemption" "differed fundamentally from French Amyraldianism, and even denied elements of Amyraldianism."[88] For example, James Ussher, John Davenant, and John Preston did not agree with French versions of the

---

"John Calvin's Soteriology," 431; McNeill, "Calvin's Efforts toward the Consolidation of Protestantism," 411–23. Cf. Berry, "Amyraldian Controversy"; Clifford, "Amyraldian Soteriology and Reformed-Lutheran *rapprochement*." Demarest calls Amyraldianism a "rapprochement with Lutheranism given its interest in justification by faith and the universality of Christ's atoning work" (Demarest, "Amyraldianism," 48). Compare the Lutheran opposition to Zanchi in Strasbourg in 1561–62 and the Lutheran-Reformed debates surrounding the Colloquy of Montbéliard in 1586 (Thomas, "Calvin and English Calvinism," 125–26; Thomas, *Extent of the Atonement*, 52–55). The following year, Beza published a statement of his view on what came later to be called limited atonement (see Godfrey, "Reformed Thought on the Extent," 140–41). For a modern, confessional Lutheran assessment of Amyraldianism, see Pieper, *Christian Dogmatics*, vol. 2, 25–26: "Also the hypothetical universalism of the Amyraldists, according to which Christ gained grace for all men, but God's will is to create faith only in the elect, practically denies the *gratia universalis*."

85. Gatiss, "Deceptive Clarity?" 194–95. In forms of hypothetical universalism, Christ died for all to save them, on the condition that they believe/repent. In its amalgamation with total depravity and unconditional election and related doctrines, no human left to himself or herself would actually believe, so God effectually works in the elect to form belief in them. "The whole point about hypothetical universalism was that it was hypothetical" (Lake, "Calvinism and the English Church 1570–1635," 59).

86. Muller, *Calvin and the Reformed Tradition*, 127–44; Muller, "Dating John Davenant's *De Galllicana controversia sententia*," 10–22.

87. Lynch, "Richard Hooker," 277.

88. Gatiss, "'Shades of Opinion within a Generic Calvinism,'" 113.

ordo decretorum ("order of the decrees").[89] Edmund Calamy held an infralapsarian view in which God elected from the *massa corrupta*, while Amyraut could be construed as teaching that God elected from the mass of (hypothetically) redeemed humanity.[90]

In sum, Amyraut's position depended upon "distinctive theological commitments which were not shared by all hypothetical universalists."[91] Amyraldianism and hypothetical universalism should not be conflated.[92] The latter came in many forms in the seventeenth century.[93] "Hypothetical universalism" was not a single doctrine, as "different species of the

---

89. Gatiss, "'Shades of Opinion within a Generic Calvinism,'" 113. Gatiss, "Synod of Dort," 162. Contra Mark Shand, Davenant was not therefore some form of proto-Amyraldian (Shand, "John Davenant," [1998], 43–69; [1998], 20–28). Amyraut believed that God elected out of the mass of redeemed humanity (based upon universal redemption), rather than from the *corrupta massa* ("corrupt mass"). See Moore, *English Hypothetical Universalism*, 218; Thomas, *Extent of the Atonement*, 189–91; Muller, "Beyond Hypothetical Universalism," 197–236. Djaballah describes Davenant as an "infralapsarian" hypothetical universalist (admittedly an anachronistic label) in contrast to "sublapsarian" hypothetical universalists like Amyraut. (Djaballah, "Controversy on Universal Grace," 197). Davenant directly critiqued the theology of Cameron (see Muller, "Davenant and Du Moulin," 136–44). On Ussher, see Gribben, "Rhetoric, Fiction, and Theology," 53–76; Snoddy, *Soteriology of James Ussher*.

90. See Gatiss, "'Shades of Opinion within a Generic Calvinism,'" 112. Yet see the Calamy material in Macleod, "Definite Atonement and the Divine Decree," 426–27.

91. Gatiss, "'Shades of Opinion within a Generic Calvinism,'" 109. Therefore, "Calamy and his position is not best labelled Amyraldian" (Gatiss, *For Us and for Our Salvation*, 93). Cf. the differentiating of Amyraut and Calamy in Letham, "Triune God, Incarnation, and Definite Atonement," 439. "While the debates on the scope of saving grace lasted several days at the Assembly, and there were a number of divines who sided with Calamy, none were driven out. A good reason for this was that Calamy's views were not seen as posing a major threat to the sovereign particularism of the decrees nor to the nature of or intent of the atonement" (ibid.). Calamy distinguished his own views from Arminianism (see Letham,, "Triune God," 439). Donald Macleod also mentions John Arrowsmith, Lazarus Seaman, and Richard Vines as other articulate hypothetical universalists at the Westminster Assembly (Macleod, "Definite Atonement and the Divine Decree," 426; cf. Troxel, "Amyraut 'at' the Assembly," 49n17). David Ponter adds Thomas Ford, William Twisse, George Walker, and Francis Rous (scribe) to this list. See Ponter, "For Whom Did Christ Die?"

92. Crisp, *Deviant Calvinism*, 184. Contra Hodge, *Atonement*, 375–80. Carl Trueman bemoans, "The contemporary use of Amyraldian is thus in general a rather sloppy and inaccurate appropriation of the term. Most modern 'Amyraldians' are more likely hypothetical universalists: they believe that Christ died for all, even though God's election is restrictive and particular" (Trueman, "Definite Atonement View," 21n4). For an example of a broad reading of "Amyraldianism," see Wenkel, "Amyraldianism."

93. Moore, *English Hypothetical Universalism*, 225.

same genus" existed.[94] Various approaches combined particular election with some form of universal redemption or universal provision of grace.[95] One should avoid classifications that are "all too neat" or simplistic.[96]

Amyraut's view of the extent of the atonement was "demanded by his unique system of theology."[97] Therefore, although "Amyraldianism" has often been attached to varying forms of "moderate" Calvinistic systems that include so-called "unlimited atonement," the label can be deceptive, since Amyraut's position was webbed with his other doctrines (not all shared by all "hypothetical universalists"), including his ordering of the decrees, his views on original sin, his distinctions between moral and natural ability, his conception of illumination, and his particular understanding of the Trinity as connected to redemption.[98]

Of course, the use of value-laden modifiers such as "moderate" (as well as "rigid," "strict," and "extreme") can be problematic.[99] Richard Baxter referred to "the middle way of Universal Redemption" that united "universal redemption" with "unconditional election," and there were plenty of proponents of varying "middle ways" or "middle positions" in his time.[100] The 1690s work entitled *An Apology for the Ministers* spoke of "a Golden Mean, a middle way . . . that Christ died only for the Elect Sinners of mankind both Sufficiently and Efficaciously, but that he died for the Non-Elect only Sufficiently but not Efficaciously."[101] Robert Baron, who spoke of a "third, middle" approach, espoused unconditional election yet insisted that Christ's death being "sufficient for all" was no mere

---

94. Crisp, *Deviant Calvinism*, 184.

95. Muller, "Davenant and Du Moulin," 130. For example, Davenant spoke of positions in the Church of England that "God having mercy on the fallen race sent his Son, who gave himself as the price of Redemption for the whole world" and "On this merit of the death of Christ is found the universal Promise of the Gospel, according to which all who believe in Christ receive remission of sins & life eternal" (as quoted in ibid., 134). See also Kang, "John Davenant," 1–24.

96. Muller, "Davenant and Du Moulin," 131.

97. Shultz, *Multi-Intentioned View of the Extent of the Atonement*, 38.

98. Gatiss, "'Shades of Opinion within a Generic Calvinism,'" 109. Cf. Shultz, *Multi-Intentioned View of the Extent of the Atonement*, 36.

99. According to Aaron Clay Denlinger, such terms are "vacuous" and "dubious" adjectives (Denlinger, "Scottish Hypothetical Universalism," 86, 100).

100. Richard Baxter, *Certain Disputations of Rights to Sacraments and the True Nature of Visible Christianity*, Preface, as discussed in Boersma, *Hot Peppercorn*; Field, "Rigide Calvinisme in a Softer Dresse," 20; Muller, "Davenant and Du Moulin," 131.

101. As quoted in Field, "*Rigide Calvinisme in a Softer Dresse*," 20.

statement of its intrinsic value, but that "Christ died for everyone to the end that everyone might be reconcilable (*reconciabiles*) to God, and that everyone's sins might be pardonable (*condonabilia*), on condition of repentance and faith in the gospel."[102] Nevertheless, most modern forms of so-called "four-point" Calvinism are "not as sophisticated as the carefully framed Calvinist universalism of a more scholastic age."[103]

102. See Denlinger, "Scottish Hypothetical Universalism," 96. Herman Witsius asserted, "That the obedience and sufferings of Christ, considered in themselves, are, on the account of the infinite dignity of the person, of that value, as to have been sufficient for redeeming not only all and every man in particular, but many myriads besides, had it so pleased God and Christ, that he should have undertaken and satisfied for them" (Witsius, *Economy of the Covenants*, vol. 1, 256). By contrast, John Davenant contrasted "mere sufficiency" and "ordained sufficiency" (Davenant, *Dissertation* II.402–3). "Christ himself is acknowledged to have died for all men sufficiently, and not by reason of the mere sufficiency or of the intrinsic value" (Davenant, *Dissertation* II.401–2; as quoted in Crisp, *Deviant Calvinism*, 190). There is a divinely "ordained sufficiency" in the atonement, but it is conditional (conditioned upon faith). "The death of Christ is represented in holy Scripture as an universal remedy, by the ordinance of God, and the nature of the thing itself, applicable for salvation to all and every individual of mankind" (Davenant, *Dissertation* II.340–41; as quoted in Crisp, *Deviant Calvinism*, 190). Yet left to themselves, humans would not believe, and thus God in a specific act of his will ordained to efficaciously form faith in the elect (cf. Macleod, "Definite Atonement and the Divine Decree," 426). Roger Nicole responds, "On the hypothetical-universalists' own showing, since no one has faith but those to whom it is efficaciously given by God, a universal redemption on condition of faith is not a blessing which issues in any concrete advantage to the non-elect. In this light the vaunted benevolence of God toward all mankind appears nugatory" (Nicole, "Case for Definite Atonement," 203). Oliver Crisp, however, has recently argued for the value of hypothetical universalism upon biblical-exegetical, historical, and systematic grounds (Crisp, *Deviant Calvinism*, 196–200). On Davenant, see Muller, "Davenant and Du Moulin."

103. Gatiss, "Deceptive Clarity?" 195—"Calvinistic universalism" referring to "hypothetical universalism" and similar approaches. Cf. Strehle, "Universal Grace and Amyraldianism," 354–57. One should probably insert a plural "Calvinist universalisms" for the singular "Calvinist universalism" (in both phrases, in the sense of provision not efficacy). Scholasticism in the period should be construed as "a method rather than a result," as "a means to an end rather than as an end in itself" (Trueman, "Necessity of the Atonement," 222). Richard Muller has defined *scholasticism* as "a highly technical and logical approach to theological system, according to which each theological topic or *locus* was divided into its components, the parts analyzed and then defined in careful propositional form" (Muller, *Dictionary of Latin and Greek Theological Terms*, 8). According to Muller, scholasticism is primarily a logical approach to organizing theology rather than a reference to specific content. In his thesis, the later Reformed dogmaticians were in essential agreement with Calvin, although they used scholastic methodology (cf. Muller, "Scholasticism in Calvin," 39–61; Muller, "Scholasticism, Reformation, Orthodoxy," 81–96). In fact, the scholastic approach was developed to preserve the essence of Reformed theology. "For Muller, a change in method

Our meanderings into Amyraut have drawn us away from the primary sources of Calvin, but they adequately demonstrate the complexities of labels such as "Calvinism" and "Amyraldianism."[104] Even the term "Calvinist" is ambiguous, in that it can be a descriptor of Calvin's own position, a term applied to his followers, and a label used of the Reformed tradition in general.[105] Carl Trueman goes further and finds the term "Calvinism" to be "profoundly unhelpful,"[106] and the reification of "Calvinism" to be "counter-productive to careful historical analysis."[107] For example, one may falsely assume that Calvin's personal theology holds some type of normative status within the Reformed tradition.[108] "We must not be sidetracked by analytical models which isolate Calvin from the western tradition as if he were some peculiar authority—he was not that even within his own narrower tradition."[109] As Muller notes, "Calvin himself viewed the term Calvinist as an insult and thought of his own theology as an expression of catholic truth."[110] The terms "Calvinist" and "Calvinism" first arose among opponents of Calvin (notably his Lutheran critics).[111] "As a matter of fact, the vast majority of sixteenth- and seventeenth-century thinkers we identify as Calvinists did not identify themselves as followers of Calvin."[112]

---

by no means implies a change in dogma" (Klauber, "Continuity and Discontinuity in Post-Reformation Reformed Theology," 467, 469, 470). Cf. Steinmetz, "Scholastic Calvin," 16–30; Muller, "Scholasticism, Reformation, Orthodoxy," 39–61; van Asselt and Dekker, *Reformation and Scholasticism*; Wisse et al., *Scholasticism Reformed*.

104. Concerning the "Calvin and the Calvinists" debate, Muller reminds us that "the simple fact" is "that none of the documents was produced in order to set the terms of debate, whether positive or negative, for various twentieth-century theological movements" (Muller, *After Calvin*, vi). Mark Garcia has constituted a new "Calvin vs. the Calvinists" approach by implying that later Reformed theologians slid back into a more Lutheran approach to matters of justification and union with Christ. See Garcia, *Life in Christ*; contrast Billings, "John Calvin's Soteriology," 446.

105. Muller, "Was Calvin a Calvinist?" 51.
106. Trueman, "Calvin and Calvinism," 226.
107. Trueman, "Reception of Calvin," 24.
108. Trueman, "Calvin and Calvinism," 225.
109. Trueman, "Calvin and Calvinism," 240.
110. Muller, "Was Calvin a Calvinist?" 54.
111. Muller, "Was Calvin a Calvinist?" 54. Cf. Billings, "John Calvin's Soteriology," 444.
112. Muller, "Was Calvin a Calvinist?" 56.

What then of Calvin himself? Calvin's relationship to Reformed theology is "complex."[113] "Calvin did not originate this [Reformed] tradition; he was not the sole voice in its early codification; and he did not serve as the norm for its development."[114] Instead of functioning as a "norm" or even as an "original" voice, Calvin served as both a recipient of previous tenets and ideas and as "an antecedent of certain lines of argument."[115] As a second-generation Reformer, Calvin inherited broad Christological and Trinitarian commitments as well as an evangelical-reformation core.[116] He did not stand alone but within the company of "other significant formulators of the Reformation."[117] Moreover, Calvin influenced social, cultural, political, and educational inheritors beyond just his theological followers.[118] In addition, Calvin's theology was largely pastorally driven and exegetically nurtured.[119] "It is not enough to regard Calvinism as a purely academic theological system."[120] It is necessary to reconstruct his theology across the breadth of his writings.[121]

Perhaps the best approach (since ultimately it is the only one available to us) is to demonstrate how Calvin addressed the specific issues he did discuss (as attempted in Chapter Two), and to refuse to make Calvin address issues or details he did not discuss.[122] Specifically, we might avoid

---

113. Trueman, "Reception of Calvin," 26.

114. Muller, "Was Calvin a Calvinist?" 68.

115. Muller, "Diversity in the Reformed Tradition" 29. Cf. Trueman, "Reception of Calvin," 27.

116. Billings, "John Calvin's Soteriology," 430–31, 441–42.

117. Muller, "Reception and Response," 184.

118. See McComish, "Calvin's Children," 1–20.

119. Billings, "John Calvin's Soteriology," 442–43, 447; see also Nettles, "John Calvin's Understanding of the Death of Christ," 294; Gunton, "Aspects of Salvation," 253. For example, editions of the *Institutes* reflect changes arising from sermon series and the exegetical work behind them (Gatiss, "Inexhaustible Fountain of All Good Things," 196; Muller, *Unaccommodated Calvin*, 115).

120. McComish, "Calvin's Children," 2.

121. Thompson, "Calvin on the Cross of Christ," 107; Muller, *Unaccommodated Calvin*, 182.

122. For example, Calvin did not intricately systematize a "multiple intentions" approach as others have done. This is not to say that such a systematic project is not noteworthy, only that a *historical* study of Calvin does not go beyond his own materials. For outlines of a "multiple intentions" view of "un/limited atonement," see Ware, "Extent of the Atonement"; Compton, "Design and Extent of Christ's Atonement"; Hammett, "Multiple-Intentions View of the Atonement." See also Shultz, "Biblical and Theological Defense of a Multi-Intentioned View"; Schultz, "God's Purposes in the

the imposition upon Calvin of anachronistic terminology such as "the four points" or "the five points," a particular "order of the decrees," etc.[123] Calvin never talked of an *ordo decretorum* structured with a hypothetical, conditional decree of universal redemption prior to an absolute decree to save the elect alone, nor of "conseils de Dieu frustratoires."[124]

As a patently anachronistic case in point, the modern acronym of *TULIP* has "contributed greatly to the confusion about Calvin and Calvinism."[125] The TULIP acronym seems to be of rather recent vintage, definitely Anglo-American in origin.[126] The application of the acronym's "highly vague and anachronistic language to the sixteenth and seventeenth centuries inevitably causes confusion."[127] "It must, incidentally be questioned as to whether such terms as 'limited' and 'universal atonement'

Atonement for the Nonelect," 145–63; Shultz, "Why a Genuine Universal Gospel Call Requires an Atonement," 111–23. For a popularized simplification based upon Ware's approach, see Driscoll and Breshears, *Death by Love*, 163–81. The eighteenth-century Scottish theologian James Fraser argued, "Christ did by one infinite, indivisible satisfaction and ransom satisfy divine justice for the sins of all mankind, though with different intentions and ends according to the different objects thereof" (Fraser, *Treatise on Justifying Faith*, 222). Normally, a "multiple-intentions" perspective also references God's cosmological designs in the death of Christ, by which he will reconcile the cosmos to himself. See Nelson, "Design, Nature, and Extent of the Atonement," 119.

123. Amyraut himself could downplay an ordering of the decrees. "In fact, he at one time remarked that the Holy Spirit has not revealed any order in the Word, adding that one will only end up in a maze of difficulties if one tries to penetrate this mystery" (Gootjes, "John Cameron," 189). See Amyraut, *Defense de la doctrine de Calvin*, 579–81.

124. Muller, "Reception and Response," 190–91. Cf. Lynch, "Richard Hooker," 293.

125. Muller, "Was Calvin a Calvinist?" 58. Crisp, *Saving Calvinism*, 28. TULIP stands for Total Depravity, Unconditional Election, Limited Atonement, Irresistible Grace, and Perseverance of the Saints.

126. Muller, "Was Calvin a Calvinist?" 58. Moore traces an appearance of TULIP in 1913, to William Vail's "The Five Points of Calvinism Historically Considered" (Moore, "Extent of the Atonement," 146n98). In an earlier work, Stewart had only traced it back to Loraine Boettner's work of 1932, *Reformed Doctrine of Predestination* (Stewart, "Points of Calvinism," 203). By his 2010 book, Stewart had pushed it back to Vail's 1913 work, through the assistance of Ched Spellman and Bart Byl (Kenneth J. Stewart, *Ten Myths about Calvinism*, 79). Vail himself documents the use of the acronym by Dr. Cleland Boyd McAfee in 1905, while pastor of the Lafayette Ave. Presbyterian Church in Brooklyn, in a popular lecture delivered before the Presbyterian Union of Newark. See Vail, "Five Points of Calvinism Historically Considered," 394; Stewart, *Ten Myths about Calvinism*, 291–92; Sinnema, "Calvin and the Canons of Dordt," 103n78.

127. Muller "Was Calvin a Calvinist?" 60.

can ever do justice to an early modern discussion and debate that did not use this language but instead had recourse to questions of the sufficiency and efficiency of Christ's satisfaction."[128] Even the word *atonement*, as an English word foreign to the continental conversations, can bring confusion to the table.[129]

Consider the following conclusions, gathered from the recent work of Richard Muller, an esteemed scholar of Reformed history. Concerning anachronistic language, "Calvin certainly never spoke of 'limited atonement.'"[130] Yet the *efficacy* of Christ's death was "limited according to the assumption of salvation by grace alone, to God's elect."[131] "Calvin was quite clear on the point: the application or efficacy of Christ's death was limited to the elect."[132] At the same time, insists Muller, "He did not often mention the traditional sufficiency-efficiency formula, and he did not address the issue, posed by Amyraut, of a hypothetical or conditional decree of salvation for all who would believe, prior to the absolute decree to save the elect."[133] And finally, according to Muller,

> He did frequently state, without further modification, that Christ expiated the sins of the world and that this "favor" is extended "indiscriminately to the whole human race," just as he also assumed, as the Canons of Dort would later declare, that God had the specific intention of saving some particular persons. Various theologians of the later Reformed tradition appealed to Calvin on all sides of the debate over hypothetical universalism.[134]

In any comparison of Calvin with later theologians, one must also appreciate the nature of the historical development of theology. As Trueman argues, "[W]e need to move beyond the language of *identity* and *difference*, and even, perhaps, to be careful in the use of *continuity* and *discontinuity*—though the latter, when understood in the correct way, is

---

128. Muller, "Diversity in the Reformed Tradition," 14.
129. Belousek, *Atonement, Justice, and Peace*, 84n5.
130. Muller, "Was Calvin a Calvinist?" 59.
131. Muller, "Was Calvin a Calvinist?" 61.
132. Muller, "Was Calvin a Calvinist?" 61. Muller adds, "And in this conclusion there was also accord among the later Reformed theologians."
133. Muller, "Was Calvin a Calvinist?" 61. Cf. Lynch, "Richard Hooker," 293.
134. Muller, "Was Calvin a Calvinist?" 61. Muller adds, "Later Reformed theology, then, is more specific on this particular point than Calvin had been—and arguably, his somewhat vague formulations point (or could be pointed) in several directions, as in fact can the formulae from the Synod of Dort" (ibid., 61–62).

not objectionable. A better approach to the question is to use the category of *development*."[135] According to Trueman, questions of continuity or discontinuity "need to be set aside, or at least adopted in a highly qualified form."[136] The quest for "continuity" and "discontinuity" can lead to "the surreptitious intrusion of anachronistic criteria into the historical task," leading to the "subordination of history to contemporary theological polemic."[137] One must recognize not only the reception of specific texts, but also the reception of ideas and concepts—often in confluent streams rather than in single trajectories.[138] Calvin's work and ideas were "adopted, adapted, and developed."[139] At the same time, a growing body of academic literature maintains that the Reformed theology of the seventeenth century was a "bigger tent" than has often been acknowledged.[140]

Kevin Kennedy has argued that "John Calvin employed a biblical hermeneutic which differed significantly from the later Reformed tradition in relation to the question of the extent of the atonement."[141] But we have seen the inherent difficulty of the implied construct—there was not a homogeneity to "the later Reformed tradition" of the movement. "Scholars have often missed its rich diversity."[142] The recent work of scholars, such as Muller, has led to a "broadening out" of our

135. Trueman, "Calvin and Calvinism," 226.

136. Trueman, "Reception of Calvin," 21. Martin Foord maintains, "When comparing Calvin to others, it cannot be done in terms of a simple continuity and discontinuity model. This mistake helped skew the so-called 'Calvin and the Calvinists' debate in recent years" (Foord, "God Wills All People to Be Saved," 79–80).

137. Trueman, "Reception of Calvin," 19, 23.

138. Trueman, "Reception of Calvin," 19. Cf. Klauber, "Continuity and Discontinuity in Post-Reformation Reformed Theology."

139. Trueman, "Reception of Calvin," 20.

140. See Muller, "Diversity in the Reformed Tradition." Stephen Strehle acknowledges that John Cameron's hypothetical universalism "remains basically Calvinistic, for Cameron still maintains that men, apart from divine grace, are dead in trespasses and sins, and volitionally incapable of responding to God's gracious provision and fulfilling the required condition" (Strehle, "Universal Grace and Amyraldianism," 347). Moreover, the "orthodox" were "obliged to acknowledge Amyraut and the Salmurian University as brethren" (ibid., 353). A. T. B. McGowan refers to Amyraldians as being "within the Reformed tradition" (McGowan, "Atonement as Penal Substitution," 206). "This debate is most hotly contested because, in so many other respects and on so many doctrinal issues, the combatants are in agreement" (ibid.).

141. Kennedy, "Hermeneutical Discontinuity between Calvin and Later Calvinism," 300; cf. 299.

142. Letham, "Faith and Assurance in Early Calvinism," 358.

understanding of early Reformed theology, "a diverse and variegated" (and even "highly diverse") tradition that was "rather diverse in its origins" and that utilized "a kind of diversity and variety of formulation."[143] Within the Reformed tradition of the sixteenth and seventeenth centuries, a spectrum of opinions existed concerning covenant theology, Eucharistic theology, the nuances of election and predestination, and the nature of faith and assurance.[144] A diversity also existed in explanations of the classic maxim of Christ's death being sufficient for all but efficient for the elect, even among the Saumurian theologians.[145] There were various ways of construing the "limited efficacy of Christ's all-sufficient work of satisfaction."[146] Furthermore, recent scholarship has highlighted the diverse forms of early modern "hypothetical universalism," including its distinctive Bremian, Dutch, English, French, Irish, Scottish, and other forms.[147] Hypothetical universalism was "a highly complex phenomenon with no one definitive formulation or uniformity of explanation."[148]

At least for some forms of hypothetical universalism, a door was open at Dort and some have even argued that a window was cracked open at Westminster.[149] Jonathan Moore insists, "The popular perception, both at the time and subsequently, that both the Canons of Dort and the Westminster Confession of Faith *excluded* hypothetical universalism was

---

143. Muller, "Diversity in the Reformed Tradition," 12, 24 cf. Lynch, "Richard Hooker," 274.

144. Letham, "Faith and Assurance in Early Calvinism," 355–84.

145. Godfrey, "Reformed Thought on the Extent of the Atonement," 133–71; Gootjes, "John Cameron," 185–95. Saumur theologians included Louis Cappel as well as John Cameron and Moïse Amyraut (see Lynch, "Richard Hooker," 276).

146. Muller, "How Many Points?" 427.

147. See Gatiss, "'Shades of Opinion within a Generic Calvinism'"; Gribben, "Rhetoric, Fiction, and Theology"; Crisp, *Deviant Calvinism*, 185; Gootjes, "John Cameron," 169–70. The French hypothetical universalists preferred terminology such as *la grâce universelle*, or *universalisme*, highlighting the grace offered in Christ (in their views). See Gootjes, "John Cameron," 169n2.

148. Moore, *English Hypothetical Universalism*, 225.

149. Crisp, *Deviant Calvinism*, 176–83; Crisp, *Saving Calvinism*, 144–46; Macleod, "Definite Atonement and the Divine Decree," 424. The Formula Consensus Helvetica condemned Amyraldianism. Muller calls the formula "a document of limited geographical reach and short-lived," and even it did not identify Amyraldianism as a heresy (Muller, "Diversity in the Reformed Tradition," 19). Compare his similar evaluation of the Articles of Morus (ibid., 17). Moore also notes that the Formula Consensus Helvetica "never attained widespread and sustained usage" (Moore, "Extent of the Atonement," 152).

never universally shared and has always been challenged right from the genesis of these documents."[150] Admittedly, opening a small window in the wording of the Westminster Confession of Faith (1646) is "altogether more difficult," and the debate is "set to continue."[151] Nevertheless, Moore argues that "the vocal and influential English Hypothetical Universalist minority pushed hard so as not to be needlessly excluded from orthodoxy at any crucial point."[152] That such a minority existed is indisputable.[153] Whether or not they succeeded is a point of dispute.[154] Richard Baxter claimed that "I have spoken with an eminent Divine, yet living,

---

150. Moore, "Extent of the Atonement," 144. Moore adds, "A majority influence at a Synod is not the same as an exclusive influence, and a minority influence or influences could potentially still have resulted in modified or necessarily more ambiguous joint codifications" (ibid.). Blocher cites Moore, maintaining that "the wording of the Westminster Confession (after the Canons of Dort) allowed the English Hypothetical Universalists to consider that their view, *in all strictness*, had not been ruled out, and to subscribe" (Blocher, "Jesus Christ the Man," 544-45). But Blocher adds that such maneuvering was "inimical" to the overall approach and tenor of Westminster, though "not impossible." See also Ferguson, "'Blessèd Assurance, Jesus Is Mine'?" 613.

151. Moore, "Extent of the Atonement," 148, 152n116. Michael Lynch has argued that the Westminster Confession of Faith allows a Davenant-form of hypothetical universalism (Lynch, "Confessional Orthodoxy and Hypothetical Universalism," 144). David Blunt has reasoned that it is "unlikely" but not "impossible" that the views of Edward Calamy (the hypothetical universalist) could be reconciled with the Westminster Confession of Faith (Blunt, "Debate on Redemption at the Westminster Assembly," 2-3). According to Blocher, "The tendency of Westminster Calvinism leads to particular redemption, but not with mathematics-like rigor" (Blocher, "Jesus Christ the Man," 454). For older attempts to wedge between Calvin and Westminster, see Rolston, *John Calvin versus the Westminster Confession;* Rolston "Responsible Man in Reformed Theology"; Torrance, "Strengths and Weaknesses of the Westminster Theology," 45-47.

152. Moore, "Extent of the Atonement," 148. Moore argues that in approaching the Westminster Standards, one must take into account the differences between Amyraldianism and other forms of Hypothetical Universalism (ibid., 152n116). Latham recognizes that "roughly one-third of the recorded speeches" at Westminster favored Hypothetical Universalism (Letham, *Westminster Assembly*, 181-82). See, however, Goodloe, *John McLeod Campbell*, 35.

153. Troxel lists Edmund Calamy, John Arrowsmith, Richard Vines, Lazarus Seaman, and Edwards Reynolds as examples of those who supported hypothetical universalism at the Westminster Assembly (Troxel, "Amyraut 'at' the Assembly," 49). David Ponter adds Thomas Ford, William Twisse, George Walker, and Francis Rous (scribe) to this list. See Ponter, "For Whom Did Christ Die?"

154. Some have argued they were successful—see Schaff, *Creeds of Christendom*, vol. 1, 772-73; Mitchell and Struthers, *Minutes of the Sessions of the Westminster Assembly*, xx, lv-lxi.

that was of the Assembly, who assured me that they purposely avoided determining the Controversie, and some of them protest themselves for the middle way of Universal Redemption."[155] While Michael Lynch has recently maintained that John Davenant's form of hypothetical universalism was permitted in the Westminster Confession of Faith, A. Craig Troxel has argued strongly that this was not the case (especially based upon Article III.6 and Article VIII.8).[156] Nevertheless, David Ponter has insisted that English Hypothetical Universalists believed their views were not prohibited by the Westminster Confession of Faith. "The suggestion that about one third of the assembly delegates would sign a document that repudiated a core element of their theology is nonsensical."[157] Muller concurs, "The Westminster Confession was in fact written with this diversity in view, encompassing confessionally the variant Reformed views on the nature of the limitation of Christ's satisfaction to the elect, just as it is written to be inclusive of the infra- and the supralapsarian views on predestination."[158]

A case for the inclusion of forms of hypothetical universalism is much easier to sustain in the case of Dort. Several delegates leaned toward or clearly favored hypothetical universalism, including members of the Bremen delegation (notably Martinius), members of the British delegation (including Samuel Ward and the influential John Davenant), and a few others.[159] The *Collegiate Suffrage* of the British delegation spoke of Christ given as a "ransom for the sins of the whole world," as his death opened an "infinite treasure of merits and spiritual blessings."[160]

155. Baxter, *Certain Disputations of Right to Sacraments and the True Nature of Visible Christianity* Bv4; as quoted in Moore, "Extent of the Atonement," 154. See also Macleod, "Definite Atonement and the Divine Decree," 427. On the concept of the "middle way" or *via media* within the context of the extent of the atonement, see Lynch, "Richard Hooker," 278–80.

156. Lynch, "Confessional Orthodoxy and Hypothetical Universalism," 127–44; Troxel, "Amyraut 'at' the Assembly," 43–55.

157. Ponter, "Robert Letham on the English Hypothetical Universalists." Cf. Fesko, *Theology of the Westminster Standards*, 201–3; Gatiss, "'Shades of Opinion within a Generic Calvinism.'"

158. Muller, *Post-Reformation Reformed Dogmatics*, vol. 1, 76–77.

159. Crisp, *Deviant Calvinism*, 179. On the British delegation to Dort, see Milton, *British Delegation and the Synod of Dort*; Shand, "English Delegation to the Synod of Dort," 37–39.

160. As quoted in Muller, "Davenant and Du Moulin," 135. See Ponter, "Collegiate Suffrage of the Divines of Great Britain." For a discussion of the synod's geographical makeup, see Dewar, "Synod of Dort," 39; Kang, "John Davenant," 10–14.

"Resolution came only through intense diplomatic activity behind the scenes."[161] The formulated theology at Dort was "the expression of a laborious theological compromise worked out between the various Calvinist traditions."[162] The Canons of Dort (1619) were carefully formulated so as to allow subscription by Davenant and Ward.[163]

Donald Sinnema delineates the particularist emphases of Dort "cloaked in universal language, especially at the insistence of the British and Bremen delegations":

> Christ's death gives entirely complete satisfaction for sins and is of infinite value, more than sufficient (*abunde sufficiens*) to atone for the sins of the whole (*totius*) world (2.3). Also, the gospel promise that whoever believes will have eternal life and the command to repent and believe ought to be declared without distinction (*promiscue*) to all (*omnibus*) nations and people (2.5). Yet, it was God's plan that the saving effectiveness (*efficacia*) of his Son's death should work itself out in all (*omnibus*) his elect in order that he might grant justifying faith to them only (*solos*); in other words, that Christ's blood should effectively (*efficaciter*) redeem from every (*omni*) people and nation all those and only those (*omnes et solos*) whom God elected from eternity (2.8).[164]

The Heidelberg Catechism (1563) response to question 37 (speaking of Christ bearing "the wrath of God against the sin of the whole human race") leaves open a door for diversity of understanding. And both the fifteenth article ("He came to be the lamb without spot, Who by sacrifice of Himself once made, should take away the sins of the world") and the thirty-first article ("The offering of Christ once made is the perfect redemption, propitiation, and satisfaction for all the sins of the whole world, both original and actual") of the Thirty-Nine Articles (1571) of the Church of England do as well.[165] Forms of non-speculative

---

161. Letham, "Faith and Assurance in Early Calvinism," 365.

162. Fornerod, "Reappraisal," 183; cf. Godfrey, "Tensions within International Calvinism."

163. See Gatiss, "Synod of Dort," 162.

164. Sinnema, "Calvin and the Canons of Dordt," 92.

165. English spelling updated. On the Anglican formularies, see Gatiss, *For Us and for Our Salvation*, 111; cf. Macleod, *Christ Crucified*, 121n28, Macleod, "Definite Atonement and the Divine Decree," 424; Lynch, "Richard Hooker," 573. The text of the Thirty-Nine Articles clearly borrows from John 1:29, although related themes recur throughout the Johannine literature (cf. John 3:16; 4:42; 6:33, 51; 1 John 2:2; 4:9–10).

hypothetical universalism such as that proposed by John Davenant never received "synodical reprimand" or "explicit confessional disapproval."[166] In fact, the view(s) of hypothetical universalism might be considered as a "significant stream" (or "streams") among the Reformed tradition(s).[167] For example, the Catechism of the Anglican *Book of Common Prayer* has been interpreted in an "unlimited atonement" fashion: "I learn to believe in . . . God the Son, Who hath redeemed me, and all mankind."[168]

Richard Muller, the doyen of post-Reformation historiography, notes that "there was a significant hypothetical universalist trajectory in the Reformed tradition from its beginnings."[169] Therefore, historical hypothetical universalism can be construed as a form of the diversity within the Reformed tradition, rather than as an abandonment of Calvinism.[170] Muller even claims that "Amyraldian hypothetical universalism can be recognized as belonging to the internal diversity of the Reformed tradition itself."[171] Views on the extent of the atonement should not therefore be considered a test of reformation doctrinal orthodoxy.[172] Oliver Crisp

---

See Daniel, *Biblical Calvinism*, 6–7. John Davenant and Samuel Ward differed with "three other" members of the British delegation at Dort, postulated by Richard Muller to be George Carleton, Thomas Goad, and Walter Balcanqual (Muller, "Davenant and Du Moulin," 132). The British Delegation argued for the omission of the banal "sufficiency-efficiency" distinction and for the reconstruction of those materials limiting the world to the *mundum electorum* (ibid., 132–33). The British delegation did not mirror the full gamut of British churchmen of the time (ibid., 133n31). According to the *Book of Common Prayer*: "Question. What dost thou chiefly learn in these articles of thy belief? Answer. First, I learn to believe in God the Father, who hath made me and all the world. Secondly, in God the Son, who hath redeemed me and all mankind. Thirdly in God the Holy Ghost, who sanctifies me, and all the elect people of God" (Cardwell, *Two Books of Common Prayer*, 345–46).

166. Muller, "Diversity in the Reformed Tradition," 24. Muller has even claimed that Du Moulin, the opponent of Amyraut, could be identified as a hypothetical universalist (Muller, *Calvin and the Reformed Tradition*, 156; Muller, "Beyond Hypothetical Universalism," 206). Allen contests this claim (Allen, *Extent of the Atonement*, 93).

167. Muller, "Diversity in the Reformed Tradition," 25.

168. Gatiss, *For Us and for Our Salvation*, 101.

169. Muller, "Diversity in the Reformed Tradition," 25. Muller adds, "it is arguably less than useful to describe its continuance as a softening of the tradition." See also Crisp, *Deviant Calvinism*, 176–83. Contrast Moore, "Extent of the Atonement," 156–57; Moore, *English Hypothetical Universalism*.

170. Field, "Rigide Calvinisme in a Softer Dresse," 21.

171. Muller, "Diversity in the Reformed Tradition," 19.

172. George, *Amazing Grace*, 94; Cf. the grudging acknowledgement of Warfield, *Calvin and Calvinism*, 363–65. Muller positions the formulations of both Cameron and

has also attempted "theological clarification" in showing that hypothetical universalism is "a viable option for those in the Reformed tradition."[173]

More historical scholarship needs to be done on the distinctive (and sometimes differing) nuances represented by the Bremian, Dutch, English, French, Irish, Scottish, and other hypothetical universalists (early modern and contemporary).[174] A coterie of scholars (building upon the scholarly foundations laid by Muller and others), including but by no means limited to Lee Gatiss, Aaron Clay Denlinger, Albert Gootjes, Michael Lynch, Jonathan Moore, David Ponter, and Oliver Crisp, seem to be leading the charge with their published investigations of the various forms of hypothetical universalisms.[175] According to Crisp, "It may also be that further work on the different versions of hypothetical universalism extant in early-modern theology would provide more resources for a constructive version of the doctrine suitable to the contemporary theological climate."[176]

Michael Lynch has recently argued that scholars have generally overlooked one specific facet of John Davenant's particular form of

---

Amyraut "within orthodoxy," thereby "evidencing the diversity of Reformed orthodox theology and continuing the direction of the recent reassessments of seventeenth-century orthodoxy" (Muller, "Diversity in the Reformed Tradition," 26; cf. Muller, "Divine Covenants, Absolute and Conditional," 36). Moore notes that "many reputable Reformed Orthodox theologians remained unconvinced by the arguments for particular redemption" (Moore, "Extent of the Atonement," 136). Moore recognizes that the "Trinitarian nature of redemption" was upheld in John Davenant's system, contrary to John Owen's counter claims (ibid., 138). Davenant proposed a system similar to a multi-intentioned position, that the salvation of the elect is not the "only or sole end" of Christ's death, because Christ "merited and offered his merits, in a different way for different persons" (Davenant, *Dissertation* II.396, 557; as quoted in Moore, "Extent of the Atonement," 137). According to Lee Gatiss, the British delegation at Dort posited a "second intention" in the cross (Gatiss, "Synod of Dort," 155–56). Contrast Article 3 of the Act of the Associate Synod at Edinburgh of 1754, declaring that Christ "died in one and the same respect, for all those for whom he in any respect died" (as quoted in Moore, "Extent of the Atonement," 151).

173. Crisp, *Deviant Calvinism*, 183.

174. "There are nuanced positions within Hypothetical Universalism that must be respected" (Macleod, "Definite Atonement and the Divine Decree," 422).

175. These and similar authors, of course, bring along their own peculiar theological angles and emphases. On the web, the primary source documentation gathered by David Ponter at calvinandcalvinism.com is incredibly informative. See also the relevant materials appearing in print in Allen, *Extent of the Atonement*.

176. Crisp, *Deviant Calvinism*, 211; Crisp, *Saving Calvinism*, 131–36.

hypothetical universalism, which included three essential elements.[177] The first element concerns redemption accomplished, "the notion of universal redemption wherein God willed Christ to make a universal remedy for all human beings applicable for reconciliation and remission of sins on the condition of faith and repentance."[178] The second element concerns the application of redemption. Only believers actually receive remission of sins and reconciliation with God. Lynch contends that scholars rightfully recognize these two elements, but Davenant's approach included a third element—that Christ's work does not have *equal* regard to the elect and the reprobate, since Christ's death purchased "the grace of effectual redemption."[179] "Davenant's third element makes it impossible that the death of Christ not be applied to certain persons, because in the death of Christ God purchased a to-be-applied effectual redemption for the elect alone."[180] This "purchased to-be-applied application destined for the elect" can be summarily regarded as "purchased redemption," so that although Christ died for all he did not die *equally* for all.[181] Rather, "Christ died with special regard for the elect."[182] In this manner, claims Lynch, Davenant's theology could be considered to be within the bounds of the Westminster Confession of Faith, including VIII.8: "To all those for whom Christ purchased redemption, He does certainly and effectually apply and communicate the same; making intercession for them, and revealing unto them, in and by the word, the mysteries of salvation."[183] Scholars naturally continue to debate this matter of Davenant's form of

---

177. For a fuller summary of Davenant's views, see Compton, "John Davenant's *Dissertation on the Death of Christ*," 167–81; Kang, "John Davenant," 1–24. Gatiss has called Davenant's view a "sophisticated form" of hypothetical universalism (Gatiss, "Synod of Dort and Definite Atonement," 155).

178. Lynch, "Confessional Orthodoxy and Hypothetical Universalism," 137.

179. Lynch, "Confessional Orthodoxy and Hypothetical Universalism," 140.

180. Lynch, "Confessional Orthodoxy and Hypothetical Universalism," 141.

181. The British delegates to Dort all signed a shared statement that included the following: "Christ therefore so died for all, that all and every one by the means of faith might obtain remission of sins, and eternal life by virtue of that ransom paid once for all mankind. But Christ so died for the elect, that by the merit of his death in special manner destinated unto them according to the eternal good pleasure of God, they might infallibly obtain both faith and eternal life" (Carleton, *Suffrage of the Divines of Great Britaine*, 47–48; English spelling updated). See also the similar statements found in Ponter, "Collegiate Suffrage of the Divines of Great Britain."

182. Compton, "John Davenant's *Dissertation on the Death of Christ*," 178.

183. Lynch, "Confessional Orthodoxy and Hypothetical Universalism," 143–44.

hypothetical universalism's positioning within or beyond the bounds of the Westminster Confession of Faith.[184]

Stepping back to place Calvin in this stream (or better, "streams") of development, perhaps an analogy may be of help. The Lombardian stew of "sufficient for all but efficient only for the elect," the porridge accepted by most of the Reformers, was poured through Calvin's own sieve. The size of the holes in his sieve, formed within his peculiar historical context, allowed "larger" admissions of universal facets to pass than would the sieves of many of his high orthodox successors. Many of the succeeding chefs within the Reformed kitchen began working with more refined sieves, constricting the universal language that was allowed to pass. On the other hand, Calvin did not explain or defend the exact nature of the gridding of his own sieve, unlike some of his successors in the Lombardian kitchen with both larger-holed and smaller-holed sieves. The nature of events compelled some later "large-holed sieve" chefs (like Amyraut) to claim Calvin on their side when they were accused of distorting the menu, even though such a direct parallel between Calvin and their own developed models was not entirely accurate. Nevertheless, they did have a place within the tradition of the Reformed kitchen, as chefs of a Lombardian stew.

Amyraut and the Amyraldians explicitly claimed to follow Calvin. Their seventeenth-century opponents critiqued their copious quotations and were reluctant to claim for themselves the label "Calvinist."[185] Pierre Du Moulin (1568–1658), Amyraut's arch-opponent, believed it was rather improper to cite Calvin as an authority, as only Scripture was the suitable authority in doctrinal controversy.[186] Du Moulin worried that use of "Calvinism" might indicate that Reformed churches viewed Calvin "as the Author of a new Religion."[187] A decade later, he continued to warn against excessive dependence upon a single thinker—a summoning of personal authority that Calvin himself would not have allowed from his Genevan pulpit but would have denounced instead.[188]

---

184. Robert Letham has argued that some forms of hypothetical universalism are allowable within Westminster's language (see Rehnman, "Particular Defense of Particularism," 24–34).

185. Muller, "Reception and Response," 182.

186. Muller, "Reception and Response," 183.

187. As quoted in Muller, "Reception and Response," 190.

188. Muller, "Reception and Response," 190.

Pierre Jurieu (1637–1713), in defending the Reformed faith against Jesuits, lamented that his opponents made Calvin "the head of a party" and endeavored "to lay his identity on us, and to call us 'Calvinists' after him."[189] A century prior, Thomas Cartwright (1535–1603) complained that his interlocutor John Whitgift "burdens us with the authority of Calvin so often."[190] According to historian Perry Miller, the New England Puritans did not consider Calvin to be the fountainhead of their theology, "nor of themselves as members of a faction of which he was the founder."[191] Yet as time went by, so-called "five-point Calvinists" not only embraced the label of "Calvinist," they insisted against various hypothetical universalists within the Reformed tradition that they alone were rightly called "Calvinists." "We need to remind ourselves," counters Muller, that "it was not by choice that Reformed catholics of the early modern era were called 'Calvinists.'"[192] Prior to these developments, the Reformers did not wear the label of "Calvinist" as a badge of honor. In fact, they were reluctant to don it at all.

---

189. As quoted in Muller, "Reception and Response," 183.
190. As quoted in Muller, "Reception and Response," 183; English spelling updated.
191. Miller, *New England Mind*, 93.
192. Muller, "Reception and Response," 184.

CHAPTER FIVE

Epilogue

CALVIN MUST BE MET on his own turf.[1] As Michael Horton cautions, "As with any other figure, it is appropriate to interpret Calvin first of all on his own terms and only then to compare and contrast him with one's own favored dogmas."[2] Andrew McGowan similarly warns, "It is in any case notoriously difficult to ask questions of a historical figure; and to seek to determine the position which Calvin might or might not have taken in any specified later controversy will always be a matter of opinion."[3] At the same time, historians have a penchant for examining not only continuities and discontinuities but also trajectories of thought, including diverse trajectories stemming from the same historical source(s).

Calvin cannot be elevated as the plumb-line of Reformed theology, and Reformation theology was a work in progress.[4] Many "significant churchmen and theologians" influenced the development of Reformed theology.[5] Carl Trueman remarks, "The last two decades have seen a definite dethroning of John Calvin as the atonement benchmark. It is now generally accepted that the Reformation was always a work in progress and that the thought of individual figures can only be used with caution as a gauge of orthodoxy."[6] Trueman therefore paints "a much more complicated situation where a variety of theologians held a variety of views, some of which differed from one another in subtle ways, others in

1. Thompson, "Calvin on the Cross of Christ," 127.
2. Horton, "Calvin's Theology of Union with Christ and the Double Grace," 79.
3. McGowan, "Was Westminster Calvinist?" 62.
4. Crisp, *Saving Calvinism*, 42.
5. Kennedy, "Was Calvin a 'Calvinist'?" 192; Crisp, *Saving Calvinism*, 42.
6. In Naselli and Snoeberger, *Perspectives on the Extent of the Atonement*, 209.

more significant matters."[7] Although one often thinks of Calvin as an innovative systematic theologian with his own particular system (because of his famous *Institutes of the Christian Religion*), "Calvin and company thought in terms of confessions, not personal contributions."[8]

Calvin was largely motivated by pastoral sensitivities as well as a desire to submit to the biblical revelation. Tension within his position may therefore be laid at the feet of his aspiration to retain pastoral and biblical faithfulness.[9]

Calvin was a student of the Scriptures. Anthony Lane affirms that Calvin was "a biblical theologian" and "an outstanding exegete," especially considering his sixteenth-century context.[10] "His constant involvement with the biblical text, together with his aversion to speculation beyond what is revealed, kept him from abandoning some of the genuine biblical tensions and paradoxes."[11] "The mark of the true disciple of Calvin," claims Lane, "is the willingness to accept biblical paradox and not to seek to reconcile it in the direction of one pole or another."[12] Some may prefer

---

7. Naselli and Snoeberger, *Perspectives on the Extent of the Atonement*, 209.

8. Naselli and Snoeberger, *Perspectives on the Extent of the Atonement*, 209. According to Charles Partee, Calvin was more of a "confessor" than a "dogmatician" (see Grow, "John Calvin contra 'Two Wills in God' Methodology"). Grow adds, "Calvin certainly had a logic and method to his theologizing, but it was driven by his ineluctable commitment to say what scripture says—even if coherence remains tenuous."

9. Tensions also arise within Calvin's discussions of God's being our enemy until we were reconciled in Christ and God already embracing us with his free favor. "The crux of the problem for Calvin is that the change that apparently takes place in God once he ceases to regard us as his enemies is at odds with the love God has of us from eternity (Penner, "Calvin, Barth, and the Subject of Atonement," 130). Calvin maintained that "God's wrath and curse always lie upon sinners until they are absolved of guilt," yet God would not have given his Son "if he had not already embraced us with his free favor" (Calvin, *Institutes* II.16.1–2). Calvin acknowledged that "some sort of [perceived] contradiction arises here," but he appealed to divine accommodation as a solution (Penner, "Calvin, Barth, and the Subject of Atonement," 130–31). See also Hay, "Heart of Wrath," 361–78; Doyle, "Penal Atonement," 103–5. Doyle reminds his readers that "The atonement does not happen outside God" (ibid., 104).

10. Lane, "Quest for the Historical Calvin," 113.

11. Lane, "Quest for the Historical Calvin," 113. "As a careful biblical scholar, Calvin demonstrated a willingness to use the vocabulary of Scripture" (Wax, "Why Calvin Is More Biblical Than Some Calvinists"). See also Kuiper, *For Whom Did Christ Die?* 86–88.

12. Lane, "Quest for the Historical Calvin," 113. See also Kuiper, *For Whom Did Christ Die?* 86–87; Blocher, "Jesus Christ *the* Man," 545. Luther seemed to have had a greater penchant for paradox (Blacketer, "Blaming Beza," 127). Stephen Holmes compares the biblical tensions inherent in discussions of the extent of the atonement with

the language of "biblical tensions" rather than "biblical paradoxes."[13] In any case, Calvin definitely aspired to a non-speculative, biblically-formed theology.[14] Matthew Harding notes that "Calvin leaves room for mystery, tension, and undisclosed realities in the mind of God concerning special revelation."[15] According to J. K. S. Reid, Calvin's "first loyalty" was directed "not to formal adherence to abstract logicality, but to the facts of the case and situation as he conceived them, or rather as he conceived the Scriptures to depict them."[16]

Moreover, Calvin's theology was also marked by its pastoral orientation.[17] Calvin considered the theologian's task to be pastoral and pedagogical rather than speculative or primarily philosophical.[18] Calvin sought to be "rhetorical, or more specifically edifying or *pastoral*," and he was concerned with "practical piety, with the actual experience and response of gratitude."[19] He sought to encourage the despairing and to warn the unbelieving.

The remainder of this epilogue will attempt to do three things. First, it will encourage contemporary theologians to consider the explanatory possibilities of a complex-intentioned approach. This section will move beyond historical investigation to contemporary constructive work.

---

biblical tensions inherent in discussions of Trinitarianism (Holmes, "Nature of the Atonement and the Extent of the Atonement," 7–17).

13. Carson, *Divine Sovereignty and Human Responsibility*. The point here is not to enter into debates about the meaning, nature, and possibility of "paradoxes" in Christian theology. One is reminded of the dispute between Cornelius van Til (who preferred the language of "paradox") and Gordon Clark (who thought that a so-called biblical paradox was "a charley horse between the ears that can be eliminated by rational massage"). See Crampton, "Does the Bible Contain Paradox?" As noted, some may consider the term "tension" to be preferable.

14. Robert Peterson praises Calvin's example "as a theologian in two areas: eschewing speculation and seeking to base his theology on the exposition of Holy Scripture" (Peterson, "Calvin on Christ's Saving Work," 247). See also Hill, *History of Christian Thought*, 203.

15. Harding, "Atonement Theory Revisited," 69.

16. Reid, "Editor's Introduction," 14. Reid added, "The logicality of his thought is dedicated not to the formation of a system, but rather to the eliciting of the meaning and the implications of those facts which, as it seemed to him, belong to the body of Christian truth" (ibid.).

17. See Gunton, "Aspects of Salvation," 253–65.

18. Battles, *Interpreting John Calvin*, 117.

19. Smit, "Justice and Divine Justice?" 95; italics original. For a revisioning of Calvin's atonement theology, see van Dyk, "How Does Jesus Make a Difference?" 205–20.

Second, the epilogue will discuss three lessons that have emerged from our historical examinations. Third, the epilogue will return to our historical investigation of Calvin in particular, by reiterating the pastoral and non-speculative nature of his approach and by reviewing five specific conclusions concerning his views.

The explanatory possibilities of a complex-intentioned approach

Calvin's approach was non-speculative regarding God's decretal will, and he turned the focus of readers to God's revealed will. According to Calvin (and similar to Luther), troubled souls are to focus upon the revealed will of God, which calls all to come and receive salvation in Christ. The general summons of the gospel are interconnected within God's complex yet unified plan as disclosed to us, even apart from any speculative ordering of the decrees. Could God's unified plan have taken into consideration the "epistemic condition" of humans (who are cognitively dependent upon his revealed Word rather than his secret eternal counsel), embracing both means and end?[20] If God intended to reach the elect through the general

---

20. See Lynch, "Richard Hooker," 290. The language of "epistemic condition" comes from Helm, "Calvin, Indefinite Language, and Definite Atonement," 113. Helm also insists that the universal gospel invitation is "sincere" rather than "deceptive or duplicitous" (ibid.). Roger Nicole, in "A Definition of the Atonement," speaks of Jesus Christ "identifying with his own" and providing a basis "for the redemption of a multitude of captives of sin," offering himself as "an expiatory sacrifice sufficient to blot out the sins of the whole world." This "good news of salvation by grace through faith is to be proclaimed indiscriminately to mankind, that is to every man, woman and child that we can possibly reach" (Nicole, *Standing Forth*, 244). Does the "good news of salvation . . . to be proclaimed indiscriminately to mankind" refer to Christ's provision for the multitude of his own or to its sufficiency for the sins of the whole world (or to both)? Is it good news for all ("every man, woman, and child that we can possibly reach"), as related to a human phenomenological perspective alone or also to a divine intent of objective provision *ex nobis* (see Ponter, "Review Essay (Part One)," 139)? Lorraine Boettner asked, "was the sacrifice of Christ merely intended to render certain the salvation of all men possible, or was it intended to render certain the salvation of those who had been given to Him by the Father?" (Boettner, *Reformed Doctrine of Predestination*, 150). One senses that this either-or question may not necessarily reflect the entirety of the matter. Boettner himself, on the next page, states that "the value of the atonement" made "the salvation of every man objectively possible," although the subjective difficulty of human inability remains (ibid., 152). Boettner concludes that there is "a certain sense in which Christ died for all men," including the facts that Christ's atonement "arrests the penalty which would have been inflicted upon the whole race because of Adam's sin; that it forms a basis for the preaching of the Gospel" (ibid., 160).

summons of the gospel (on account of their "epistemic condition"), then one could speak of his unified plan being *complex*, weaving together his decree of election with his intention to reach the elect through the efficacious call of the Spirit using the "word of truth" of the universal promises (sincere and not duplicitous!) of grace truly available to all in Christ and generally presented through gospel proclamation.[21] All of this did not "just happen" but only because God himself saw fit to "*choose* to bring his grace to sinners ... by saying that Christ died for the world" even as he *chose* the elect.[22]

By building upon materials in Calvin yet moving beyond his explicit discussions in order to build or "construct" theology, we may be able theoretically to distinguish between a multi-intentioned view of the atonement and a complex-intentioned view of the atonement. To be clear, this distinction is not found in Calvin, and would therefore be anachronistic if placed overtly upon him. Nevertheless, the distinction may perhaps help to further contemporary discussions. On the one hand, people may have multiple intentions that are unrelated to one another. For instance, a couple may intend to work extra hours in the family business throughout the summer, to visit Chicago in September, and to visit Brazil in November. These three intentions may stand as distinct, unrelated intentions. On the other hand, people may have multiple yet interwoven intentions, in which case some type of internal connection relates the intentions to one another. For example, a couple may intend to work extra hours in the family business throughout the summer partly in order to raise funds to visit Chicago and Brazil, and they may plan to visit Chicago partly in order to stop by the Brazilian consulate for travel paperwork, and they may plan to visit Brazil partly in order to purchase goods for the family business. Strands of intentionality interweave the multiple intentions within a unified plan, and a unity of will and purpose coordinates the complex-intentioned plan.

---

21. I.e., Eph 1:13 in the context of Eph 1:3–13. Calvin declared, "God commands nothing in pretense, but seriously exhibits what he wills and approves of" (as quoted in Lynch, "Richard Hooker," 288). Lynch also highlights the perspective of Polanus, that God does not mock but seriously (*serio*) wishes the reprobate to come (ibid.).

22. Helm, "Calvin, Indefinite Language, and Definite Atonement," 113; italics added. The use of this quotation is not to imply that Helm agrees with the framework presented here.

The concept of "complex intentionality" may be a consideration for contemporary theologians, regardless of Calvin's own historical views.[23] Leaving aside historical considerations and debates for a moment, we may briefly consider the matter. Various contemporary theologians have explicitly emphasized a "multiple intentions" or "multi-intentioned" approach to the atonement within a framework characterized by "unconditional election."[24] Contemporary "multiple-intentions" theologians tend to discuss the additional role of Christ's death in reconciling the cosmos, often citing Col 1:19–20.[25] Calvin and the early Reformers did not emphasize a cosmological intention in Christ's death to the degree that some contemporary "multiple-intentions" theologians have done.[26]

---

23. Jeffrey Johnson refers to a concept of "complex intentionality," though not fully in the same manner (Johnson, *He Died for Me*).

24. Ware, "Extent of the Atonement"; Shultz, *Multi-Intentioned View of the Extent of the Atonement*; Hammett, "Multiple Intentions View of the Atonement."

25. See also Rom 8:18–22; 1 Cor 15:24–28; 2 Cor 5:18–21; Phil 2:9–11. See Kuiper, *For Whom Did Christ Die?* 95–100; Shultz, "Reconciliation of All Things in Christ," 442–59. T. F. Torrance, though not in the "multiple-intentions" camp, remarks, "The universal range of the redemptive work of Christ takes in not only all humanity, but the whole created universe of space and time, including all things (*ta panta*) visible and invisible, earthly and heavenly alike" (Torrance, "Atonement," 249). On the other hand, Torrance was not a universalist (Habets, "Doctrine of Election in Evangelical Calvinism," 340–41). See also Peterson, "To Reconcile to Himself All Things," 37–46. T. F. Torrance has espoused a modified Barthian view of Christ's work (including the atonement) centered in the incarnation (Torrance, *Atonement*, 182; Habets, "Doctrine of Election in Evangelical Calvinism," 334–54). "It was his whole life, and above all that life poured out in supreme sacrifice of death on the cross, that made atonement for sin, and constituted the price of redemption for all mankind" (Torrance, "Atonement," 240). For a critique of Barth, see Williams, "Karl Barth and the Doctrine of the Atonement," 249–70; cf. Kuiper, *For Whom Did Christ Die?* 77. While Kuiper binds Christ's atoning death with his intercessory work (so that the former cannot be wider in final scope of intention than the latter), Torrance binds Christ's atoning death with the incarnation (see ibid., 64). "Atonement and incarnation cannot be separated from one another, and therefore the range of his representation is the same in both" (Torrance, "Atonement," 245). Torrance insists, however, that due to the irrational and inextricable nature of sin, not all will be saved (ibid., 245, 248). See Molnar, "Thomas F. Torrance and the Problem of Universalism." For a critique of Torrance, see Letham, "Triune God, Incarnation, and Definite Atonement," 444–59.

26. For example, the double intentionality of David Pareaus (1548–1622) taught the divine intention of Christ dying for all in respect to sufficiency, and the divine intention of Christ dying for the elect alone as to efficiency (efficacy). But Paraeus did not highlight a cosmological intention. See Allen, *Extent of the Atonement*, 89. Allen, "Calvin and the Extent of the Atonement," 2. Edmund Calamy, an English hypothetical universalist, spoke directly of "absolute intention for the elect, conditional intention for the reprobate in case they do believe" (see Troxel, "Amyraut 'at' the Assembly," 49).

Moreover, as we have noted above, Calvin's penchant can be described as "non-speculative" regarding the ordering of the eternal decrees and similar concerns. But Calvin's words do seem to reflect how the sufficiency of Christ's provision gave opportunity to all despairing individuals to take consolation in God's gift of grace for them, and the same provision left unbelievers without excuse for their unbelief, as they rejected the grace provided for them.

One wonders if contemporary constructive endeavors representing a "multiple intentions" approach could place more emphasis upon the *complex interrelationship* of divinely appointed means along with a foundational unconditional election and a resultant efficacious call. One could maintain that in the historical outworking of the unified plan, the Holy Spirit customarily forms faith in the elect (those chosen in eternity past through unconditional, divine choice) *by means of* pointing them to the all-sufficient provision and the universal promises in the general offer.[27] Christ's work in the gospel provides a foundation for faith *ex nobis*. Taking this into account, the universal facet of provision within a complex-intentioned plan is not merely "abstract and irrelevant."[28] Rather the means and ends are complexly interwoven, as reflected in what finite humans do have access to—God's revealed will.

In a special and particular manner Christ loves the church and gave himself for her, purchasing her with his own blood.[29] He laid down his life for his sheep.[30] In securing his treasure (and as seen through one prism, in order to secure his treasure), Christ bought the whole field.[31]

---

27. Perspectivally framed by progressive revelation and one's historical position in relation to the cross. See also Williams, *Heart of Piety*, 101–41.

28. See Owen in Trueman, "Atonement and the Covenant of Redemption," 212.

29. Eph 5:25; Acts 20:28; cf. Rom 8:32; Rev 5:9. As a sidenote, theologians who teach that the church did not commence until after Christ's death and resurrection should believe that Christ died for more people than the members of the universal church alone (even though Acts 10:28 and Eph 5:25–27 are customarily used as arguments for "limited atonement"). If Old Testament saints were not members of the church and yet they, too, were saved by Christ's atonement (Heb 12:22–24), then another intention was at work beyond Christ's giving himself for his Bride and thus purchasing the church. Those who believe that the church is composed of all believers of all times would not face this particular issue, of course (cf. Piper, *Five Points*, 49–50).

30. John 10:15; cf. John 15:13–14.

31. Matt 13:44. See the use of the analogy in Daniel, *History and Theology of Calvinism*, 363; cf. Macleod, "Definite Atonement and the Divine Decree," 428; Williams, *Heart of Piety*, 191. Of course, in Jesus' parable, the illustration is used toward a different end, concerning the kingdom of heaven.

God manifested his love by sending his Son into the world, for the sins of humanity as proclaimed in the gospel offer.[32] This divine provision secured the objective promises of the gospel *ex nobis* as a foundation of faith. At the same time, Calvary's payment is not an automatic pecuniary one, as an application within personal history applies Christ's work to an individual.[33] Christ's work is applied by faith, and God particularly ordained to form faith in elect sinners (who would not believe if left to themselves) through the proclaimed gospel promises and the efficacious work of the Spirit.[34]

---

32. 1 John 4:9-10; 2:2. As discussed earlier, Calvin differed in his own interpretation of 1 John 2:2 (see Chapter Three of this present work).

33. Cf. Knox, *Doctrine of God*, 109; Lynch, "*Quid Pro Quo* Satisfaction?" Consider the counsel of Robert Dabney: "Christ's satisfaction is not a pecuniary equivalent, but only such a one as enables the Father, consistently with His attributes, to pardon, if in His mercy He sees fit. The whole avails of the satisfaction to a given man is suspended on his belief. There would be no injustice to the man, if he remaining an unbeliever, his guilt were punished twice over, first in his Savior, and then in Him" (Dabney, *Lectures in Systematic Theology*, 521; cf. Lynch, "*Quid Pro Quo* Satisfaction?" 58). See as well the comparisons of pecuniary and judicial/penal satisfaction in Hodge, *Atonement*, 368-69; and Hodge, "For Whom Did Christ Die?" 553-58; cf. Gerrish, *Thinking with the Church*, 188-89; Boettner, *Reformed Doctrine of Predestination*, 151-52. See also the discussion of Andrew Fuller's critique of commercialism in Thomas, *Atonement Controversy*, 132-33. On the "pecuniary" vs. "forensic" distinction, see Crisp, *Deviant Calvinism*, 224. A "pecuniary" satisfaction is a commercial transaction that automatically remits the debt. A "forensic" satisfaction demands discretionary judgment in application. In a "forensic" view, "there is an element of divine discretion that obtains so that the benefits of Christ's work do not necessarily apply ipso facto" (ibid., 224-25). For a response, see Williams, "Definite Atonement of Penal Substitutionary Atonement," 468-71. Williams argues that a pecuniary vs. penal distinction does not alleviate the tensions of hypothetical universalism, since such a distinction "relies on a defective ontology that separates things as they are in themselves from God's determinations regarding those things" (ibid., 471). This could beg the question of what God intended and determined, including a non-speculative "complex-intentioned" view (see my discussion in this chapter). Williams, of course, locates "the specificity and particularity" of the atonement in the sacrifice of Christ itself (ibid., 480). Cf. Williams, "Punishment God Cannot Twice Inflict," 480-86, 506. Williams claims that the hypothetical universalist is the one who turns the sacrifice into a pecuniary one, since "money can simply be refused and returned, but penal suffering can never be undone" (ibid. 511). See also Tay, *Priesthood of Christ*, 48. By contrast, Thomas Nettles defends an application of a pecuniary (commercial) conceptual framework and language to definite atonement (Nettles, "Review").

34. We do not mean here to enter into discussions concerning the death of infants, but only refer to the regular means of divine working (cf. the relevant caveats found in Crisp, *Deviant Calvinism*, 101n5; 201n29). Calvin's own view of infants and salvation is debated, as reflected in Stagg, *Calvin, Twisse and Edwards*.

In the gospel and its objective promises, Christ offers himself to all as a real provision. Since God intended this sufficiency to be "available for everyone," one can be gospel-centered in one's approach by pointing individuals to the objective truths of the gospel outside of us (*ex nobis*).[35] Someone does not have to believe first that he is elect in order to know that Christ died for him; rather, he knows that he is elect through believing in Christ who died for him. A person must only know that she is a sinner in order to know that Christ's death is available for her.[36]

Therefore, instead of "multiple intentions" alone (a listing of multiple purposes that can be considered as standing distinct, and thus implicitly unconnected from one another), could one speak of a *complex-intentioned* atonement (of intentions complexly interwoven together in both unified design and implementation) as reflected in the revealed will of God?[37] The divine intentions cohere in plan and execution, as do the means and ends.[38] The provision of the death of Christ supports a divinely intentioned truth *ex nobis*, and the Spirit uses the objective promise found in the general offer as a ground in the formation of faith in the elect through his efficacious call.[39] The universal facets of the atonement provide warrant and encouragement for approaching God through Christ

---

35. See Williams, *Heart of Piety*, 142–66. Thomas notes, "In line with the whole thrust of the Protestant Reformation, Calvin regarded the work of redemption as performed *extra nos*. It is a work of God complete in itself and to which we can add nothing" (Thomas, *Extent of the Atonement*, 28).

36. Contrast Packer, *Introductory Essay*, 20; Packer, "Saved by His Precious Blood," 132.

37. Thus preserving an emphasis upon the unified plan of God in his eternal purpose. Besides the universal and particular aspects to the atonement, there is also a cosmic one (Hammett, "Multiple Intentions View of the Atonement," 199).

38. R. B. Kuiper, who believed in a "scriptural universalism" that included Christ dying "for" the non-elect in the sense of "in behalf of" but not "in the place of," argued: "Nevertheless, it can be shown that the Calvinist, and he alone, precisely because of his particularism is in a position to do full justice to Scriptural universalism. The particular design of the atonement and its universal design in no way contradict each other. They support and strengthen each other. In final analysis they stand and fall together. The Calvinist can be, must be, and inconsistencies aside, will be an ardent universalist because he is a zealous particularist" (Kuiper, *For Whom Did Christ Die?* 79).

39. Cf. Calvin, *Institutes* III.2.15. It is not in believing that we are elect that we know that Christ died for us in particular. It is rather in believing that Christ died for us that we know in particular that we are elect. Contrast Turretin's two stages in faith as described in Blocher, "Jesus Christ *the* Man," 569.

in faith, and are used by the Spirit in the formation and strengthening of faith in the elect.[40]

In such a constructed framework, if for no other reason (and there are others), Christ died for all because he intended to form within chosen ones a faith anchored in divine promises of an objective provision *ex nobis*.[41] The gospel summons is thus undergirded by the divinely ordained sufficiency of Christ's satisfaction, standing behind the grace offered to all.[42] In this understanding, God's design was complex-intentioned, such that the Triune God ordained for Christ to procure a universal satisfaction to be applied to the elect in particular through faith in the universal promises of the gospel.[43] Moreover, in a *complex-intentioned* view, these divine intentions are interwoven in God's unified design. The multiple intentions do not merely stand side-by-side without connection. Coming from his own perspective, the Reformed theologian Rienk Kuiper declared: "The particular design of the atonement and its universal design in no way contradict each other. Nor do they merely complement each other. They support and strengthen each other. In the final analysis, they stand and fall together."[44]

---

40. See Williams, *Heart of Piety*, 140–41.

41. Contrast Macleod, "Definite Atonement and the Divine Decree," 428. This does not mean that we know all the intricacies and inter-connections within the unified plan of God's eternal divine counsel, but we do know facets of connection as reflected in his revealed will.

42. Muller uses similar phraseology of Davenant's view (Muller, "Davenant and Du Moulin," 157). On the other hand, "Davenant can hardly be called a forerunner of Amyraut!" (ibid.). Gatiss speaks of "ordained sufficiency" and "conditional intentionality" in Davenant (Gatiss, "Synod of Dort and Definite Atonement," 157).

43. Others have used "complex" language of Calvin's thought in a different manner. J. T. McNeill spoke of the "variety and subtlety" of Calvin's thought, "a resourcefulness that is not overmastered by an anxious consistency," and even a "*complexio oppositorum*" (McNeill, *History and Character of Calvinism*, 202). McNeill declared, "The simple effort to utter the truths of the Bible may have made Calvin hesitate to force its meanings to a consistent pattern" (ibid.).

44. Kuiper, *For Whom Did Christ Die?* 78–79. "According to the Reformed faith the divine design of the atonement is indeed in an important respect limited. But the Reformed faith also insists that in other important respects it is universal" (ibid., 78). In Kuiper's view, a "scriptural universalism" "does justice to all the Scriptural data bearing on the subject" because "the particularist view of the design of the atonement is in harmony with the universalistic passages of Holy Scripture" (ibid., 62–64). This "scriptural universalism'" includes (1) the universal suitableness and sufficiency of the Atonement, (2) common grace, (3) the universal and sincere offer of salvation, (4) the salvation of the world, in the sense of the cosmos including non-human facets

One may posit an intricate, complex-intentioned atonement as a reflection of the divine plan of an infinitely wise God. As Curt Daniel explains, "The universal and particular aspects of the atonement have been eternally married to each other, and what God has joined together let no man put asunder."[45] This unified plan awaits an eschatological culmination, weaving all facets into its tapestry. In the eschaton, God's redeemed, new humanity will thrive in the restored new heavens and new earth, reflecting the cosmic facet of God's plan.[46] In the successive outworking of salvation, Gods' plan will be fully realized, as all things will be reconciled to himself.[47]

(ibid., 78–100). "Therefore, the statement, so often heard from Reformed pulpits, that Christ died only for the elect must be rated a careless one" (ibid., 78). In Kuiper's view, Christ died "for" the non-elect as well, in the sense of "in behalf of" but not in the sense of "in the place of" (ibid., 78). One senses a hurdle in Kuiper's mind seemingly related to the combination of substitutionary atonement and an implied understanding of the so-called "double-payment" objection. For a discussion of the relationship between the atonement and common grace, see Baek, *Atonement as the Judicial Basis of Common Grace*. For a response to the claim that a "universal redemption" within Calvin's theology would annul his understanding of "substitutionary atonement," see Kennedy, *Union with Christ and the Extent of the Atonement*, 6–7, 57–61. "By placing all of the benefits of our salvation in the person of Christ, and by making our union with Christ through faith the key to our reception of the benefits of salvation, Calvin was able to hold to a view of the atonement that was both universal and substitutionary" (ibid., 147). Contrast Packer, "What Did the Cross Achieve?" 37; Murray, *Redemption Accomplished and Applied*, 59–75. Calvin affirmed, "First, we must understand that as long as Christ remains outside of us, and we are separated from him, all that he has suffered and done for the salvation of the human race remains useless and of no value for us. Therefore, to share with us what he has received from the Father, he had to become ours and to dwell within us. . . . For, as I have said, all that he possesses is nothing to us until we grow into one body with him. It is true that we obtain this by faith" (Calvin, *Institutes* III.1.1). "For the faithless have no profit at all by the death and passion of our Lord Jesus Christ, but rather are so much the more damnable, because they reject the mean that God had ordained: and their unthankfulness shall be so much the more grievously punished, because they have trodden under foot the blood of our Lord Jesus Christ, which was the ransom for their souls. Therefore it stands us on hand to receive the promises of the Gospel by faith, if we desire that Jesus Christ should communicate himself unto us, and that he should bring us to the possession and enjoyment of the benefits which he hath purchased for us: so as they belong not to any other than such as are members of his body, and are grafted into him, and receive him by faith" (Calvin, *Sermons on Galatians*, 39; English spelling updated).

45. Daniel, *History and Theology of Calvinism*, 377.

46. Piper, "'My Glory I Will Not Give to Another,'" 655. Kuiper, *For Whom Did Christ Die?* 96–100.

47. Blocher, "Jesus Christ *the* Man," 580–81; cf. 1 Cor 15:28; Col 1:19–20.

Is there anything *inherently* illogical in proposing that the Trinitarian members shared a complexly interwoven, unified plan?[48] Roger Nicole insisted "that holding to universal atonement does terrible damage to the unity of the counsel of God. It is to separate the Father and the Holy Spirit from the Son, when the very essence of God is that there is one purpose in which they are united."[49] If the Father's *sole* intention was particular application to the elect, and if the Son's *sole* intention was a universal provision, and if the Spirit's *sole* intention was a particular effectual call, then incongruities would exist within the Trinitarian intentions.[50] But what if the three Trinitarian members were completely united not in one restricted intent alone but in a complex-intentioned yet unified design and implementation? Would not all three members, although undertaking distinct roles in the outworking of salvation, have harmoniously formed such a unified plan in eternity past and also be consistently implementing it within history (at Calvary and in individual lives) and in the eschaton, all interwoven in a complex yet complementary manner?[51]

48. Contra Troxel, "Amyraut 'at' the Assembly," 54.

49. Nicole, "Particular Redemption," 172. See also Johnson, *He Died for Me*.

50. Gibson, "Glorious, Indivisible, Trinitarian Work of God in Christ," 368; Letham, "Triune God, Incarnation, and Definite Atonement," 440, 444; Horton, "Traditional Reformed View," 120, 127. According to Robert Letham, "the most serious problem" with a universal atonement view is that it "threatens to tear apart the Holy Trinity" (Letham, *Work of Christ*, 237).

51. See the discussion of the Trinitarian Members in Kennedy, *Union with Christ and the Extent of the Atonement*, 106–16. This approach also addresses the matter of individuals who lived before Christ's death, and it avoids the a-historic "double payment" argument commonly posed by "strict" particular redemptionists. See Eph 2:1–13; Daniel, *History and Theology of Calvinism*, 370–71; Compton, "John Davenant's Dissertation on the Death of Christ," 175–76. In his strong assessment, Oliver Crisp calls the "double payment" argument a "failure" (Crisp, *Deviant Calvinism*, 238; cf. the lengthy discussion in ibid., 213–33). See also Shedd, *Dogmatic Theology*, vol. 2, 443–44; Williams, *Heart of Piety*, 113–14; Allen, *Atonement*, 247–52. For an attempt at preserving the argument through modification ("a more nuanced understanding . . . that renders the double payment version safe to handle"), see Williams, "Punishment God Cannot Twice Inflict," 483–518. Williams acknowledges that a double payment argument that depends upon commercial concepts is problematic, and he alternatively describes the punishment afflicted as "suffering inflicted as a fitting answer to sin" (ibid., 484, 486). Williams insists, "Payment God cannot twice demand; punishment God cannot twice inflict. Christ's blood has spoken an answer to the sins of his people, including their sins of unbelief. Nothing more remains to be said" (ibid., 515). Williams prefers merging the metaphors of God as ruler and creditor (ibid., 493), and he argues that Christ's atonement can be both "unquantifiable" punishment (infinitely valuable due to the hypostatic union) and inherently "definite" (ibid., 499). Contrast

If the Trinitarian members work in "indivisible harmony" and in a unified concert of plan and implementation, then a complex-intentioned framework cannot be "inherently incoherent."[52]

Various contemporary theologians have coalesced the biblical data in a similar fashion, demonstrating that at least some theologians find such a fusion logically conceivable.[53] Curt Daniel explains, "There are general and particular aspects about the work of each member of the Trinity."[54] John Hammett maintains, "The Father may send Christ to the

---

Lynch, "*Quid Pro Quo* Satisfaction?"

52. Contrast Letham, "Triune God, Incarnation, and Definite Atonement," 444.

53. See Cunningham, *Reformers and the Theology of the Reformation*, 399. While critiquing hypothetical universalism, Blocher concedes, "All could agree that a duality harmoniously affects the roles of Father, Son, and Spirit" (Blocher, "Jesus Christ *the Man*," 567). See also Clifford, "Calvin & Calvinism," 67; Clifford, *Amyraut Affirmed*, 51–52.

54. Daniel, *History and Theology of Calvinism*, 371. See also Elliott, "Availability and Application of the Atonement," 40. Daniel adds, "The Father loves all men as creatures, but gives special love only to the elect. The Spirit calls all men, but efficaciously calls only the elect. Similarly, the Son died for all men, but died in a special manner for the elect. We must keep the balance with each of these" (Daniel, *History and Theology of Calvinism*, 371). To add to Daniel's comments, the Spirit inspired the Scriptures with their general call of the gospel. Therefore, the Spirit neither "underperforms" nor "brings disharmony into the Trinity," even though not all hear the gospel (cf. the critique in Jonathan Gibson, "Glorious, Indivisible, Trinitarian Work of God in Christ," 369). The Trinity is unified in the work of *general* revelation through the starry heavens (Ps 19:1–4), even though congenitally blind individuals never see the celestial bodies. Nor is there "a deep Trinitarian dysfunction with deleterious implications for our doctrine of God," as charged by Sinclair Ferguson (Ferguson, "'Blessèd Assurance, Jesus Is Mine'?" 629). Ferguson declares that the members of the Trinity "are at one" in hypothetical universalism, but this Trinitarian unity cannot be sustained because "the Father sets forth his Son as a real propitiation for the sins of some for whom that propitiation never actually propitiates" (ibid.). Yet even the temporary staying of the immediate, full infliction of God's wrath upon unbelievers flows from a common grace rooted in Christ's death (Kuiper, *For Whom Did Christ Die?* 82–84), and the objective provision of propitiation is applied through faith even in the elect. On the other hand, hypothetical universalists, multi-intentioned atonementists, and similar proponents must indeed consider the issue of the unevangelized within their systems (see Ferguson, "'Blessèd Assurance, Jesus Is Mine'?" 629; Strange, "Slain for the World?" 592, 594n25). Calvin seems to have recognized this very necessity, ruminating as follows: "Thus we see three degrees of the love that God has shown us in our Lord Jesus Christ. The first is in respect of the redemption that was purchased in the person of him that gave himself to death for us, and became accursed to reconcile us to God his Father. That is the first degree of love, which extends to all men, inasmuch as Jesus Christ reaches out his arms to call and allure all men both great and small, and to win them to him. But there is a special love for those to whom the gospel is preached: which is

cross both to save some and provide forgiveness for all; Christ in dying accomplished both; and the Spirit in applying the benefits of Christ's death only to some also acted in harmony with the will of Father and Son. Thus, Christ's atonement may have multiple intentions without in any way contradicting the unity of the divine will."[55] Gary Shultz asserts that the "multiple-intentions" view "holds consistently to both unconditional election and an atonement that paid for the sins of all people by asserting that God the Father had multiple intentions for the atonement, and sent God the Son to accomplish these multiple purposes. The atonement not only accomplishes the Father's elective purposes, but his purposes for the creation and the nonelect as well. The Holy Spirit then works among the nonelect and the elect on the basis of the atonement, fulfilling the Father and the Son's intentions. Each person of the Trinity has general and particular intentions for creation, which means the unity of the Trinity is upheld by the multi-intentioned view."[56]

A *complex*-intentioned approach strengthens this unity. The claim, then, would *not* be that Christ "expanded the divine intention when he died," but that the Father, Son, and Spirit were all eternally and historically united in the complex-intentioned-yet-unified design and

---

that God testifies to them that he will make them partakers of the benefit that was purchased for them by the death and passion of his Son. And forasmuch as we be of that number, therefore we are double bound already to our God: here are two bonds which hold us as it were [closely] tied to him. Now let us come to the third bond, which depends upon the third love that God shows us: which is that he not only causes the gospel to be preached to us, but also makes us to feel the power thereof, so as we know him to be our Father and Saviour, not doubting but that our sins are forgiven us for our Lord Jesus Christ's sake, who brings us the gift of the Holy Spirit, to reform us after his own image" (Calvin, *Sermons on Deuteronomy*, 167). There is a narrowing of these three "degrees" of love, as if pictured by three concentric circles in target-like alignment: Christ objectively available, evangelistically proclaimed, and efficaciously received. Although he is available to all, not all hear the gospel, and not all who hear the gospel receive it through God's working.

55. Hammett, "Multiple-Intentions View of the Atonement," 173; "A multi-intentioned view holds that God the Father, in sending his Son to die on the cross, had both particular and general intentions for the atonement. In accordance with the Father's will, the Son then died to fulfill these multiple intentions. Based upon the Son's atoning death on the cross, the Spirit then works to apply the atonement in both particular and in general ways. God's multiple intentions in the atonement indicate that the atonement is in some ways for all people, but that it is for the elect in certain ways in which it is not for all people. God's particular intention in the atonement was to secure the salvation of the elect" (Shultz, *Multi-Intentioned View of the Atonement*, 8; cf. Shultz, "Biblical and Theological Defense of a Multi-Intentioned View," 226).

56. Shultz, *Multi-Intentioned View of the Extent of the Atonement*, 125.

implementation.⁵⁷ Nor is the claim that Christ died for all with "self-conscious ineffectiveness," but rather he consciously, intentionally, and certainly *provided* a universal redemption; and he also consciously, intentionally, and certainly *secured* the salvation of the elect whom the Father had chosen and whom the Spirit would efficaciously call *through* the resulting general gospel offer.⁵⁸ The secured application is anchored in (and interwoven with) a finished provision.⁵⁹ It is not logically contradictory to claim that all three members of the Godhead were united in a complex-intentioned design and implementation.⁶⁰

In this discussion of complex-intentionality, we have ventured beyond the individual statements found in Calvin by positing a possible pattern of constructive synthesis.⁶¹ We do not claim that Calvin himself purposed to develop systematically a "complex-intentioned" theology.⁶² A complex-intentioned view of the atonement is not systematically delineated by Calvin, although building blocks may emerge from his disparate materials. As acknowledged, this first discussion of the epilogue has moved beyond historical investigation. We have shifted from an inductive gathering of relevant statements in the primary-source texts to a synthetic attempt to trace a framework that might possess explanatory power for contemporary theologians.⁶³ Nevertheless, even apart

57. Compare Snoeberger, "Introduction," 11.

58. Compare Snoeberger, "Introduction," 11.

59. In some forms of hypothetical universalism, Christ's death secured "the grace of effectual redemption" for the elect alone. Put slightly differently, Christ's death purchased "a to-be-applied effectual redemption for the elect alone." In Lynch's view, Davenant distinguished between "an application destined and an application made" (see Lynch, "Confessional Orthodoxy and Hypothetical Universalism," 139–41).

60. Some critics have claimed that penal substitution by its very nature implies a division in the nature of the Trinity. For a response to this claim, see Jeffery et al., *Pierced for Our Transgressions*, 279–86.

61. Cf. van Buren, *Christ in Our Place*, 50. "In the preaching of salvation through Christ to lost men, no greater wrong could be imposed than to reduce truths that are throbbing with glory, light, and blessing to mere philosophical contemplation" (Chafer, "For Whom Did Christ Die?" 310).

62. Cf. Muller, "Davenant and Du Moulin," 140.

63. On an emerging framework in Calvin as "the bare bones of the argument," Reid declared, "the universality of the grace of Christ is symbolized by a promiscuous preaching of the Gospel; the universality of the Mediator is paralleled by the universality of the call to penitence and faith. But at this point the harmony ends; the offer of salvation is made equally to all, but salvation itself is for those who are elect. It is the bare bones of the argument, then, that are exposed, even if the result manifests a

from the historical question of Calvin's own views, perhaps a complex-intentioned view of the atonement warrants further investigation and critical assessment. Whether or not Calvin would recognize a more systematic complex-intentioned view as reflecting or approaching his own perspectives, a complex-intentioned approach as a further refinement of a multiple-intentions approach is worth further consideration, whether for adaptation or critique.

Three lessons

Let us now turn to particular lessons learned more directly from this historical study. In doing so, we move from a contemporary or constructive explanatory arrangement back toward lessons surfacing from the historical investigations. In general, this historical study has reminded us that we can all learn to listen more carefully and to speak more precisely. Yet three specific considerations also come to mind, gleaned from our historical examinations. I must emphasize that these considerations have surfaced *through* the historical explorations and the interpretation of the primary sources; I do not claim that these three considerations were explicitly taught *by* Calvin himself. Nevertheless, it would even seem that those who believe in a "strict" form of definite atonement could agree with the following three descriptive conclusions. First, the honored TULIP acronym fails to reflect the full complexities of the topic in historical embodiment. Second, the history of the Reformed tradition reflects a continuing and complex diversity in the matter of the extent of the atonement. Third, more refined reflection could assist many contemporary discussions of the relationship between sufficiency and divine intention.

i. TULIP is inadequate

First, the honored TULIP acronym fails to reflect the full complexities of the topic in historical embodiment. One is reminded of Michael Lynch's recent review of a collected volume defending "definite atonement." Lynch expressed his frustration by declaring, "The most glaring deficiency of the book is its ambiguity over the definition of definite atonement."[64] Lynch

---

certain awkward untidiness. There is no attempt to compel harmony or to systematize by force" (Reid, "Editor's Introduction," 13–14).

64. Lynch, Review of *From Heaven He Came and Sought Her*, 353. I reproduce

claims that within some passages of the volume, the notion of "definite atonement" entailed Christ being punished for the sins of the elect alone, while in other contexts "definite atonement" appeared to be shorthand for "an intention to apply redemption to the elect alone."[65] If Dort left a door open for various forms of hypothetical universalism, the latter conceptualization ("an intention to apply redemption to the elect alone") has placed a welcome mat in front of the door, inviting both hypothetical universalists and non-speculative multiple-intentionists to enter—even though many of the contributors to the volume, if queried, would not consider these others to believe in "definite atonement," as they understand the doctrine.[66]

Richard Muller maintains that if "limited atonement" means that Christ's satisfaction is efficient only for the elect, then *all* forms of seventeenth-century hypothetical universalism (including Amyraldianism) could be construed as alternative forms of "limited atonement."[67] Lee Gatiss, in a volume defending "definite atonement," claims that Davenant's approach *ultimately* aligns itself with "five-point Calvinism" and that others "who take a less 'strict,' non-Genevan view on this issue may also lay claim, historically speaking, to all five petals of the TULIP (though not in the oversimplified way in which the acronym is sometimes defined)."[68] Garry Williams (although an opponent of hypothetical universalism) even avers that Davenant's explanation of hypothetical universalism "may mean that he has a more definite account of the atonement than advocates of definite atonement, such as Dabney and Fuller, who locate the specificity exclusively in the application of Christ's work."[69] This kind

---

Lynch's assessments here for the sake of illustration, not necessarily for the sake of agreeing or disagreeing with his critique of the volume's "glaring" deficiency.

65. Lynch, Review of *From Heaven He Came and Sought Her*, 353. "Generally speaking, the book's *de facto* definition often amounts to little more than this: God intended or designed to savingly apply the benefits of the death of Christ to the elect alone. That God designed the death of Christ to be savingly applied only to the elect is hardly controversial among any confessional Reformed theologian, whether he or she affirms hypothetical universalism or not. Instead, the book only obfuscates the real issue that advocates of definite atonement should be arguing, namely, that Christ made a satisfaction only for the sins of the elect" (ibid.).

66. Confessional Lutheran theologians combine a *universa gratia* with unconditional election, along with the Spirit's personal work of grace.

67. Muller, "Was Calvin a Calvinist?" 61n21.

68. Gatiss, "Synod of Dort and Definite Atonement," 163.

69. Williams, "Punishment God Cannot Twice Inflict," 510n81.

of reasoning illustrates the irony reflected in others who posit a mutually exclusive polarization between a purported "five-point Calvinism" in Calvin and a non-speculative "hypothetical universalism" as found in Davenant and others.[70]

In sum, whatever one believes about Calvin's own view, the use of TULIP to box in so-called "five-point Calvinists" vs. "four-point Calvinists" is an overly simplistic and even misleading approach, when viewed through the complexities of history. Therefore, one wonders why the historical topic of Calvin's own view sometimes elicits a reactionary backlash based upon such reductionistic categorizations.[71] The more one understands the nuances of various authors in the sixteenth- and seventeenth-century Reformed tradition(s), the more an elaborate spectrum becomes apparent. There is no simple, clean-cut scheme of classification or labeling that does justice to all the particular iterations in all their elaborations.

Michael Horton believes that using TULIP as a summary of the main teachings of Reformed or Calvinist theology is "simplistic to the point of being unhelpful."[72] Authors like Kenneth Stewart, Donald Sinnema, and Oliver Crisp have recognized the weaknesses of using TULIP as a reductionistic cipher to solve all atonement riddles.[73] The acronym is a heuristic device, of recent vintage and of limited value. According to Sinnema, "When the 'Five Points of Calvinism' are popularly formulated in the acronym TULIP, the result is an unnuanced oversimplification and distortion that does not well represent Calvin or even the Canons [of Dort]."[74] When the acronym is used as a polemical weapon in popular-

---

70. If one puts Pierre Du Moulin's anti-Amyraldian form of non-speculative hypothetical universalism into the mix, matters become even more complicated (Muller, "Davenant and Du Moulin").

71. For instance, one scholar who had heard wind of but had not read my work claimed that I had drunk too deeply at the "Calvin vs. Calvinism" well and that Muller's work had proved that Calvin indeed taught "limited atonement." Yet Muller himself eschews the latter claim as anachronistic. And Muller himself, at times, speaks of a universal provision in Calvin's thought (Muller, *Calvin and the Reformed Tradition*, 279). Whether I am inebriated with a Kendall-like well springing from outdated forty-year-old scholarship without drawing from recent sources springing from the likes of Muller I must leave for others to decide, after having read this volume.

72. Horton, "Traditional Reformed View," 112.

73. Stewart, *Ten Myths about Calvinism*, 75–96; Sinnema, "Calvin and the Canons of Dordt," 102–3; Crisp, *Deviant Calvinism*, 236–37; Crisp, *Saving Calvinism*, 129–49.

74. Sinnema, "Calvin and the Canons of Dordt," 103. Alan Sell counsels that the nature of the "five points" as responses to the Remonstrance should "caution us against thinking that they represent the *sum* of Calvinism" (Sell, *Great Debate*, 14).

level discourses, rather than as a blossoming testimony to divine grace, the irony is only compounded.

ii. The diversity of the Reformed tradition concerning the extent of the atonement

Second, the history of the Reformed tradition reflects a continuing and complex diversity in the matter of the extent of the atonement. Ever since the Reformation, a *variety* of voices (indeed, an elaborate *spectrum* of voices) has always existed, representing a collection of family resemblances. In particular, recent scholarship has underscored the diverse forms of "hypothetical universalism" and their kin in the early modern era. John Davenant and Moïse Amyraut may have been theological cousins, but they were not identical twins.

Members of the extended Reformed family have not always crossed their Calvinistic t's and dotted their Calvinistic i's in the same manner. Beyond the examples discussed in the previous chapters, this is illustrated by the cases of Robert Dabney and William Shedd, two nineteenth-century Presbyterian systematic theologians who were both particular redemptionists. Shedd maintained that Christ's death was unlimited in passive intrinsic value yet limited in active intended application.[75] Accordingly, he cited the Lombardian formula, as is commonly done.[76] More peculiarly, Shedd spoke of an "unlimited" atonement along with a "limited" redemption.[77] "Atonement is unlimited, and redemption is limited. This statement includes all the Scripture texts: those which assert that Christ died for all men, and those which assert that he died for his people. He who asserts unlimited atonement, and limited redemption, cannot well be misconceived. He is understood to hold that the sacrifice of Christ is unlimited in its value, sufficiency, and publication, but limited in its effectual application."[78] Shedd also declared, "There are no claims of justice not yet satisfied; there is no sin of man for which an unlimited atonement has not been provided."[79]

---

75. Shedd, *Dogmatic Theology*, vol. 2, 469.
76. Shedd, *Dogmatic Theology*, vol. 2, 468.
77. Shedd, *Dogmatic Theology*, vol. 2, 466, 470. See Snoeberger, "Introduction," 15.
78. Shedd, *Dogmatic Theology*, vol. 2, 470.
79. Shedd, *Dogmatic Theology*, vol. 2, 482. According to Charles Hodge, "Christ, therefore, did not die equally for all men. He laid down his life for his sheep; He gave

Dabney explicitly opposed hypothetical universalism.[80] Yet Dabney posited unlimited expiation along with particular redemption. He declared, "Hence, when men use the word atonement, as they often do, in the sense of expiation, the phrases 'limited atonement,' 'particular atonement,' have no meaning. Redemption is limited, i.e., to true believers, and is particular. Expiation is not limited."[81] "As it [expiation] is applied in effectual calling, it becomes personal, and receives a limitation. But in itself, limitation is irrelevant to it."[82] Expiation is "single, unique, complete; and, in itself considered, has no more relation to one man's sins than another."[83] Dabney added, "We are bound to assert that, while the expiation is infinite, redemption is particular."[84] Christ paid the "penal debt of the world."[85] Yet, Dabney insisted, God did not intend to save all through Christ's death.[86] Clearly variant approaches have applied theological vocabulary in differing ways.

iii. The need for further reflection on sufficiency and divine intention

Third, more refined reflection could assist many contemporary discussions of the relationship between sufficiency and divine intention, among

---

Himself for his Church. But in perfect consistency with all this, He did all that was necessary, so far as a satisfaction to justice is concerned, all that is required for the salvation of all men" (Hodges, *Systematic Theology*, vol. 2, 556-57). A generation ago, Norman Douty asserted, "But though God's design in Christ's death was dual, we must not think that the death itself was[;] . . . the sense in which Christ died for the elect and non-elect was single, but His object in doing so was double[;] . . . His death had a *special* reference to the elect, but we strongly deny that it had an exclusive reference to them" (Douty, *Did Christ Die Only for the Elect?* 44, 49-50).

80. Dabney, *Lectures in Systematic Theology*, 235, 519-20. Dabney demurs of Amyraldianism that "it tends towards assigning a sequence to the parts of the decree, as it subsists in God's mind" (ibid., 520). Dabney responds, "He [God] thinks and purposes it as one contemporaneous, mutually connected whole" (ibid.).

81. Dabney, *Lectures in Systematic Theology*, 528. Cf. Dabney, *Five Points of Calvinism*, 60.

82. Dabney, *Lectures in Systematic Theology*, 528.

83. Dabney, *Lectures in Systematic Theology*, 528.

84. Dabney, *Five Points of Calvinism*, 61.

85. Dabney, *Christ Our Penal Substitute*, 24.

86. "If God ever intended to save any soul in Christ, . . . that soul will certainly be saved. . . . But some souls will never be saved; therefore some souls God never intended to be saved by Christ's atonement" (Dabney, *Lectures in Systematic Theology*, 521).

both high and moderate Calvinists.⁸⁷ There are a few contemporary high Calvinists who deny the Lombardian formula that posits a sufficiency broader (in some sense) than the intended efficiency of the atonement: "Christ's death was sufficient for all, but efficient only for the elect."⁸⁸ Most Calvinists along the spectrum, however, acknowledge a "sufficiency for all," although often in a manner in need of further reflection or refinement. Consider but one example, passages from a self-proclaimed and renowned spokesperson for so-called "five-point Calvinism"—John Piper. We interact here with his popular-level volume entitled *The Five Points: Towards a Deeper Experience of God's Grace*.⁸⁹ Piper acknowledges the difficulties and ambiguities inherent in the use of the TULIP acronym, but retains it as the means of structuring his discussion.⁹⁰

Piper declares that "The atonement of Christ is *sufficient* for all humans and *effective* for those who trust him."⁹¹ Piper adds, "But the *full, saving effectiveness* of the atonement that Jesus accomplished is limited to those for whom that saving effect was prepared. . . . Thus Christ died for all people, but not for all in the same way."⁹² Is the "total sufficiency of the

---

87. See Allen, *Extent of the Atonement*, xix–xxviii.

88. For instance, Jim Scott Orrick asserts: "Even some Five-Point Calvinists for whom I have the utmost respect teach something about the extent of the atonement with which I disagree. They teach that the atonement was sufficient for all, but efficient only for the elect. I maintain that the Scriptures teach that the sufficiency and the efficiency of the atonement are coequal . . ." (Orrick, *Mere Calvinism*, 92).

89. This is not to deny that John Piper has at other times written technical work for academic audiences.

90. "These five points are focused on the central act of God's saving sinners. Nor do I make the claim that these titles for the five doctrines of grace are the best titles. Like any shorthand version of a doctrine, they are all liable to misunderstanding" (Piper, *Five Points*, 13). Piper's short-hand explanation of "limited atonement" in the "Preface" is that God sent "Jesus to atone for the sins of the elect" (ibid., 14).

91. Piper, *Five Points*, 16; italics original. Cf. Horton: "We declare not only generally to all but particularly to each person that Christ's death is sufficient to save him or her" (Horton, "Traditional Reformed View," 132). "Because the death of Christ is sufficient for everyone, no one is left out except those who refuse this gift" (ibid., 181).

92. Piper, *Five Points*, 16; italics original. Cf. Nicole, who finds the statement "Jesus Christ died for your sins" problematic, preferring instead: "God in his unfathomable mercy has been pleased to love sinners such as you and me, and he invites you to repent and believe in Jesus Christ. If you do so, you will find that the work of Christ avails you, and you will be saved" (Nicole, "Covenant, Universal Call and Definite Atonement," 410). As another example, Andrew Naselli acknowledges his belief in particular redemption. Yet he explains, "A Calvinist can tell unbelievers, 'Jesus died for you,' because unbelievers generally understand the conjunction 'for' in that sentence to

atonement" that is available "for all people," such that "Christ died for all people" (although "not for all in the same way"), an *unintended* result?[93] Does it *merely happen* to be so, or did *God intend* it to be so? As Rienk Kuiper (a Reformed theologian) reasoned, "If the atonement was suitable for all and sufficient for all, it goes without saying that God designed that it should be such."[94]

So if God designed and *intended* the "availability" of salvation *for* everyone, but only *intended* the effectual salvation of the elect, does God have multiple intentions? The positioning of the italicized "*And*" in the original of the following passage could easily lend itself to a multi-intentioned reading of Piper's own view—a design of "the availability of total sufficiency" and a design of limited accomplished application: "The availability of the total sufficiency of the atonement is for all people. Whosoever will—whoever believes—will be covered by the blood of Christ. *And* there is a divine design in the death of Christ to accomplish the promises of the new covenant for the chosen bride of Christ."[95]

---

mean that the benefits of Jesus' death are available if they repent and believe" (Naselli, "John Owen's Argument for Definite Atonement," 76). By contrast, the English hypothetical universalist John Preston declared, "Go and tell every man without exception, that there is good news for him, Christ is dead for him, and if he will take him, and accept of his righteousness, he shall have it; restrain it not, but go and tell every man under Heaven" (Moore, "Calvin versus the Calvinists?" 333; English spelling updated).

93. Piper, *Five Points*, 16.

94. Kuiper, *For Whom Did Christ Die?* 80. Kuiper continues, "And Berkhof says discerningly, although not altogether lucidly: '... But after the extent of the atonement had been made the object of special study, Reformed theologians generally refused to state the truth in that form, because it was apt to give the impression that Christ in dying intended that all men should share in the proper effects of His atoning death. They prefer to say that the death of Christ viewed objectively and apart from His design and purpose, was inherently sufficient for all, though efficacious only for the elect.' It hardly needs to be noted that Berkhof cannot mean to say that God did not design that the atonement should be objectively sufficient for all. God most assuredly designed that, for He purposed all that is" (ibid., 80–81).

95. Piper, *Five Points*, 16; italics original. Piper's statement, connecting definite atonement with the new covenant, raises other questions related to the historical outworking of redemption in the Old Testament. Piper equates purchasing the faith of the elect with securing the blessings of the new covenant for his people (ibid., 41), while affirming that the new covenant was not yet established in the Old Testament (ibid., 44; Jer 31:31–34). Piper's connection of the doctrine of "limited atonement" to new covenant blessings and "the new covenant people" adds further layers to be explained. He states, "The upshot of this understanding of the new covenant is that there is a definite atonement for the new covenant people" (ibid., 45).

Furthermore, if "Christ died for all people, but not for all in the same way" (as Piper states), how does this compare with John Davenant's views?[96] Consider the following in Piper's *Five Points*, how his explanation in this specific passage seems to approach Davenant's sentiments: "We do not deny that Christ died to save all in *some sense*. Paul says in 1 Timothy 4:10 that in Christ God is 'the Savior of all people, especially of those who believe.' What we deny is that the death of Christ is for all men in the *same* sense. God sent Christ to save *all* in some sense. And he sent Christ to save those who believe in *a more particular sense*."[97] I am not claiming that Piper's full view reflects Davenant's theology. I am simply pointing out the need for further reflection and refinement in much of contemporary discourse.[98]

This leaves remaining the question of what Piper means by "availability"? *What* precisely is *it* that is "available" "for all people" (Piper)?[99] To what objective, external referent do the words in the verbalized free offer of the gospel point?[100] Piper refers to the availability of the "total sufficiency of the atonement" in Christ's death, but what exactly is meant by this "total sufficiency"? More clarity is desired within such popular-level discourse, often divorced from the intricacies of historical theology.[101] Through the centuries, theologians have wrangled over distinct types of

---

96. See Lynch, "Confessional Orthodoxy and Hypothetical Universalism," 137–41. Mark Coppenger asserts: "I think the big point is lost in the scuffle over details, namely that Christ knew what his death was and was not accomplishing ultimately—the salvation of only a minority of mankind—and he assented to do this" (Coppenger, "Review Essay on *Whosoever Will*," 162).

97. Piper, *Five Points*, 40.

98. Piper seems to equate "For whom did he [Christ] die?" and "Whose sin did he atone for?" with "For whom did he purchase all the benefits of salvation?" (including repentance and faith as "blood-bought gifts," within the context) (ibid., 38). Various hypothetical universalists would not see these as equivalent questions.

99. Piper, *Five Points*, 16. Cf. Shedd, *Dogmatic Theology*, vol. 2, 466–67.

100. Piper explains that "Christ is the foundation of the free offer of the gospel. . . . In that sense God sent Jesus for everyone" (Piper, *Five Points*, 40). "Christ died to provide an absolutely reliable and valid offer of forgiveness to all, such that everyone, without exception, who trusts Christ would be saved" (ibid. 41). Allen responds to Piper's perspective: "The issue is God offering something to the non-elect that does not exist for them to receive" (Allen, *Extent of the Atonement*, 762).

101. Piper relates the "five points of Calvinism" to the Canons of Dort (Piper, *Five Points*, 12). As we have argued in Chapter Four, historical theologians recognize that the Canons of Dort purposely cast a net broad enough to include some forms of hypothetical universalism.

"sufficiency."[102] Moreover, some scholars argue that the sufficiency/efficiency distinction within the Lombardian formula took on divergent meaning in the web and flow of historical change and development.[103]

In any case, it seems that more reflection and refinement could aid discussions of the relationship between sufficiency and divine intentionality in much of modern discourse. Precise language is necessary to distinguish between alternative viewpoints, historically considered. Muller explains,

> Calvin taught that the value, virtue, or merit of Christ's work served as sufficient payment for the sins of all human beings, and provided the basis for the divine promise that all who believe will be saved, assuming that believers are recipients of God's grace and that unbelievers are "left without excuse"—as also did, granting different nuancings of the relation of divine intentionality to the value of sufficiency of Christ's death, Theodore Beza, the Canons of Dort, John Davenant, Pierre Du Moulin, Moise Amyraut, and a host of other often forgotten and sometimes

---

102. Owen could state: "It was, then, the purpose and *intention* of God that his Son should offer a sacrifice of infinite worth, value, and dignity, sufficient in itself for the redeeming of all and every man, if it had pleased the Lord to employ it for that purpose" (Owen, *Works of John Owen*, vol. 10, 295). Owen added, "Sufficient we say, then, was the sacrifice of Christ for the redemption of the whole world, and for the expiation of all the sins of all and every man in the world" (ibid., 295-96). Owen described this value of the sacrifice of Christ as "its own internal sufficiency" (ibid., 296). "This is its own true internal perfection and *sufficiency*. That it should be *applied* unto any, made a price for them, and become beneficial to them, according to the worth that is in it, is external to it, doth not arise from it, but merely depends upon the *intention* and will of God" (ibid.; italics added). A duality of *intention* (Owen himself uses the word of two factors) thus exists within this lengthy passage. Yet, of course, Owen strongly positioned himself against hypothetical universalism—while Christ's sacrifice was intended to be of intrinsic sufficient value (an abstract sufficiency in principle not focused upon actual persons), it was not intended in reality as a price or ransom or satisfaction for all. "Therefore, it is denied that the blood of Christ was a sufficient price and ransom for all and every one, not because it was not sufficient," because "the blood of Christ was sufficient to have been made a price for all" (ibid., 296). "It was in itself of infinite value and sufficiency to *have been made a price* to have bought and purchased all and every man in the world" (ibid., 296; italics original). But in reality it was not a price for all "from the intention of God and Christ" (ibid.). Owen's construction seems rooted, in part at least, in his objection arising from his understanding of double payment (contrast Crisp, *Deviant Calvinism*, 213-33, 238).

103. Allen, *Extent of the Atonement*, 27-31.

maligned Reformed writers of the next two centuries, among them both particularists and hypothetical universalists.[104]

Theologians of all stripes along the spectrum should agree that the word *sufficiency* retains a level of ambiguity that must be parsed out.[105] At a minimum, might not concepts from theological forebears, such as an "ordained sufficiency" or a "mere sufficiency" (or "bare sufficiency"), a sufficiency in design or a sufficiency in principle, an "actual sufficiency" of satisfaction or a "hypothetical sufficiency" or "conditional sufficiency" of abstraction, an "extrinsic sufficiency" of provision of satisfaction or an "intrinsic sufficiency" of infinitude of value at least *inform* continuing conversations?[106] We are reminded that the intricacies of the discussion are not new, and others have wrestled with the same tensions. Whether or not we agree with them, we may listen to and perhaps even profit from their conceptual refinements. Previous theologians may help sharpen our contemporary discussions. No matter one's view, clarity and precision of language should be welcomed by all.

Calvin's approach

We now return a final time to Calvin's own historical views. In sum, putting all of Calvin's statements "together into a satisfying, coherent whole is genuinely challenging."[107] Paul Helm has insisted that Calvin was *committed* to the doctrine of definite atonement, although he did not *commit*

---

104. Muller, *Calvin and the Reformed Tradition*, 105. Unbelievers are not recipients of God's efficacious grace, although Calvin insisted that they do reject "the grace offered" to them in Christ (Calvin, John 3:17, *Gospel according to St John 1–10*, 76).

105. Allen, *Extent of the Atonement*, 88, 94.

106. Cf. Crisp, *Saving Calvinism*, 136; Nicole, "Particular Redemption," 166–69; Allen, *Extent of the Atonement*, 88–89, 92, 94; Allen, "Calvin on the Extent of the Atonement," 2, 12–13, 16; Allen, *Atonement*, 272–73. For an example of how important defining terms can be (and how authors sometimes use terms differently), compare Johnson, *He Died for Me* and Allen, "Response to Jeffrey Johnson's Book Review." As an example of a further complication, Gary Williams argues for the "infinite value" and "unquantifiable value" of Christ's suffering because "it was the suffering of his humanity hypostasized in union with his divine person" (Williams, "Punishment God Cannot Twice Inflict," 499). Williams contends for a combination of "unquantifiable punishment" and "inherently definite atonement" (ibid.). Contrast Lynch, "*Quid Pro Quo* Satisfaction?"

107. Gatiss, *For Us and for Our Salvation*, 74.

himself to the doctrine.[108] By contrast, our study has complicated any such particularist-only approach by demonstrating that some of Calvin's statements, on a *prima facie* level, stand *committed* to a universal facet to Christ's gospel work, even as other statements remain *committed* to particularist emphases. The tension deserves to be explained in some manner, even if only cautiously.

In fact, the tension within Calvin's own writings is further deepened by underscoring the revelation of God's universal saving desire, even while acknowledging the "secret" decree of reprobation.[109] Individuals may take heart in approaching God through Christ, because God sincerely desires the salvation of all persons.[110] Recognition of this divine desire in the revealed word of the gospel can encourage those prone to despair. The result is pastorally valuable, although acknowledgement of God's ardent desire to save all may complicate the attempt to reconcile the building blocks present in Calvin. Anthony Lane explains, "Calvin was prepared to recognize both God's universal love for all mankind and his desire for all to repent and his purpose that some only should be saved. To the feeble human mind these are irreconcilable."[111] A common solution to relieve the inherent tension involves splicing between the decretive and desiderative will of God.[112] Calvin himself acknowledges that God's will is really "one and undivided," although it is set before us as "double."[113]

---

108. Helm, *Calvin and the Calvinists*, 18.

109. See Sinnema, "Calvin's View of Reprobation"; Sinnema, "Are the Canons of Dordt a True Reflection . . . ?"

110. Calvin, 2 Pet 3:9, *Epistle of Paul the Apostle to the Hebrews and the First and Second Epistles of St Peter*, 364.

111. Lane, "Quest for the Historical Calvin," 113.

112. See Blocher, "Jesus Christ *the* Man," 565. "We have found that God himself expresses an ardent desire for the fulfillment of certain things which he has not decreed in his inscrutable counsel to come to pass. This means that there is a will to the realization of what he has not decretively willed, a pleasure towards that which he has not been pleased to decree. This is indeed mysterious, and why he has not brought to pass, in the exercise of his omnipotent power and grace, what is his ardent pleasure lies hid in the sovereign counsel of his will" (Murray "Free Offer of the Gospel," 131).

113. Calvin, Matt 23:37, *Harmony of the Gospels*, vol. 3, 69; Calvin, *Institutes*, I.18.3. Muller therefore concludes, "Such distinctions indicate differences between the fullness of divine willing *ad intra* and the manner and extent of revelation *ad extra*, but they in no way imply two distinct wills *ad intra*" (Muller, *Calvin and the Reformed Tradition*, 271).

A result of Calvin's focus upon God's revealed will is that "those who do not come are without excuse."[114] Those who reject the gospel truly reject the grace of God offered and provided for them, and as a result are justly condemned for their unbelief.[115] According to Muller, "Calvin taught that the value, virtue, or merit of Christ's work served as sufficient payment for the sins of all human beings, and provided the basis for the divine promise that all who believe will be saved, assuming that believers are recipients of God's grace and that unbelievers are 'left without excuse.'"[116] Within Calvin's own predestinarian theology, the provision of the atonement grounds the "double culpability" of unbelievers, who reject the gracious work of Christ.[117]

As one interprets God's revealed will as a reflection of his saving desire, yet ever with the secret decree of reprobation remaining in the background, the tension becomes palpable.[118] Nevertheless, Calvin chose to embrace a scriptural conceptualization of God's saving desire, and he chose to draw attention to the revealed will of the gospel's general summons.[119] On a pastoral level, Calvin focused upon Christ as the mirror of our election.

One could argue that God's revealed will meets us in our human "epistemic condition," and God's initiative of grace took our "epistemic condition" into account within a unified plan.[120] The complexities and ambiguities are ultimately entrusted to God in the fullness of his character,

---

114. Calvin, Matt 23:37, *Harmony of the Gospels*, vol. 3, 69–70.

115. Calvin, 2 Pet 2:1, *The Epistle of Paul the Apostle to the Hebrews and the First and Second Epistles of St Peter*, 346; Calvin, 1 John 5:16, *Gospel according to St John 11–21 and the First Epistle of John*, 310.

116. Muller, *Calvin and the Reformed Tradition*, 105.

117. Calvin, *Sermons on Isaiah's Prophecy*, 141.

118. Grebe, *Election, Atonement and the Holy Spirit*, 14. Sam Waldon quotes the Canons of Dort, "As many as are called by the gospel are unfeignedly called. For God has most earnestly and truly declared in His Word what is acceptable to Him, namely, that those who are called should come to Him. He also seriously promises rest of soul and eternal life to all who come to Him and believe" (Article 8, third and fourth head). Waldron asserts, "God not only commands but also desires the salvation of everyone who hears the gospel, whether they are elect or not." Yet he confesses that, within his own particularist system, "this is a difficult question involving deep mysteries" (Waldon, "Biblical Confirmation of Particular Redemption," 149).

119. Ben Pugh claims that later Calvinists subordinated God's free love to his sovereign will, although this approach does not reflect the ordering of Calvin's own structuring of his *Institutes* (Pugh, *Atonement Theories*, 81).

120. See Crawford, *Doctrine of Holy Scripture Respecting the Atonement*, 193–95.

who expects us to live in the light of his revealed will. For this reason, scholars may speak of the "non-speculative" nature of Calvin's approach. Muller reasons that "there is also a body of material, *including statements made by Calvin, most notably in commentaries and sermons,* that points toward several non-speculative forms of hypothetical universalism . . . as argued within the bounds of the traditional formula, *sufficienter pro omnibus, efficienter pro electis* [sufficiently for all, efficiently for the elect], but that fails to point to the more speculative form of hypothetical universalism found in Amyraut's model of multiple divine decrees."[121] Muller further claims that Calvin's relevant statements were not unique among his contemporaries in the Reformation: "Clear statements of nonspeculative hypothetical universalism can be found (as Davenant recognized) in Heinrich Bullinger's *Decades* and commentary on the Apocalypse, in Wolfgang Musculus' *Loci communes,* in [Zacharias] Ursinus' catechetical lectures, and in [Girolamo] Zanchi's *Tractatus de praedestinatione sanctorum,* among other places."[122]

Forming a coherent synthesis of Calvin's often complicated exegetical, theological, and polemical materials on the death of Christ is a challenging endeavor.[123] Nevertheless, the composite materials in Calvin seem more than sufficient to doubt that he had committed himself to so-called "limited atonement" (admittedly, an anachronistic label) in a strict sense.[124] Various materials also seem sufficient, taken at face value, to maintain that Calvin taught some so-called "unlimited" or "universal" facet(s) in the death of Christ (in the sense of sufficiency of intended provision). The composite materials *at least* "demonstrate how freely Calvin used universal language to describe the atonement," unlike many of his theological descendants.[125] Nevertheless, the materials in Calvin do not seem sufficient to build a *full* systematic synthesis of his view on the matter, which he never explicitly discussed in detail. For instance, Calvin did not speculate concerning an intricate system of ordered, multiple decrees

---

121. Muller, *Calvin and the Reformed Tradition,* 104; italics added.

122. Muller, "Review of English Hypothetical Universalism," 150. For example, Bullinger affirmed, "Therefore I say, the sins of all men of the world of all ages have been expiated by his death" (as quoted in Thomas *Extent of the Atonement,* 75). On Ursinus, see Lynch, "*Quid Pro Quo* Satisfaction?" 62.

123. Cf. Nettles, "John Calvin's Understanding of the Death of Christ," 293, from the perspective of definite atonement.

124. Allen, *Extent of the Atonement,* 96.

125. Kennedy, "Was Calvin a 'Calvinist'?" 196.

nor did he provide a detailed distinction between an "antecedent will" and a "consequent will" (as found in Amyraut's ruminations).[126] These later developments cannot and should not be directly pinned on Calvin.

While retaining his non-speculative bent, Calvin webbed his language of universal provision with the general summons of the gospel and with the fact that unbelievers are left without excuse for their unbelief. The unified divine plan, as partially known from the situatedness of our epistemic condition, is complexly interwoven in a non-speculative manner. Although Calvin did not speculate in an Amyraldian fashion about Christ's universal provision within the framework of God's decretal will, he did interconnect the universal provision with the indiscriminate call in the revealed will of God.[127] Similarly, he repeatedly emphasized that unbelievers are left without excuse, because they reject the grace truly provided. These strands are interwoven with one another in a non-speculative manner.

Details can indeed get complicated, as one moves away from oversimplified categorizations of theologies into the splicing of refined variables.[128] Through the centuries, in addressing issues of the atonement, varying theologians have decided to place seeming tension(s) in differing locations. Should the gospel be preached to all, including the universal duty of repentant faith? Is God's gospel offer available to all? If so, did he make an objective provision for all, or is there an "availability" in a verbal offer without an objective provision founding it? If Christ died for all, did he die for all with equal intent, or with unequal intent? Was Christ's death for the non-elect an actual satisfaction for their sins, or only related to common grace and/or temporal benefits, such as postponement of judgment? Was Christ's death "sufficient for all" in an abstract sense of infinite value or was his death "sufficient for all" as a provision of universal satisfaction? If there is a sufficient, real provision for all, did this flow from divine intent? If so, how does this intent square with God's

---

126. The logical ordering of the decrees (as distinct from a chronological ordering of the decrees) may beg deeper questions, including the reading of discursive reasoning into God. At one juncture, Amyraut could assert that there is actually but one divine decree, "formed in God in one and the self-same Moment, without any succession of Thought, or Order of Priority and Posteriority" (cited in Quick, *Synodicon in Gallia Reformata*, vol. 2, 355, as quoted in Macleod, "Definite Atonement and the Divine Decree," 428–29).

127. Allen, *Extent of the Atonement*, 85.

128. Muller differentiates between those historians inclined to be "groupers" and those inclined to be "splicers."

particular intention of election? Were there perhaps multiple intentions or a complexly-webbed yet unified divine plan? Did Christ's death in some manner procure saving faith for the elect? Are repentance and faith "blood-bought gifts" purchased by Christ's death? Is God's gospel offer available to all without his sincerely desiring that it be accepted by all? If he sincerely desires that it be accepted by all, how does this harmonize with his particular will of election? How does all this fit with God's eternal decree? Does he desire the salvation of all because he desires repentant belief in all, even though he does not will this in his eternal decree? Can God possess both a decretive will and a desiderative will (or desire)? Can God have both a secret will and a revealed will, or both possess a decretive will and display a preceptive will? Or are these simply ways of phenomenologically talking about God's unified plan from our human epistemic perspective? What role does divine accommodation to human thought or language play?[129] Such questions could be multiplied.[130]

There is no wonder that a range of theological paradigms have developed throughout history—and why referencing "the traditional Reformed view of definite atonement" is reductionistic.[131] As but one example, where does Rienk Kuiper's theology land in the midst of the questions gathered in the previous paragraph? Kuiper, a former professor at Westminster Theological Seminary and president of Calvin Theological Seminary, insisted,

> When the Reformed theology describes the universal offer of salvation as sincere, it does not merely mean that the human preacher, who obviously cannot distinguish with certainty between the elect and the non-elect, must for that reason issue to all men indiscriminately a most sincere offer of eternal life and an equally sincere invitation to accept that offer. It most assuredly means that, but it means incomparably more. The Reformed

---

129. As Ford Lewis Battles insisted, divine accommodation "would seem (even when Calvin does not explicitly advert to it) his fundamental way of explaining how the secret, hidden God reveals himself to us" (Battles, *Interpreting John Calvin*, 131). Battles underscores that Calvin used the verb *accommodare* and its synonym *attemperare* but never the noun *accommodatio* (ibid., 35, 117, 120, 130).

130. "Too often Reformed historiography has obsessed at a superficial level about whether or not a particular theologian did or did not state that Christ did or did not 'die for all' or 'for the world' or some such other ambiguous statement, without actually examining their respective positions on the nature of the atonement itself" (Moore, "Extent of the Atonement," 132).

131. Contrast Piper, "'My Glory I Will Not Give to Another,'" 657.

theology insists that God Himself, who has determined from eternity who are to be saved and who are not, and therefore distinguishes infallibly between the elect whom He designed to save by the death of Christ and the reprobate whom He did not design to save, makes on the ground of the universally suitable and sufficient atonement a most sincere, *bona fide*, offer of eternal life, not only to the elect but to all men, urgently invites them to everlasting life, and expresses the ardent desire that every person to whom this offer and this invitation come accept the offer and comply the invitation.[132]

In fact, according to Kuiper's citation of Calvin, "God desires nothing more earnestly."[133]

A number of pages earlier, Kuiper approvingly quoted Charles Hodge, "The righteousness of Christ, the merit of his obedience and death, is needed for justification by each individual of our race, and therefore is needed by all. . . . He rendered the obedience required by all, and suffered the penalty which all had incurred; and therefore his work is equally suited to all."[134] One could try to mesh these materials in Kuiper (and Kuiper's fuller work) with the listing of relevant questions in the previous paragraph, and attempt to ascertain where Kuiper might have landed in the spectrum of possible answers.[135] One begins to realize the inherent complexities—theologians can espouse a range of options and explanations.

Conclusion

In closing, our historical examination has hopefully demonstrated the reductionistic simplicity of a "limited atonement" vs. "unlimited atonement" bifurcation in contemporary parlance (represented by a simplified TULIP test) that does not take into account the intricate spectrum of

---

132. Kuiper, *For Whom Did Christ Die?* 86.

133. See Kuiper, *For Whom Did Christ Die?* 94. Calvin, Ezek 18:23, *Commentaries on the First Twenty Chapters of the Book of the Prophet Ezekiel*, vol. 2, 246.

134. Kuiper, *For Whom Did Christ Die?* 79; Hodge, "For Whom Did Christ Die?" 545. On Charles Hodge's views of the extent of the atonement, see Allen, *Extent of the Atonement*, 330–32. Contrast Allen's assessment of Archibald Alexander Hodge's views in ibid., 372–77.

135. Jeffrey Johnson places Kuiper among "moderate Calvinists" (Johnson, *He Died for Me*). Kuiper lists four facets of his "Scriptural universalism," including a cosmic dimension (Kuiper, *For Whom Did Christ Die?* 78–100).

manifold views. We may quibble about where Calvin's statements place him within the diverse spectrum of Reformed theologians. But we simply *cannot* know with certainty how Calvin would assess all the intricate varieties within a spectrum that developed after him, nor how he would decipher his own exact place within it. To attempt to do so would be anachronistic, of course. One cannot overlook the influential developments (and therefore refinements and explanatory exactitudes) of the last five hundred years. Later thinkers were forced to provide answers to questions that had not reached the front of the queue in Calvin's own day.

We can only reasonably estimate where Calvin would stake his claim, if transported by time-machine from his era into our own with no opportunity for adjustment or contextual acclimation.[136] Rather than trying to find an exact parallel of Calvin's construction in a later edifice, we might rather think of the blocks of Calvin's construction being used to build later structures (sometimes with a more exact or tightly-fitting construction, sometimes with differing blocks made prominent, sometimes with some original blocks rearranged, and sometimes with entirely new blocks added). When one further remembers that Calvin was not the only architect of his own generation, one better understands how later architects designed differing constructions using similar yet customized sets of building materials.[137] The ambiguity of Calvin's original sketch plans led Beza and Amyraut to build different structures, even though both claimed to be faithful to the original blueprints found in Calvin.

In conclusion, if we wish to return to *terra firma* regarding Calvin's own views, we may emphasize the following five points. *First*, in virtually any scholarly interpretation, Calvin was not inclined to speak as consistently or vigorously about limited atonement as some contemporary discussions are prone to do. Any counterclaim to this statement would not only lack sufficient primary-source evidence but could also be construed as inherently anachronistic. Therefore, those who insist upon an explicit and consistent support for limited atonement do not directly follow Calvin himself in the matter.[138]

---

136. Helm, *Calvin: A Guide for the Perplexed*, 10–11.

137. "This alerts us to the reality that Calvin, given his procedure, is open to multi-appropriations, which would explain why, in the history, there in fact are multiform articulations on Calvin's theological trajectories" (Grow, "John Calvin contra 'Two Wills in God' Methodology"). Grow later refers to the "multiform appropriation of Calvin."

138. Daniel, "Hyper-Calvinism and John Gill," 827.

Second, Calvin at times spoke in ways that *some* strict "limited atonement" proponents would now critique or at least find problematic *if uttered by others* today.[139]

Third, Calvin at times (many times!) used *the language* of a general provision in Christ's death.[140] Yet scholars propose differing interpretations of this universal language as found in Calvin. Some deny a provision of an objective, universal sufficiency, while others do not. Some claim that Calvin was only speaking in a phenomenological manner due to the limitations of the human situation, not from the divine perspective of what God in Christ's death provided.[141] Others posit the accommodation of a "revealed" will in the gospel summons in such a manner that no actual universal redemption or universal satisfaction stands objectively behind the "linguistic device" of the gospel offer.[142] Others propose that Calvin merely maintained the "classical" assertions of sufficiency and efficiency within the Lombardian formula in an indistinct manner, without thought of refinement (due to his historical context).[143] Others, however, find within Calvin's work a divinely intentioned, objective provision of universal redemption or universal satisfaction in some manner co-existing with particular election (an "ordained sufficiency").[144]

What I have proposed here is that Calvin's understanding of Christ's death as a word for the world reflected his supposition of a universally sufficient sacrifice. It seems to me that the most natural reading of the cumulative weight of evidence found in Calvin's universal language materials is that Christ made a sufficient satisfaction for all (see my Chapter

---

139. "It is true that at times Calvin uses general terms with respect to the design of Christ's death in a more unguarded manner than would *now* be done by one of his consistent disciples" (Hodge, *Atonement*, 390).

140. As Muller affirms, "He [Calvin] did frequently state, without further modification, that Christ expiated the sins of the world and that this 'favor' is extended 'indiscriminately' to the whole human race, just as he also assumed, as the Canons of Dort would later declare, that God had the specific intention of saving some particular persons" (Muller, "Was Calvin a Calvinist?" 61).

141. See Ponter, "Review Essay (Part One)," 139, 151; Ponter, "Review Essay (Part Two)," 256.

142. See Ponter, "Review Essay (Part One)," 145; Ponter, "Review Essay (Part Two)," 266.

143. Rouwendal, "Calvin's Forgotten Classical Position."

144. In other words, Christ laying down the price of redemption for unbelievers (including apostates) is not merely a matter of human phenomenology (Ponter, "Review Essay (Part Two)," 255).

Two).¹⁴⁵ Behind the proclaimed offer of the gospel stands a divinely intended, objective provision *extra nobis*, thus leaving unbelievers without excuse, as they are guilty of rejecting the grace truly provided. As Calvin insisted, "Although Christ suffered for the sins of the world, and is offered by the goodness of God without distinction to all men, yet not all receive him."¹⁴⁶ Moreover, in Calvin's thought, the Spirit forms faith in the elect customarily through the efficacious personalization of the gospel promises (as found in the proclamation of Christ's objective provision). Thus, Christ died for the sins of all but with an unequal intent/purpose (in full consideration), because of the divine design to apply the redemption effectually to the elect alone. All of this is united in God's eternal plan (his secret will), though we only ascertain facets through God's revelation to us (his revealed will). The Trinity is united in the eternal decree and historical implementation of God's unified plan.

Fourth, the ascertaining of Calvin's exact view is complex and shows no signs of resolution to the satisfaction of all.¹⁴⁷ The remaining "ambiguity of his position" will continue to result in "considerable debate."¹⁴⁸ This probably goes without saying.

Fifth, while some have critiqued the seemingly endless discussions of the topic (producing more heat than light, it is claimed), nevertheless discernible shifts resulting from these complicated—often sophisticated—historical discussions have actually refined recent scholarship. For instance, the last few decades have witnessed shifts in the related topic of "Calvin and the Calvinists," by (a) mitigating the role of Calvin as one theologian among a robust assemblage of theologians and (b) highlighting a measure of diversity within the early Reformed movement.¹⁴⁹ As Aaron Clay Denlinger explains, "Recognition among scholars of

---

145. See the abundance of primary source materials assembled in Chapter Two.

146. Calvin, Rom 5:18, *Epistles of Paul the Apostle to the Romans and to the Thessalonians*, 18.

147. Nelson, "Design, Nature, and Extent of the Atonement," 123.

148. Sinnema, "Calvin and the Canons of Dordt," 93, 96.

149. Letham, "Faith and Assurance in Early Calvinism," 383–84. Edwin E. M. Tay refers to the ongoing "reappraisal" of the "Calvin against the Calvinists" thesis. He concludes that "proponents of the reappraisal argue that there is essential continuity between Reformation thought and that of Protestant orthodoxy, affirm the presence of discontinuous elements, albeit of a non-essential nature, and acknowledge the fluidity of intellectual and theological thought in a way that allows for a tradition to be expressed in a plurality of ways within an ongoing process of development" (Tay, *Priesthood of Christ*, 7).

considerable diversity among Reformed divines (who were committed, nonetheless, to common, core doctrines) has followed from recognition that no single individual—most obviously Calvin—ever served as the absolute measure of right or wrong doctrine."[150] These recent developments prove that continued discussions are not necessarily unproductive.

Richard Muller, the eminent scholar of Reformed historiography, concludes: "Calvin, nevertheless, assumed that Christ's death paid the price for all sin and that all who believe the gospel will be saved."[151] Muller affirms that Calvin "consistently points to Christ's death as full payment for the sins of the world, undergirding, as it were, the indiscriminate proclamation of the gospel."[152] Muller adds, "In the case of the doctrine of Christ's satisfaction for sin, since Christ paid for the price of all sin and accomplished a redemption capable of saving the whole world, his benefits are clearly placed before, proferred, or offered to all who hear: what Calvin does not indicate is any sort of universalizing intentionality flowing from the sufficiency into the actual efficacy of this offering."[153]

Of course, in Calvin's thought, those who do believe do so only because of God's particular and effectual grace.[154] Muller insists, "The actual issues relevant to the debate were (1) the divine intention concerning the sufficiency of Christ's satisfaction, specifically, the relationship between the hypothetical, 'if all would believe,' and the infinite value or merit of Christ's death, namely, its 'sufficiency' for all sin; (2) the divine intention concerning the effective application of salvation to individuals,

150. Denlinger, "Scottish Hypothetical Universalism," 101. Cf. Mullan, "Theology in the Church of Scotland," 595–617.

151. Muller, *Calvin and the Reformed Tradition*, 279. Muller continues, "Indeed, once the confusing terminology of limited and unlimited atonement is set aside and the theologians of the era permitted to speak in their own language, a rather complex picture emerges of different approaches to the issue of the value, merit, or sufficiency of Christ's satisfaction and its relationship to a limited application, including several rather different kinds of hypothetical universalism, all within the bounds established by the Reformed confessions" (ibid., 271–72).

152. Muller, *Calvin and the Reformed Tradition*, 82. In the sentences preceding, Muller affirms that nowhere does Calvin "indicate a divine intention to save all people or to send Christ to save all people—in fact, he consistently points toward the limit of salvation to the elect" (ibid.).

153. Muller, *Calvin and the Reformed Tradition*, 105.

154. According to David Allen, one can thus speak of a "dual intentionality" that affirmed "elements of universalism and particularism in the design of the atonement" (Allen, *Extent of the Atonement*, 67). Allen directly interacts with Muller's recent work in ibid., 85–94.

specifically, the grounds of limitation of the efficiency or efficacy of Christ's work; and (3) the relationship between the value or sufficiency and efficiency of Christ's satisfaction and the universal or, more precisely, indiscriminate proclamation and call of the gospel."[155] In the end, Calvin's non-speculative approach within its historical context (framed by his exegetical and pastoral purposes) may not answer all these questions completely to one's full satisfaction.

In this epilogue, we have built upon two principles found within Muller's assessment of Calvin's theology ("Christ's death paid the price for all sin" and "the divine intention concerning the effective application of salvation to individuals") by constructing a basic framework of a non-speculative, "complex-intentioned" view of the atonement, as reflected in the revealed will of God.[156] We argue that such an approach reflects a pattern that one could interpret as *emerging* from Calvin, even if he did not delineate or develop such a view systematically. One can take the bare bones of propositions found in Calvin's writings and arrange them into such a skeletal framework. One can add some sinews of the putative interconnections between the statements. But whether the specific pattern that is fleshed out mirrors the webbing of explanation residing in Calvin's own mind, or whether Calvin would recognize a reflection of his own fullness of theology, will undoubtedly remain in dispute.

Moreover, even if such a non-speculative, complex-intentioned approach reflects a framework emerging from a reading of Calvin, it should not therefore be construed as prescriptive for systematic theology.[157] Ultimately, Calvin's own theology drives one back to his methodology, and therefore back to the scriptural sources, which served as his authority.[158]

One welcomes the candor of Henri Blocher, in a recent essay supporting "definite atonement" within a monumental volume contending

155. Muller, *Calvin and the Reformed Tradition*, 77.

156. Muller, *Calvin and the Reformed Tradition*, 77 and 105.

157. Nor should one assume that the "emerging" framework found within the epilogue necessarily reflects my own theology or that of any institution, church, or fellowship with which I am associated.

158. "Calvin himself never imagined that his own work would provide the single necessary starting point and criterion for any future theological reflection—that honour was reserved for Scripture alone—nor did he consider his writings to have drawn a line under everything which preceded them" (Trueman, *Claims of Truth*, 11–12). Cf. Lane, "Calvin versus Calvinism Revisited," 33–34; Coppenger, "Review Essay on *Whosoever Will*," 167; Lightner, *Death Christ Died*, 33; Daniel, *History and Theology of Calvinism*, 377; Nettles, "John Calvin's Understanding of the Death of Christ," 293.

for the same.¹⁵⁹ Blocher rightly acknowledges, "What Calvin really thought and taught on the matter is a hotly disputed issue."¹⁶⁰ Blocher then confesses his own "frustration" with Calvin's writings.¹⁶¹ He hypothesizes that Calvin personally held to limited atonement but "deliberately avoided taking sides" by stating a fully developed position, and "maybe Calvin *refrained* from developing one."¹⁶² Blocher muses: "*If* he deliberately avoided taking sides, we may imagine motives. His concern for Protestant unity was paramount; he may have feared that the issue would be divisive. He may have concluded that the biblical evidence was not clear-cut (he shunned speculation). He may have felt that the precise point in debate did not *preach* well. We may even mention the 'existential' slant in Calvin's theology."¹⁶³

While evaluating the extant evidence differently than Blocher, we can still appreciate his guarded approach, acknowledging Calvin's biblical foundations and pastoral motivations. We have argued that a non-speculative, "complex-intentioned" understanding of the atonement may *emerge* from the building blocks of Calvin's relevant statements, even if he himself did not fit the stones together to build a finished edifice. We have maintained that Calvin spoke of a universal provision in Christ's death (in some sense) along with a firm emphasis upon the intended application to the elect alone (rooted in God's eternal, unconditional election). Although coming from a different angle, we nevertheless agree with Blocher that Calvin refrained from delineating a fully developed and systematic approach to the relationship (and even tension) between his disparate statements.

---

159. Blocher, "Jesus Christ *the* Man," 541–82.

160. Blocher, "Jesus Christ *the* Man," 550.

161. "A hundred times, while rambling through Calvin's writings, I have felt the same frustration: now a magnificent opportunity for him to clarify his position—and he bypasses it" (Blocher, "Jesus Christ *the* Man," 551).

162. Blocher, "Jesus Christ *the* Man," 551, 551n45; italics original.

163. Blocher, "Jesus Christ *the* Man," 551. Calvin's desire for Protestant unity led him to sign his name to the *Variata* form of the Augsburg Confession of Faith, including Article III, which declared that Christ "truly suffered, was crucified, dead, and buried, that he might reconcile the Father unto us, and might be a sacrifice, not only for original guilt, but also for all actual sins of men." See Billings, "John Calvin's Soteriology," 431; McNeill, "Calvin's Efforts toward the Consolidation of Protestantism," 411–23.

No doubt, this present study will not be the final say in this highly contested topic.[164] Yet sometimes the scholarly engagement does advance even amidst the lateral movement of back-and-forth volleys.[165] Despite any shortcoming, I hope this work inches the conversation forward with more historical light than polemical heat.

---

164. "We sit on the shoulders of giants. To dream of solving at one stroke an issue that has divided them for centuries is foolish" (Blocher, "Jesus Christ *the* Man," 542).

165. In this sense, responses and counter-responses serve as more than mere ping-pong entertainment (cf. Helm, "Calvin, Indefinite Language, and Definite Atonement," 100n12). Paul Helm laments, "The game of pitting definite against indefinite language seems about to peter out, only for the same data to be revisited once more" (ibid., 100n11). Yet sometimes more light does emerge from the continuing exchange.

Bibliography

Allen, David L. *The Atonement: A Biblical, Theological, and Historical Study of the Cross of Christ*. Nashville: B&H Academic, 2019.

———. "Calvin and the Extent of the Atonement: 21st Century Research." Paper presented at the Evangelical Theological Society Meeting (Providence, RI), November 19, 2017. http://drdavidlallen.com/wp-content/uploads/2017/11/Allen-ETS-Paper-Calvin-and-the-Extent-of-the-Atonement.pdf.

———. *The Extent of the Atonement: A Historical and Critical Review*. Nashville: B&H Academic, 2016.

———. "Response to Jeffrey Johnson's Book Review of My Book *The Extent of the Atonement*." https://drdavidlallen.com/calvinism/response-to-jeffrey-johnsons-book-review-of-my-book-the-extent-of-the-atonement.

Allen, R. Michael. "The Perfect Priest: Calvin on the Christ of Hebrews." In *Christology, Hermeneutics and Hebrews: Profiles from the History of Interpretation*, edited by Jon C. Laansma and Daniel J. Treier, 120–34. Library of New Testament Studies. London: T. & T. Clark, 2012.

Allison, Gregg. "A History of the Doctrine of the Atonement." *The Southern Baptist Journal of Theology* 11 (2007) 4–19.

Amyraut, Moïse. *Defense de la doctrine de Calvin sur le sujet de l'élection et de la reprobation*. Saumur, France: Isaac Desbordes, 1644.

Anderson, James William. "The Grace of God and the Non-Elect in Calvin's Commentaries and Sermons." ThD diss., New Orleans Baptist Theological Seminary, 1976.

Archbald, Paul. "A Comparative Study of John Calvin and Theodore Beza on the Doctrine of the Extent of the Atonement." PhD diss., Westminster Theological Seminary, 1998.

Armstrong, Brian G. *Calvinism and the Amyraut Heresy: Protestant Scholasticism and Humanism in Seventeenth-Century France*. Madison, WI: University of Wisconsin Press, 1969.

———. "*Duplex cognitio Dei*, or? The Problem and Relation of Structure, Form and Purpose in Calvin's Theology." In *Probing the Reformed Tradition*, edited by Elsie Anne McKee and Brian G. Armstrong, 135–53. Louisville, KY: Westminster/John Knox, 1989.

———. "*Semper Reformanda*: The Case of the French Reformed Church, 1559–1620." In *Later Calvinism: International Perspectives*, edited by W. Fred Graham, 119–40. Sixteenth Century Essays and Studies 22. Kirksville: Sixteenth Century Journal, 1994.

Ascol, Thomas K. "Redemption Defined." In *John Calvin: A Heart for Devotion, Doctrine, & Doxology*, edited by Burk Parsons, 157–68. Orlando: Reformation Trust, 2008.

Augustine. *Augustine: Later Works*. Translated by John Burnaby. Library of Christian Classics 8. Philadelphia: Westminster, 1955.

Backus, Irena. *Historical Method and Confessional Identity in the Era of the Reformation, 1378–1615*. Studies in Medieval and Reformation Thought 94. Leiden: Brill, 2003.

Baek, John Hoongkyu. "The Atonement as the Judicial Basis of Common Grace." ThM thesis, Gordon-Conwell Theological Seminary, 2009.

Balserak, Jon, and Jim West, eds. *From Zwingli to Amyraut: Exploring the Growth of Reformed Traditions*. Göttingen: Vandenhoeck & Ruprecht, 2017.

Banman, Rebekah A. "Union with the Incarnate Saviour: Exploring the Soteriological Implications of the Incarnation and the Atonement in Dialogue with John Calvin and Thomas F. Torrance." MA thesis, Providence Theological Seminary, 2011.

Barro, Antonio Carlos. "Election, Predestination and the Mission of God." In *John Calvin and Evangelical Theology: Legacy and Prospect in Celebration of the Quincentenary of John Calvin*, edited by Sun Wook Chung, 181–98. Louisville, KY: Westminster John Knox, 2009.

Battles, Ford Lewis. "God Was Accommodating Himself to Human Capacity." *Interpretation* 31 (1977) 19–38.

———. *Interpreting John Calvin*. Edited by Robert Benedetto. Grand Rapids: Baker, 1996.

Bauder, Kevin. "Limited Atonement: Evaluating the Argument." https://religiousaffections.org/articles/in-the-nick-of-time/limited-atonement-evaluating-the-argument.

Baylor, T. Robert. "'With Him in Heavenly Realms': Lombard and Calvin on Merit and the Exaltation of Christ." *International Journal of Systematic Theology* 17 (2015) 152–75.

Beach, J. M. "Calvin's Treatment of the Offer of the Gospel and Divine Grace." *Mid-America Journal of Theology* 22 (2011) 55–76.

Beeke, Joel R. *Assurance of Faith: Calvin, English Puritanism, and the Dutch Second Reformation*. New York: Lang, 1991.

———. "Does Assurance Belong to the Essence of Faith? Calvin and the Calvinists." *The Master's Seminary Journal* 5 (1994) 43–71.

———. *The Quest for Full Assurance: The Legacy of Calvin and His Successors*. Edinburgh: Banner of Truth, 1999.

———. "William Perkins and His Greatest Case of Conscience: 'How a man may know whether he be the child of God, or No.'" *Calvin Theological Journal* 41 (2006) 255–78.

Beeke, Joel R., ed. *Calvin for Today*. Grand Rapids: Reformation Heritage, 2009.

Bell, M. Charles. *Calvin and Scottish Theology: The Doctrine of Assurance*. Edinburgh: Handsel, 1985.

———. "Calvin and the Extent of the Atonement." *Evangelical Quarterly* 55 (1983) 115–23.

———. "Was Calvin a Calvinist?" *Scottish Journal of Theology* 36 (1983) 535–40.

Belousek, Darrin W. Snyder. *Atonement, Justice, and Peace: The Message of the Cross and the Mission of the Church*. Grand Rapids: Eerdmans, 2011.

Berry, H. E. "The Amyraldian Controversy and Its Implications for the Lutheran-Reformed Unity in the Doctrine of Grace." BDiv thesis, Concordia Theological Seminary, 1970.

Billings, J. Todd. "John Calvin's Soteriology: On the Multifaceted 'Sum' of the Gospel." *International Journal of Systematic Theology* 11 (2009) 428–47.

———. "Union with Christ and the Double Grace: Calvin's Theology and Its Early Reception." In *Calvin's Theology and Its Reception: Disputes, Developments, and New Possibilities*, edited by Todd Billings and I. John Hesselink, 49–71. Louisville, KY: Westminster John Knox, 2012.

Billings, J. Todd, and I. John Hesselink. *Calvin's Theology and Its Reception: Disputes, Developments, and New Possibilities.* Louisville, KY: Westminster/John Knox, 2012.

Bizer, Ernst. *Frühorthodoxie und Rationalismus.* Theologische Studien 71. Zürich: EVZ, 1963.

Blacketer, Raymond A. "Blaming Beza." In *From Heaven He Came and Sought Her: Definite Atonement in Historical, Biblical, Theological, and Pastoral Perspective*, edited by David Gibson and Jonathan Gibson, 121–42. Wheaton, IL: Crossway, 2013.

———. "Definite Atonement in Historical Perspective." In *The Glory of the Atonement: Biblical, Historical & Practical Perspectives*, edited by Charles E. Hill and Frank A. James III, 304–23. Downers Grove, IL: InterVarsity, 2004.

———. "The Three Points in Most Parts Reformed: A Reexamination of the So-Called Well-Meant Offer of Salvation." *Calvin Theological Journal* 35 (2000) 37–65.

Blocher, Henri. "The Atonement in John Calvin's Theology." In *The Glory of the Atonement: Biblical, Historical & Practical Perspectives*, edited by Charles E. Hill and Frank A. James III, 279–303. Downers Grove, IL: InterVarsity, 2004.

———. "Biblical Metaphors and the Doctrine of the Atonement." *Journal of the Evangelical Theological Society* 47 (2004) 629–45.

———. "Jesus Christ the Man." In *From Heaven He Came and Sought Her: Definite Atonement in Historical, Biblical, Theological, and Pastoral Perspective*, edited by David Gibson and Jonathan Gibson, 121–42. Wheaton, IL: Crossway, 2013.

Blunt, David. "Debate on Redemption at the Westminster Assembly." *British Reformed Journal* 13 (1996) 5–10.

Boersma, Hans. "Calvin and the Extent of the Atonement." *Evangelical Quarterly* 64 (1992) 333–55.

———. *A Hot Peppercorn: Richard Baxter's Doctrine of Justification in Its Seventeenth-Century Context of Controversy.* Zoertermeer, Netherlands: Uitgeverij Boekencentrum, 1993.

Boettner, Lorraine. *The Reformed Doctrine of Predestination.* Phillipsburg, NJ: Presbyterian and Reformed, 1932.

Boice, James Montgomery, and Philip Graham Ryken. *The Doctrines of Grace: Rediscovering the Evangelical Gospel.* Wheaton, IL: Crossway, 2002.

Bond, David. "Amyraldianism and Assurance." In *Christ for the World: Affirming Amyraldianism*, edited by Alan C. Clifford, 92–108. Norwich, UK: Charenton Reformed, 2007.

Bonet-Maury, Gaston. "Jean Cameron, pasteur de l'église de Bordeaux et professeur de théologie à Saumur." In *Études de théologie et d'histoire*, edited by Auguste Sabatier, 77–117. Paris: Librairie Fischbacher, 1901.

———. "John Cameron: A Scottish Protestant Theologian in France." *Scottish Historical Review* 7 (1910) 325–45.

Bouwsma, William J. *John Calvin: A Sixteenth-Century Portrait.* New York: Oxford University Press, 1988.

———. "The Quest for the Historical Calvin." *Archiv für Reformationsgeschichte* 77 (1986) 47–57.
Bray, John S. *Theodore Beza's Doctrine of Predestination*. Nieuwkoop, Netherlands: De Graaf, 1975.
Byrne, Tony. "Paradox and Mystery." http://theologicalmeditations.blogspot.com/2005/06/paradox-and-mystery.html.
———. "Theological Meditations." https://www.theologicalmeditations.blogspot.com.
Calkins, Wolcott. *John Calvin's Calvinism*. Oberlin: Bibliotheca Sacra, 1909.
Calvin, John. *The Acts of the Apostles 1–13*. Translated by John W. Fraser and W. J. G. McDonald. Edited by David W. Torrance and Thomas F. Torrance. Calvin Commentaries. Edinburgh: Oliver and Boyd, 1965.
———. *The Acts of the Apostles 14–28*. Translated by John W. Fraser. Edited by David W. Torrance and Thomas F. Torrance. Calvin Commentaries. Grand Rapids: Eerdmans, 1966.
———. "Clear Explanation of Sound Doctrine Concerning the True Partaking of the Flesh and Blood of Christ in the Holy Supper in Order to Dissipate the Mists of Tileman Heshusius." In *Tracts and Treatises on the Doctrine and Worship of the Church*, vol. 2, translated by Henry Beveridge, edited by Thomas F. Torrance, 495–572. Grand Rapids: Eerdmans, 1958. Also available in *Calvin: Theological Treatises*, translated by J. K. S. Reid, 257–324. Philadelphia: Westminster, 1954.
———. *Commentaries on the Catholic Epistles*. Translated and edited by John Owen. Calvin's Commentaries. Grand Rapids: Eerdmans, 1948
———. *Commentaries on the First Twenty Chapters of the Book of the Prophet Ezekiel*. 2 vols. Translated by Thomas Myers. Calvin's Commentaries. Grand Rapids: Eerdmans, 1948.
———. *Commentaries on the Twelve Minor Prophets: Joel, Amos, Obadiah, Jonah, Micah, Nahum*. Translated by John Owen. 4 vols. Calvin's Commentaries. Grand Rapids: Baker, 1984.
———. *A Commentary on Jeremiah*. 5 vols. Translated by John Owen. Geneva Series Commentary. Edinburgh: Banner of Truth, 1989.
———. *Commentary on the Book of the Prophet Isaiah*. 4 vols. Translated by William Pringle. Calvin's Commentaries. Grand Rapids: Eerdmans, 1947.
———. *Commentary on the Gospel according to John*. 2 vols. Translated by William Pringle. Calvin's Commentaries. Grand Rapids: Eerdmans, 1949.
———. *Concerning the Eternal Predestination of God*. Translated by J. K. S. Reid. Louisville, KY: Westminster/John Knox, 1961.
———. "Confession of Faith in Name of the Reformed Churches of France." In *Tracts and Treatises on the Doctrine and Worship of the Church*, vol. 2, translated by Henry Beveridge, edited by Thomas F. Torrance, 137–62. Grand Rapids: Eerdmans, 1958.
———. *The Deity of Christ and Other Sermons*. Translated by Leroy Nixon. Audubon, NJ: Old Paths, 1997.
———. *The Epistle of Paul the Apostle to the Galatians, Ephesians, Philippians and Colossians*. Translated by T. H. L. Parker. Edited by David W. Torrance and Thomas F. Torrance. Calvin's Commentaries. Grand Rapids: Eerdmans, 1965.
———. *The Epistle of Paul the Apostle to the Hebrews and the First and Second Epistles of St Peter*. Translated by William B. Johnston. Edited by David W. Torrance and Thomas F. Torrance. Calvin's Commentaries. Edinburgh: Oliver and Boyd, 1963.
———. *The Epistles of James and Jude*. Translated by A. W. Morrison. Edited by David W. Torrance and Thomas F. Torrance. [Bound with vol. 3 of *A Harmony of the Gospels*.] Calvin's Commentaries. Grand Rapids: Eerdmans, 1972.

———. *The Epistles of Paul the Apostle to the Romans and to the Thessalonians*. Translated by Ross Mackenzie. Edited by David W. Torrance and Thomas F. Torrance. Calvin's Commentaries. Grand Rapids: Eerdmans, 1960.

———. *Faith Unfeigned: Four Sermons Concerning Matters Most Useful for the Present Time with a Brief Exposition of Psalm 87*. Translated by Robert White. Edinburgh: Banner of Truth, 2010.

———. "Forms of Prayer for the Church." In *Calvin's Tracts, Containing Treatises on the Sacraments, Catechism of the Church of Geneva, Forms of Prayer, and Confessions of Faith*, vol. 2, translated by Henry Beveridge, 100–112. Edinburgh: Calvin Translation Society, 1849.

———. *The Gospel according to St John 1–10*. Translated by T. H. L. Parker. Edited by David W. Torrance and Thomas F. Torrance. Calvin's Commentaries. Grand Rapids: Eerdmans, 1959.

———. *The Gospel according to St John 11–21 and the First Epistle of John*. Translated by T. H. L. Parker. Edited by David W. Torrance and Thomas F. Torrance. Calvin's Commentaries. Edinburgh: Oliver and Boyd, 1961.

———. *A Harmony of the Gospels: Matthew, Mark and Luke*, vol. 1. Translated by A. W. Morrison. Edited by David W. Torrance and Thomas F. Torrance. Calvin's Commentaries. Grand Rapids: Eerdmans, 1972.

———. *A Harmony of the Gospels: Matthew: Mark and Luke*, vol. 2. Translated by T. H. L. Parker. Edited by David W. Torrance and Thomas F. Torrance. Calvin's Commentaries. Grand Rapids: Eerdmans, 1972.

———. *A Harmony of the Gospels: Matthew, Mark and Luke*, vol. 3. Translated by A. W. Morrison. Edited by David W. Torrance and Thomas F. Torrance. Calvin's Commentaries. Grand Rapids: Eerdmans, 1972.

———. *Institutes of the Christian Religion*. Translated by Ford Lewis Battles. Edited by John T. McNeill. Philadelphia: Westminster, 1960.

———. *Institutes of the Christian Religion*. Translated by Henry Beveridge. Grand Rapids: Eerdmans, 1964.

———. "Last Admonition to Joachim Westphal." In *Tracts and Treatises on the Doctrine and Worship of the Church*, vol. 2, translated by Henry Beveridge, edited by Thomas F. Torrance, 345–494. Grand Rapids: Eerdmans, 1958.

———. "The Prayer Which John Calvin Ordinarily Made at the Ending of His Sermons." In *The Complete Works of Rev. Thomas Smythe, D.D.*, vol. 9, edited by J. Wm. Flynn, 730–31. Columbia: Bryan, 1911.

———. *The Second Epistle of Paul the Apostle to the Corinthians and the Epistles to Timothy, Titus and Philemon*. Translated by T. A. Smail. Edited by David W. Torrance and Thomas F. Torrance. Calvin's Commentaries. Grand Rapids: Eerdmans, 1964.

———. *A Selection of the Most Celebrated Sermons of John Calvin, Minister of the Gospel and One of the Principal Leaders in the Protestant Reformation*. New York: Forbes, 1830.

———. *Sermons on Deuteronomy*. Translated by Arthur Golding. Edinburgh: Banner of Truth, 1987.

———. *Sermons on Galatians*. Translated by Arthur Golding. Audubon, NJ: Old Paths, 1995.

———. *Sermons on Isaiah's Prophecy of the Death and Passion of Christ*. Translated and edited by T. H. L. Parker. London: Clarke, 1956.

———. *Sermons on Job*. Translated by Arthur Golding. Edinburgh: Banner of Truth, 1993.

———. *Sermons on the Acts of the Apostles, Chapters 1–7*. Translated by Rob Roy McGregor. Edinburgh: Banner of Truth, 2008.

———. *Sermons on the Beatitudes*. Translated by Robert White. Edinburgh: Banner of Truth, 2006.

———. *Sermons on the Book of Micah*. Translated and edited by Benjamin Wirt Farley. Phillipsburg, NJ: P&R, 2003.

———. *Sermons on the Epistle to the Ephesians*. Translated by Arthur Golding. London: Banner of Truth, 1973.

———. *Sermons on the Epistles to Timothy and Titus*. Translated by Laurence Tomson. Edinburgh: Banner of Truth, 1983.

———. *Sermons on the Hundred and Nineteenth Psalm*. Translated by Thomas Stocker. Audubon, NJ: Old Paths, 1996.

———. *Theological Treatises*. Translated by J. K. S. Reid. Library of Christian Classics 22. Philadelphia: Westminster, 1954.

Cammenga, Ronald. "John Calvin Research Bibliography." *Protestant Reformed Theological Journal* 51 (2017) 68–96.

Campos, Heber Carlos de Jr. "Calvino e os Calvinistas da Pós-Reforma." *Fides reformata* 14 (2009) 11–31.

Cardwell, Edward, ed. *The Two Books of Common Prayer: Set Forth by Authority of Parliament in the Reign of King Edward the Sixth*. 3rd ed. Oxford: Oxford University Press, 1852.

Carleton, George. *The Suffrage of the Divines of Great Britaine, Concerning the Five Articles Controverted in the Low Countries*. London: Robert Milbourne, 1629.

Carson, D. A. *The Difficult Doctrine of the Love of God*. Wheaton, IL: Crossway, 2000.

———. *Divine Sovereignty and Human Responsibility: Biblical Perspectives in Tension*. Reprint, Eugene, OR: Wipf & Stock, 2002.

Chafer, Lewis Sperry. "For Whom Did Christ Die?" *Bibliotheca Sacra* 137 (1980) 310–26.

Chambers, Neil Andrew. "A Critical Examination of John Owen's Argument for Limited Atonement in 'The Death of Death in the Death of Christ.'" ThM thesis, Reformed Theological Seminary, 1998.

Clark, R. Scott. "Election and Predestination: The Sovereign Expressions of God." In *Theological Guide to Calvin's Institutes: Essays and Analysis*, edited by David W. Hall and Peter A. Lillback, 90–122. Phillipsburg, NJ: P&R, 2008.

Clark, Richard E. "The Calvinism of Arminius." MA thesis, New Orleans Baptist Theological Seminary, 2018.

Clifford, Alan C. "Amyraldian Theology and Reformed-Lutheran *rapprochement*." In *From Zwingli to Amyraut: Exploring the Growth of European Reformed Traditions*, edited by Jon Balserak and Jim West, 157–78. Göttingen: Vandenhoeck & Ruprecht, 2017.

———. *Amyraut Affirmed, or "Owenism a Caricature of Calvinism."* Norwich, UK: Charenton Reformed, 2004.

———. *Atonement and Justification: English Evangelical Theology 1640–1790, an Evaluation*. Oxford: Clarendon, 1990.

———. "Calvin & Calvinism, Amyraut et al." In *John Calvin 500: A Reformation Affirmation*, edited by Alan C. Clifford, 37–79. Norwich, UK: Charenton Reformed, 2001.

———. *Calvin Celebrated: The Genevan Reformer and His Huguenot Sons*. Norwich, UK: Charenton Reformed, 2009.

———. *Calvinus: Authentic Calvinism, a Clarification*. Rev. ed. Norwich, UK: Charenton Reformed, 2007.

———. "Geneva Revisited or Calvinism Revised: The Case for Theological Reassessment." *Churchman* 100 (1986) 323–31.

———. "The Gospel and Justification." *Evangelical Quarterly* 57 (1985) 247–67.

———. "John Calvin and the *Confessio Fidei Gallicana*." *Evangelical Quarterly* 58 (1986) 195–206.

———. "Justification: The Calvin-Saumur Perspective." *Evangelical Quarterly* 79 (2007) 331–48.

———. "Mulling Muller on Calvin and Amyraut." https://pdfs.semanticscholar.org/952a/3f6bd6023fe9865007c8623f794bd6481f24.pdf?_ga=2.152086713.1663574870.1571163732-1516855895.1568613098

Cole, Henry. *Calvin's Calvinism*. London: Wertheim and Macintosh, 1857.

Compton, Jared M. "John Davenant's *Dissertation on the Death of Christ*: A Review Essay." *Detroit Baptist Seminary Journal* 21 (2016) 167–82.

Compton, R. Bruce. "The Design and Extent of Christ's Atonement." Paper presented at the Bible Faculty Leadership Summit, Maranatha Baptist University (Waterton, WI), June 27, 2019.

Coppenger, Mark T. "Review Essay on *Whosoever Will*." *Southwestern Journal of Theology* 55 (2012) 159–71.

Costley, Stephen L. "Answering Roger Nicole on 1 Timothy 2:5." http://controversialcalvinism.blogspot.com/2008/12/roger-nicole-1timothy-25.html.

———. "Controversial Calvinism." http://controversialcalvinism.blogspot.com.

———. "Did Christ's Sacrifice *Actually* Save?" http://controversialcalvinism.blogspot.com/2009/06/did-christs-sacrifice-actually-save.html.

———. "Understanding Calvin's Argument against Heshusius." http://calvinandcalvinism.com/?p=215.

Cottret, Bernard. *Calvin Biographie*. Paris: Jean-Claude Lattès, 1995.

Courthial, Pierre. "The Golden Age of Calvinism." Translated by Jonathan Jack. In *John Calvin: His Influence in the Western World*, edited by W. Stanford Reid, 73–92. Grand Rapids: Zondervan, 1982.

Crampton, W. Gary. "Does the Bible Contain Paradox?" http://www.trinityfoundation.org/PDF/The%20Trinity%20Review%200076a%20DoestheBibleContainParadox.pdf.

Crawford, Thomas J. *The Doctrine of the Holy Scripture Respecting the Atonement*. Edinburgh: Blackwood, 1871.

Crisp, Oliver D. *Deviant Calvinism: Broadening Reformed Theology*. Minneapolis: Fortress, 2014.

———. *Saving Calvinism: Expanding the Reformed Tradition*. Downers Grove, IL: IVP Academic, 2016.

Crisp, Oliver D., and Fred Sanders, eds. *Locating Atonement: Explorations in Constructive Dogmatics*. Grand Rapids: Zondervan, 2015.

Cunningham, William. *The Reformers and the Theology of the Reformation*. Carlisle, PA: Banner of Truth, 1967.

Dabney, Robert L. *Christ Our Penal Substitute*. Richmond, VA: Presbyterian Committee of Publication, 1898.

———. *The Five Points of Calvinism*. 1895. Reprint, Harrisonburg, VA: Sprinkle, 1992.

———. *Lectures in Systematic Theology*. 1878. Reprint, Grand Rapids: Zondervan, 1972.

Daniel, Curt D. *Biblical Calvinism: An Introduction to the Doctrines of Grace.* Madison, WI: Haynes, 1994.

———. "Extract from Curt Daniel." Appendix 2 in *Calvin and English Calvinism to 1649*, by R. T. Kendall, 231–38. Carlisle, UK: Paternoster, 1997.

———. *The History and Theology of Calvinism.* Dallas: Scholarly Reprints, 1993.

———. "Hyper-Calvinism and John Gill." PhD diss., University of Edinburgh, 1983.

Dantine, Johannes. "Das christologie Problem in Rahmen der Prädestinationslehre von Theodore Beza." *Zeitschrift für Kirchengeschichte* 77 (1966) 81–96.

———. "Les Tabelles sur la doctrine de la predestination par Théodore de Bèze." *Revue de théologie et de philosophie* 16 (1996) 365–67.

Demarest, Bruce A. "Amyraldianism." In the *Evangelical Dictionary of Theology*, edited by Daniel J. Treier and Walter A. Elwell, 48. 3rd ed. Grand Rapids: Baker Academic, 2017.

———. *The Cross and Salvation.* Foundations of Evangelical Theology 1. Wheaton, IL: Crossway, 1997.

Denlinger, Aaron Clay. "'Men of Gallio's Naughty Faith?': The Aberdeen Doctors on Reformed and Lutheran Concord." *Church History and Religious Culture* 92 (2012) 57–83.

———. "Scottish Hypothetical Universalism: Robert Baron (c. 1596–1639) on God's Love and Christ's Death for All." In *Reformed Orthodoxy in Scotland: Essays on Scottish Theology 1560–1775*, edited by Aaron Clay Denlinger, 83–102. London: Bloomsbury Academic, 2015.

Dewar, Michael. "The Synods of Dort, the Westminster Assembly and the French Reformed Church 1618–1643." *Churchman* 104 (1990) 38–42.

Djaballah, Amar. "Calvin and the Calvinists: An Examination of Some Recent Views." *Reformation Canada* 5 (Spring 1982) 7–20.

———. "Controversy on Universal Grace: A Historical Survey of Moïse Amyraut's *Brief Traité de la predestination*." In *From Heaven He Came and Sought Her: Definite Atonement in Historical, Biblical, Theological, and Pastoral Perspective*, edited by David Gibson and Jonathan Gibson, 165–200. Wheaton, IL: Crossway, 2013.

Douty, Norman F. *Did Christ Die Only for the Elect? A Treatise on the Extent of Christ's Atonement.* Eugene, OR: Wipf and Stock, 1998.

Doyle, Robert Colin. "The Context of Moral Decision Making in the Writings of John Calvin—The Christological Ethics of Eschatological Order." PhD diss., University of Aberdeen, 1981.

———. "Penal Atonement: The Orthodox Teaching of the Fathers and Three Conversations with John Calvin [Part 2]." *Reformed Theological Review* 65 (2006) 93–105.

Duby, Steven J. "The Cross and the Fullness of God: Clarifying the Meaning of Divine Wrath in Penal Substitution." *Scottish Bulletin of Evangelical Theology* 29 (2011) 165–76.

Edmondson, Stephen. *Calvin's Christology.* New York: Cambridge University Press, 2004.

Elliott, Michael B. "The Availability and Application of the Atonement Based on the High Priestly Work of Jesus Christ." ThM thesis, The Master's Seminary, 2011.

Elwell, Walter. "Atonement, Extent of." In the *Evangelical Dictionary of Theology*, edited by Daniel J. Treier and Walter A. Elwell, 100–101. 3rd ed. Grand Rapids: Baker Academic, 2017.

Emmert, Kevin P. "The Softer Face of Calvinism." *Christianity Today* (Oct. 23, 2014). http://www.christianitytoday.com/ct/2014/september-web-only/softer-face-of-calvinism.html.

Estes, Elizabeth Colmant. "Reincorporating Christus Victor in the Reformed Theology of Atonement." *Perspectives* 32 (2017) 6–10.

Faber, Jelle. "The Saving Work of the Holy Spirit in Calvin." In *Calvin and the Holy Spirit: Papers and Responses Presented at the Sixth Colloquium on Calvin & Calvin Studies*, edited by Peter De Klerk, 1–11. Grand Rapids: Calvin Studies Society, 1989.

Fackre, Gabriel. "Divine Perseverance." In *What about Those Who Have Never Heard?* edited by John Sanders, 71–95. Downers Grove, IL: InterVarsity, 1995.

Ferguson, Reid. "Responsive Reiding." http://www.responsivereiding.com.

Ferguson, Sinclair. "'Blessèd Assurance, Jesus Is Mine'? Definite Atonement and the Cure of Souls." In *From Heaven He Came and Sought Her: Definite Atonement in Historical, Biblical, Theological, and Pastoral Perspective*, edited by David Gibson and Jonathan Gibson, 607–31. Wheaton, IL: Crossway, 2013.

Ferguson, William Stark. "The Nature of the Connection between Election and Atonement in the Theology of John Calvin." MCS thesis, Regent College, 1986.

Fesko, J. V. *Beyond Calvin: Union with Christ and Justification in Early Modern Reformed Theology (1517–1700)*. Reformed Historical Theology 20. Göttingen: Vandenhoeck & Ruprecht, 2012.

———. *Diversity within the Reformed Tradition: Supra- and Infralapsarianism in Calvin, Dort and Westminster*. Jackson: Reformed Academic, 1999.

Field, David P. *"Rigide Calvinisme in a Softer Dresse": The Moderate Presbyterianism of John Howe (1630–1705)*. Edinburgh: Rutherford House, 2004.

Fields, Paul W., et al. "2014 Calvin Bibliography." Grand Rapids: The H. Henry Meeter Center, 2014.

Foord, Martin. "God Wills All People to Be Saved—Or Does He? Calvin's Reading of 1 Timothy 2:4." In *Engaging with Calvin: Aspects of the Reformer's Legacy for Today*, edited by Mark D. Thompson, 179–203. Nottingham, UK: Apollos, 2009.

Frame, John M. Review of *Calvinism and the Amyraut Heresy*, by Jonathan Armstrong. *Westminster Theological Journal* 34 (1972) 186–92.

Fraser, James. *A Treatise on Justifying Faith*. Edinburgh: Gray, 1749.

Fuller, Morris J. *The Life, Letters & Writings of John Davenant, D.D., 1572–1641, Lord Bishop of Salisbury*. London: Methuen, 1897.

Garcia, Mark A. *Life in Christ: Union with Christ and Twofold Grace in Calvin's Theology*. Studies in Christian History and Thought. Carlisle, UK: Paternoster, 2008.

Gardoski, Ken. "The Will of God and the Death of Christ: A Case for the Universal Scope of the Atonement." *Journal of Ministry and Theology* 15 (2011) 68–109.

Gatiss, Lee. "A Deceptive Clarity? Particular Redemption in the Westminster Standards." *Reformed Theological Review* 69 (2010) 180–96.

———. *For Us and for Our Salvation: "Limited Atonement" in the Bible, Doctrine, History, and Ministry*. London: Latimer Trust, 2012.

———. "Grace Tasted Death for All: Thomas Aquinas on Hebrews 2:9." *Tyndale Bulletin* 63 (2012) 217–36.

———. "The Inexhaustible Fountain of All Good Things: Union with Christ in Calvin on Ephesians." *Themelios* 34 (2009) 194–206.

———. "'Shades of Opinion within a Generic Calvinism': The Particular Redemption Debate at the Westminster Assembly." *Reformed Theological Review* 69 (2010) 101–18.

———. "The Synod of Dort and Definite Atonement." In *From Heaven He Came and Sought Her: Definite Atonement in Historical, Biblical, Theological, and Pastoral Perspective*, edited by David Gibson and Jonathan Gibson, 143–63. Wheaton, IL: Crossway, 2013.

Geisler, Norman. *Chosen but Free: A Balanced View of Divine Election*. 2nd ed. Minneapolis: Bethany House, 2001.

George, Timothy. *Amazing Grace: God's Pursuit, Our Response*. Wheaton, IL: Crossway, 2011.

———. *Theology of the Reformers*. Nashville: Broadman, 1988.

Gerrish, Brian A. "Atonement and 'Saving Faith.'" *Theology Today* 17 (1960) 181–91.

———. *Grace and Gratitude: The Eucharistic Theology of John Calvin*. Minneapolis: Fortress, 1993.

———. *Thinking with the Church: Essays in Historical Theology*. Grand Rapids: Eerdmans, 2010.

Gerstner, John R. "The Atonement and the Purpose of God." In *Atonement*, edited by Gabriel N. E. Fluhrer, 49–66. Phillipsburg, NJ: P&R, 2010.

Gibson, David, and Jonathan Gibson, eds. *From Heaven He Came and Sought Her: Definite Atonement in Historical, Biblical, Theological, and Pastoral Perspective*. Wheaton, IL: Crossway, 2013.

Gibson, Jonathan. "The Glorious, Indivisible, Trinitarian Work of God In Christ." In *From Heaven He Came and Sought Her: Definite Atonement in Historical, Biblical, Theological, and Pastoral Perspective*, edited by David Gibson and Jonathan Gibson, 331–73. Wheaton, IL: Crossway, 2013.

Godfrey, W. Robert. "Reformed Thought on the Extent of the Atonement to 1618." *Westminster Theological Journal* 37 (1975) 133–71.

———. "Tensions within International Calvinism: The Debate on the Atonement at the Synod of Dort, 1618–1619." PhD diss., Stanford University, 1974.

Goodloe, James L., IV. *John McLeod Campbell: The Extent and Nature of the Atonement*. Studies in Reformed Theology and History 3. Princeton, NJ: Princeton Theological Seminary, 1997.

Gootjes, Albert. "Calvin and Saumur: The Case of Claude Pajon (1626–1685)." In *The Reception of John Calvin and His Theology in Reformed Orthodoxy*, edited by Andreas J. Beck and William A. den Boer, 203–14. Leiden: Brill, 2011.

———. "John Cameron (ca. 1579–1625) and the French Universalist Tradition." In *The Theology of the French Reformed Churches: From Henri IV to the Revocation of the Edict of Nantes*, edited by Martin I. Klauber, 169–96. Reformed Historical-Theological Studies. Grand Rapids: Reformation Heritage, 2014.

———. "L'héritage de John Cameron en France au XVIIe siècle: Les origines de la pensée de Claude Pajon (1626–1685)." *Bulletin annuel de l'Institut d'histoire de la Réformation* 32 (2010–11) 51–70.

———. "Scotland and Saumur: The Intellectual Legacy of John Cameron in Seventeenth-Century France." In *Reformed Orthodoxy in Scotland: Essays on Scottish Theology 1560–1775*, edited by Aaron Clay Denlinger, 175–90. London: Bloomsbury Academic, 2015.

Gordon, Amy Glassner. "The First Protestant Missionary Effort: Why Did It Fail?" *International Bulletin of Missionary Research* (1984) 12–18.

Grebe, Matthias. *Election, Atonement and the Holy Spirit: Through and Beyond Barth's Theological Interpretation of Scripture*. Cambridge: James Clarke, 2014.

Greenbury, James. "Calvin's Understanding of Predestination with Special Reference to the *Institutes*." *Reformed Theological Review* 54 (1995) 121–34.

Gribben, Crawford. "Rhetoric, Fiction, and Theology: James Ussher and the Death of Jesus Christ." *The Seventeenth Century* 20 (2005) 53–76.

Grohman, Donald Davis. "The Genevan Reactions to the Saumur Doctrine of Hypothetical Universalism, 1635–1685." ThD diss., Knox College, University of Toronto, 1971.

Grow, Bobby. "John Calvin contra 'Two Wills in God' Methodology." *The Evangelical Calvinist*. https://growrag.wordpress.com/2012/02/22/john-calvin-contra-two-wills-in-god-methodology.

Grudem, Wayne. *Systematic Theology: An Introduction to Biblical Doctrine*. Grand Rapids: Zondervan, 2000.

Guelzo, Allen C. *Edwards on the Will: A Century of American Theological Debate*. Middletown, CT: Wesleyan University Press, 1989.

Gumerlock, Francis X. *Fulgentius of Ruspe on the Saving Will of God: The Development of a Sixth-Century African Bishop's Interpretation of 1 Timothy 2:4 during the Semi-Pelagian Controversy*. Lewiston, NY: Edwin Mellen, 2009.

Gunton, Colin. "Aspects of Salvation: Some Unscholastic Themes from Calvin's *Institutes*." *International Journal of Systematic Theology* 1 (1999) 253–65.

Habets, Myk. "Doctrine of Election in Evangelical Calvinism." *Irish Theological Quarterly* 73 (2008) 334–54.

Habets, Myk, and Bobby Grow, eds. *Evangelical Calvinism: Essays Resourcing the Continuing Reformation of the Church*. Eugene, OR: Pickwick, 2012.

Hall, Basil. "Calvin against the Calvinists." In *John Calvin*, edited by G. E. Duffield, 19–37. Appleford, UK: Sutton Courtenay, 1966.

Hall, David W., and Peter A. Lillback, eds. *A Theological Guide to Calvin's Institutes: Essays and Analysis*. Phillipsburg, NJ: P&R, 2008.

Hall, Joseph H. "The Marrow Controversy: A Defense of Grace and the Free Offer of the Gospel." *Mid-America Journal of Theology* 10 (1999) 239–57.

Hammett, John S. "Multiple-Intentions View of the Atonement." In *Perspectives on the Extent of the Atonement: Three Views*, edited by Andrew David Naselli and Mark A. Snoeberger, 143–94. Nashville: B&H Academic, 2015.

Hammond, Jackson. "Satisfaction and Substitution: An Atonement for All Cultures." *Journal of Theta Alpha Kappa* 43 (2019): 48–59.

Harding, Matthew S. "Atonement Theory Revisited: Calvin, Beza, and Amyraut on the Extent of the Atonement." *Perichoresis* 11 (2013) 49–73.

Hardt, Tom G. A. "Justification and Easter: A Study in Subjective and Objective Justification in Lutheran Theology." In *A Living Legacy: Essays in Honor of Robert Preus*, edited by Kurt E. Marquart et al., 52–78. Fort Wayne: Concordia Theological Seminary, 1985.

Harmon, Matthew Paul. "Moyse Amyraut's Six Sermons: Directions for Amyraldian Studies." ThM thesis, Westminster Theological Seminary, 2008.

Hart, Trevor. "Humankind in Christ and Christ in Humankind: Salvation as Participation in Our Substitute in the Theology of John Calvin." *Scottish Journal of Theology* 42 (1989) 67–84.

Hartog, Paul. "Calvin: Still Making Points with Baptists." *Baptist Bulletin* 75.4 (2009) 10–13.

———. "Calvin's Preface to Chrysostom's Homilies as a Window into Calvin's Own Priorities and Perspectives." *Perichoresis* 17 (2019) 57–72.

———. "Naselli and Snoeberger's *Perspectives on the Extent of the Atonement: Three Views*." *The Christian Librarian* 58 (2015) 126–28.

———. "Strivens' *Philip Doddridge and the Shaping of Evangelical Dissent*." *The Christian Librarian* 60 (2017) 111–12.

Hastie, Peter. "Straight Talk on John Calvin: Paul Helm Talks to Peter Hastie." *The Briefing* (June 3, 2009). https://matthiasmedia.com/briefing/2009/06/straight-talk-on-john-calvin-paul-helm-talks-to-peter-hastie.

Hay, Andrew R. "The Heart of Wrath: Calvin, Barth, and Reformed Theories of Atonement." *Neue Zeitschrift für systematische Theologie und Religionsphilosophie* 55 (2013) 361–78.

Haykin, Michael A. G. "The *esse* of Reformed: A Current Question." *Historia Ecclesiastica*. http://andrewfullercenter.org/articles/blog/2009/11/the-esse-of-reformed-a-current-question.

Haykin, Michael A. G., and C. Jeffrey Robinson, Sr., "How Very Important This Corner Is: The Calvinistic Missions to France and Brazil." In *To the Ends of the Earth: Calvin's Missional Vision and Legacy*, 65–74. Wheaton, IL: Crossway, 2014.

Helm, Paul. *Calvin: A Guide for the Perplexed*. Guides for the Perplexed. London: T. & T. Clark, 2008.

———. *Calvin and the Calvinists*. Edinburgh: Banner of Truth, 1982.

———. "Calvin and the Covenant: Unity and Continuity." *Evangelical Quarterly* 55 (1983) 65–81.

———. "Calvin, English Calvinism and the Logic of Doctrinal Development." *Scottish Journal of Theology* 34 (1981) 179–85.

———. "Calvin, Indefinite Language, and Definite Atonement." In *From Heaven He Came and Sought Her: Definite Atonement in Historical, Biblical, Theological, and Pastoral Perspective*, edited by David Gibson and Jonathan Gibson, 97–119. Wheaton, IL: Crossway, 2013.

———. "Faith, Atonement, and Time." In *John Calvin's Ideas*, 389–416. Oxford: Oxford University Press, 2004.

———. "The Logic of Limited Atonement." *Scottish Bulletin of Evangelical Theology* 3 (1985) 47–54.

Hendryx, John. "The Amyraldian View Undone." http://www.reformationtheology.com/2006/11/the_amyraldian_view_undone.php.

———. "Is it God's Desire for All Men to Be Saved?" http://www.monergism.com/thethreshold/articles/onsite/desireallsaved.html.

Hesselink, I. John. "Calvin on the Atonement: A Reexamination." In *Tools for Understanding: Essays in Honor of Donald J. Bruggink*, edited by James Hart Brumm, 295–319. The Historical Series of the Reformed Church in America 60. Grand Rapids: Eerdmans, 2008.

Hill, Jonathan. *The History of Christian Thought*. Downers Grove, IL: InterVarsity, 2003.

Hodge, Archibald Alexander. *The Atonement*. Philadelphia: Presbyterian Board of Education, 1867.

Hodge, Charles. "For Whom Did Christ Die?" In *Systematic Theology*, vol. 2, 544–62. Grand Rapids: Eerdmans, 1946.

Hogg, David S. "'Sufficient for All, Efficient for Some': Definite Atonement in the Medieval Church." In *From Heaven He Came and Sought Her: Definite Atonement in Historical, Biblical, Theological, and Pastoral Perspective*, edited by David Gibson and Jonathan Gibson, 75–95. Wheaton, IL: Crossway, 2013.

Holmes, Stephen R. "The Nature of Theology and the Extent of the Atonement." *Perichoresis* 16 (2018) 3–18.

Holtrop, Philip C. *The Bolsec Controversy on Predestination, from 1551 to 1555: The Statements of Jerome Bolsec and the Responses of John Calvin, Theodore Beza and Other Reformed Theologians*. Lewiston, NY: Edwin Mellen, 1993.

Horton, Michael S. "Calvin's Theology of Union with Christ and the Double Grace: Modern Reception and Contemporary Possibilities." In *Calvin's Theology and Its Reception: Disputes, Developments, and New Possibilities*, edited by Todd Billings and I. John Hesselink, 72–94. Louisville, KY: Westminster/John Knox, 2012.

———. *For Calvinism*. Grand Rapids: Zondervan, 2011.

———. "Traditional Reformed View." In *Five Views on the Extent of the Atonement*, edited by Adam J. Johnson, 112–33. Counterpoints: Bible & Theology. Grand Rapids: Zondervan Academic, 2019.

Howson, Barry H. *Erroneous and Schismatical Opinions: The Question of Orthodoxy Regarding the Theology of Hanserd Knollys (c. 1599–1691)*. Studies in the History of Christian Thought. Leiden: Brill, 2001.

Hughes, Seán, F. "The Problem of 'Calvinism': English Theologies of Predestination c. 1580–1630." In *Belief and Practice in Reformation England: A Tribute to Patrick Collinson from His Students*, edited by Susan Wabuda and Caroline Litzenberger, 229–49. Aldershot, UK: Ashgate, 1998.

Jeffery, Steve, et al. *Pierced for Our Transgressions: Rediscovering the Glory of Penal Substitution*. Wheaton, IL: Crossway, 2007.

Jinkins, Michael. "Theodore Beza: Continuity and Regression in the Reformed Tradition." *Evangelical Quarterly* 64 (1992) 131–54.

Johnson, Jeffrey D. *He Died for Me: Limited Atonement and the Universal Gospel*. Conway, AR: Free Grace, 2017.

Johnson, Marcus. "New or Nuanced Perspective on Calvin? Reply to Thomas Wenger." *Journal of the Evangelical Theological Society* 51 (2008) 543–58.

Johnson, Phil. "The Nature of the Atonement: Why and for Whom did Christ Die?" http://www.biblebb.com/files/MAC/SC03-1027.htm.

Kang, Hyo Ju. "John Davenant, a Champion of the '*Via Media*' at the Synod of Dort?" *Journal of Academic Perspectives* 3 (2017) 1–24.

Kendall, R. T. *Calvin and English Calvinism to 1649*. Oxford: Oxford University Press, 1979; Rev. ed. Carlisle, UK: Paternoster, 1997.

———. "The Puritan Modification of Calvin's Theology." In *John Calvin: His Influence in the Western World*, edited by W. Stanford Reid, 199–214. Grand Rapids: Zondervan, 1982.

Kennedy, Kevin Dixon. "Hermeneutical Discontinuity between Calvin and Later Calvinism." *Scottish Journal of Theology* 64 (2011) 299–312.

———. *Union with Christ and the Extent of the Atonement in Calvin*. New York: Lang, 2002.

———. "Was Calvin a 'Calvinist'? John Calvin on the Extent of the Atonement." In *Whosoever Will: A Biblical-Theological Critique of Five-Point Calvinism*, edited by David L. Allen and Steve W. Lemke, 191–212. Nashville: B&H Academic, 2010.

Kickel, Walter. *Vernunft und Offenbarung bei Theodor Beza: Zum Problem der Verhältnisses von Theologie, Philosophie und Staat*. Neukirchen-Vluyn: Neukirchener Verlag, 1967.

Kieser, Ty. "Multiple Intentions, Indivisible Operations, and Christ's Atoning Work: Bruce Ware and John Owen on the Triune Shape of the Atonement and Its Extent." MDiv paper. Trinity Evangelical Divinity School, 2012. https://www.academia.edu/13706725/Multiple_Intentions_Indivisible_Operations_and_Christ_s_Atoning_Work_John_Owen_on_the_Triune_Shape_and_the_Extent_of_the_Atonement?email_work_card=view-paper.

Klauber, Martin I. "Continuity and Discontinuity in Post-Reformation Reformed Theology: An Evaluation of the Muller Thesis." *Journal of the Evangelical Theological Society* 33 (1990) 467–75.

Klooster, Fred H. *Calvin's Doctrine of Predestination*. 2nd ed. Grand Rapids: Baker, 1977.

Knox, D. Broughton. *The Doctrine of God*, vol. 1 of *Selected Works*. Edited by Tony Payne. Kingsford, Australia: Matthias Media, 2000.

Kuiper, Rienk B. *For Whom Did Christ Die? A Study of the Divine Intent of the Atonement*. Grand Rapids: Eerdmans, 1959.

Kuyper, Abraham. "Calvinism a Life-System." In *Lectures on Calvinism: The Stone Lectures of 1898*, 9–40. Grand Rapids: Eerdmans, 1961.

Lake, Donald M. "He Died for All: The Universal Dimensions of the Atonement." In *Grace Unlimited*, edited by Clark Pinnock, 31–50. Minneapolis: Bethany Fellowship, 1975.

Lake, Peter G. "Calvinism and the English Church 1570–1635." *Past and Present* 114 (1987) 32–76.

Lane, Anthony N. S. "Calvin versus Calvinism Revisited." *Foundations* 42 (1999) 32–35.

———. "Calvin's Doctrine of Assurance." *Vox Evangelica* 11 (1979) 32–54.

———. "Calvin's Doctrine of Assurance Revisited." In *Tributes to John Calvin: A Celebration of His Quincentenary*, edited by David W. Hall, 270–313. Phillipsburg, NJ: P&R, 2010.

———. "The Quest for the Historical Calvin." *Evangelical Quarterly* 55 (1983) 95–113.

———. *A Reader's Guide to Calvin's Institutes*. Grand Rapids: Baker Academic, 2009.

———. "Review of *Calvin and English Calvinism to 1649*, by R. T. Kendall." *Themelios* 6 (1980) 29–31.

Laplanche, François. *Orthodoxie et prédication: L'œuvre d'Amyraut et la querelle de la grâce universelle*. Paris: Presses Universitaires de France, 1965.

Leahy, Frederick S. "Calvin and the Extent of the Atonement." *Reformed Theological Journal* 8 (1992) 54–64.

Letham, Robert. "Faith and Assurance in Early Calvinism: A Model of Continuity and Diversity." In *Later Calvinism: International Perspectives*, edited by W. Fred Graham, 355–84. Sixteenth Century Essays and Studies 22. Kirksville: Sixteenth Century Journal, 1994.

———. "Saving Faith and Assurance in Reformed Theology: Zwingli to the Synod of Dort." 2 vols. PhD diss., University of Aberdeen, 1979.

———. "The Triune God, Incarnation, and Definite Atonement." In *From Heaven He Came and Sought Her: Definite Atonement in Historical, Biblical, Theological, and Pastoral Perspective*, edited by David Gibson and Jonathan Gibson, 437–60. Wheaton, IL: Crossway, 2013.

———. *The Westminster Assembly: Reading Its Theology in Historical Context*. Westminster Assembly and the Reformed Faith. Phillipsburg, NJ: P&R, 2009.

———. *The Work of Christ*. Downers Grove, IL: InterVarsity, 1993.

Lightner, Robert P. *The Death Christ Died: A Case for Unlimited Atonement*. Des Plaines: Regular Baptist, 1967.

———. "For Whom Did Christ Die?" In *Walvoord: A Tribute*, edited by Donald K. Campbell, 157–68. Chicago: Moody, 1982.

Lillback, Peter A. *The Binding of God: Calvin's Role in the Development of Covenant Theology*. Grand Rapids: Baker, 2001.

Lovell, Nathan. "The Love of God in Time and Eternity: Accounting for Particularity in Reformed Soteriology." http://www.academia.edu/7623273/The_Love_of_God_in_Time_and_Eternity_Accounting_for_Particularity_in_Reformed_Soteriology.

Lynch, Michael J. "Confessional Orthodoxy and Hypothetical Universalism: Another Look at the Westminster Confession of Faith." In *Beyond Calvin: Essays on the Diversity of the Reformed Tradition*, edited by W. Bradford Littlejohn and Jonathan Tomes, 127–44. Lincoln, NE: Davenant Trust, 2017.

———. "*Quid Pro Quo* Satisfaction? An Analysis and Response to Garry Williams on Penal Substitutionary Atonement and Definite Atonement." *Evangelical Quarterly* 89 (2018) 51–70.

———. Review of *From Heaven He Came and Sought Her: Definite Atonement in Historical, Biblical, Theological, and Pastoral Perspective*, edited by David Gibson and Jonathan Gibson. *Calvin Theological Journal* 49 (2014) 352–54.

———. Review of *Perspectives on the Extent of the Atonement: Three Views*. *Calvin Theological Journal* 51 (2016) 345–47.

———. "Richard Hooker and the Development of English Hypothetical Universalism." In *Richard Hooker and Reformed Orthodoxy*, edited by W. Bradford Littlejohn and Scott N. Kindred-Barnes, 273–93. Göttingen: Vandenhoeck & Ruprecht, 2017.

Macleod, Donald. "Amyraldus Redivivus: A Review Article." *Evangelical Quarterly* 81 (2009) 210–29.

———. *Christ Crucified: Understanding the Atonement*. Downers Grove, IL: IVP Academic, 2014.

———. "Definite Atonement and the Divine Decree." In *From Heaven He Came and Sought Her: Definite Atonement in Historical, Biblical, Theological, and Pastoral Perspective*, edited by David Gibson and Jonathan Gibson, 401–35. Wheaton, IL: Crossway, 2013.

Marshall, I. Howard. *Aspects of the Atonement: Cross and Resurrection in the Reconciling of God and Humanity*. Milton Keynes, UK: Paternoster, 2007.

Maxfield, John A. "Luther, Zwingli, and Calvin on the Significance of Christ's Death." *Concordia Theological Quarterly* 75 (2011) 91–110.

McComish, William. "Calvin's Children." In *Tributes to John Calvin: A Celebration of His Quincentenary*, edited by David W. Hall, 1–20. Phillipsburg, NJ: P&R, 2010.

McCormack, Bruce L. "For Us and Our Salvation: Incarnation and Atonement in the Reformed Tradition." *Greek Orthodox Theological Review* 43 (1998) 281–316.

McDonald, H. D. *The Atonement of the Death of Christ: In Faith, Revelation, and History*. Grand Rapids: Baker, 1984

McGowan, Andrew T. B. *Always Reforming: Explorations in Systematic Theology*. Downers Grove, IL: IVP Academic, 2006.

———. "The Atonement as Penal Substitution." In *Always Reforming: Explorations in Systematic Theology*, edited by A. T. B. McGowan, 183–210. Downers Grove, IL: IVP Academic, 2006.

———. "Calvin on Limited Atonement." In *The Federal Theology of Thomas Boston*, 48–58. Edinburgh: Rutherford House, 1997.

———. "Was Westminster Calvinist?" In *Reformed Theology in Contemporary Perspective: Westminster: Yesterday, Today—and Tomorrow?* edited by Lynn Quigley, 46–65. Edinburgh: Rutherford House, 2006.

McNeill, John T. "Calvin's Efforts toward the Consolidation of Protestantism." *Journal of Religion* 8 (1928) 411–23.

———. *The History and Character of Calvinism*. New York: Oxford University Press, 1954.

McPhee, Ian. "Conserver or Transformer of Calvin's Theology? A Study of the Origins and Development of Theodore Beza's Thought 1550–1570." PhD diss., University of Cambridge, 1979.

Miller, Perry. *The New England Mind: From Colony to Province*. Cambridge: Harvard University Press, 1953.

Milton, Anthony, ed. *The British Delegation and the Synod of Dort (1618–1619)*. Church of England Record Society 13. Woodbridge, UK: Boydell, 2005.

Mitchell, Alex F., and John Struthers, eds. *Minutes of the Sessions of the Westminster Assembly of Divines*. Edinburgh: Blackwood, 1874.

Molnar, Paul D. "Thomas F. Torrance and the Problem of Universalism." *Scottish Journal of Theology* 68 (2015) 164–86.

Moltmann, Jürgen. "Zur Bedeutung des Petrus Ramus für Philosophie und Theologie im Calvinismus." *Zeitschrift für Kirchengeschichte* 68 (1957) 295–318.

Moore, Jonathan D. "Calvin versus the Calvinists? The Case of John Preston (1587–1628)." *Reformation & Renaissance Review* 6 (2004) 327–48.

———. *English Hypothetical Universalism: John Preston and the Softening of Reformed Theology*. Grand Rapids: Eerdmans, 2007.

———. "The Extent of the Atonement: English Hypothetical Universalism versus Particular Redemption." In *Drawn into Controversie: Reformed Theological Diversity and Debates within Seventeenth-Century British Puritanism*, edited by Michael A. G. Haykin and Mark Jones, 124–61. Göttingen: Vandenhoeck & Ruprecht, 2011.

Mullan, David. "Theology in the Church of Scotland 1618–c. 1640: A Calvinist Consensus?" *Sixteenth Century Journal* 26 (1995) 595–617.

Muller, Richard A. *After Calvin: Studies in the Development of a Theological Tradition*. Oxford: Oxford University Press, 2003.

———. "Beyond Hypothetical Universalism: Moïse Amyraut (1596–1664) on Faith, Reason, and Ethics." In *The Theology of the French Reformed Churches: From Henri IV to the Revocation of the Edict of Nantes*, edited by Martin I. Klauber, 197–216. Reformed Historical-Theological Studies. Grand Rapids: Reformation Heritage, 2014.

———. "Calvin and the 'Calvinists': Assessing Continuities and Discontinuities between the Reformation and Orthodoxy." *Calvin Theological Journal* 30 (1995) 345–75; 31 (1996) 125–60.

———. *Calvin and the Reformed Tradition: On the Work of Christ and the Order of Salvation*. Grand Rapids: Baker Academic, 2012.

———. "Calvin, Beza and the Later Reformed on the Assurance of Salvation and the 'Practical Syllogism.'" In *Calvin and the Reformed Tradition: On the Work of Christ and the Order of Salvation*, 244–76. Grand Rapids: Baker Academic, 2012.

———. *Christ and the Decree: Christology and Predestination in Reformed Theology from Calvin to Perkins*. Grand Rapids: Baker, 2008.

———. "Dating John Davenant's *De Gallicana controversia sententia* in the Context of Debate over John Cameron: A Correction." *Calvin Theological Journal* 50 (2015) 10–22.

———. "Davenant and Du Moulin: Variant Approaches to Hypothetical Universalism." In *Calvin and the Reformed Tradition: On the Work of Christ and the Order of Salvation*, 126–60. Grand Rapids: Baker Academic, 2012.

———. *Dictionary of Greek and Latin Theological Terms: Drawn Principally from Protestant Scholastic Theology*. Grand Rapids: Baker, 1985.

———. "Diversity in the Reformed Tradition: A Historiographical Introduction." In *Drawn into Controversie: Reformed Theological Diversity and Debates within Seventeenth-Century British Puritanism*, edited by Michael A. G. Haykin and Mark Jones, 11–30. Göttingen: Vandenhoeck & Ruprecht, 2011.

———. "Divine Covenants, Absolute and Conditional: John Cameron and the Early Orthodox Development of Reformed Covenant Theology." *Mid-America Journal of Theology* 17 (2006) 11–56.

———. "*Duplex cognitio dei* in the Theology of Early Reformed Orthodoxy." *Sixteenth Century Journal* 10 (1979) 51–61.

———. *God, Creation, and Providence in the Thought of Jacob Arminius: Sources and Directions of Scholastic Protestantism in the Era of Early Orthodoxy*. Grand Rapids: Baker, 1991.

———. "How Many Points?" *Calvin Theological Journal* 28 (1993) 425–33.

———. "John Calvin and Later Calvinism." In *The Cambridge Companion to Reformation Theology*, edited by David Bagchi and David C. Steinmetz, 130–49. Cambridge: Cambridge University Press, 2004.

———. "The Placement of Predestination in Reformed Theology: Issue or Non-Issue?" *Calvin Theological Journal* 40 (2005) 184–210.

———. *Post-Reformation Reformed Dogmatics*. 2nd ed. 4 vols. Grand Rapids: Baker, 2003.

———. "Reception and Response: Referencing and Understanding Calvin in Post-Reformation Calvinism." In *Calvin and His Influence, 1509–2009*, edited by Irena Backus and Philip Benedict, 182–201. New York: Oxford University Press, 2011.

———. Review of *English Hypothetical Universalism: John Preston and the Softening of Reformed Theology*, by Jonathan D. Moore. *Calvin Theological Journal* 43 (2008) 149–50.

———. "Revising the Predestination Paradigm: An Alternative to Supralapsarianism, Infralapsarianism, and Hypothetical Universalism." Fall Lecture Series at Mid-America Reformed Seminary (Dyer, IN), November 5–6, 2008.

———. "Scholasticism in Calvin: A Question of Relation and Disjunction." In *The Unaccommodated Calvin: Studies in the Foundation of a Theological Tradition*, 39–61. New York: Oxford University Press, 2000.

———. "Scholasticism, Reformation, Orthodoxy, and the Persistence of Christian Aristotelianism." *Trinity Journal* 19 (1998) 81–96.

———. "A Tale of Two Wills? Calvin and Amyraut on Ezekiel 18:23." *Calvin Theological Journal* 44 (2009) 211–25.

———. "'To Grant this Grace to All People and Nations': Calvin on Apostolicity and Mission." In *For God So Loved the World: Missiological Reflections in Honor of Roger S. Greenway*, edited by A. C. Leder, 211–32. Belleville, ON: Essence, 2006.

———. "Toward the *Pactum Salutis*: Locating the Origins of a Concept." *Mid-America Journal of Theology* 18 (2007) 11–65.

———. *The Unaccommodated Calvin: Studies in the Foundation of a Theological Tradition*. New York: Oxford University Press, 2002.

———. "Was Calvin a Calvinist?" In *Calvin and the Reformed Tradition: On the Work of Christ and the Order of Salvation*, 51–69. Grand Rapids: Baker Academic, 2012.

Murray, John. "The Atonement and the Free Offer of the Gospel." In *Collected Writings of John Murray*, vol. 1, 59–85. Carlisle, PA: Banner of Truth, 1976.

———. "Calvin on the Extent of the Atonement." *The Banner of Truth* 234 (March 1983) 20–22.

———. "The Free Offer of the Gospel." In *Collected Writings of John Murray*, vol. 4, 113–32. Carlisle, PA: Banner of Truth, 1982.

———. *Redemption Accomplished and Applied*. Grand Rapids: Eerdmans, 1955.

Naselli, Andrew David. "John Owen's Argument for Definite Atonement in *The Death of Death in the Death of Christ*: A Summary and Evaluation." *The Southern Baptist Journal of Theology* 14 (2010) 60–82.

Naselli, Andrew David, and Mark A. Snoeberger, eds. *Perspectives on the Extent of the Atonement: Three Views*. Nashville: B&H Academic, 2015.

Nelson, David P. "The Design, Nature, and Extent of the Atonement." In *Calvinism: A Southern Baptist Dialogue*, edited by E. Ray Clendenen and Brad J. Waggoner, 115–38. Nashville: B&H Academic, 2008.

Nettles, Thomas J. "John Calvin's Understanding of the Death of Christ." In *Whomever He Wills: A Surprising Display of Sovereign Mercy*, edited by Matthew M. Barrett and Thomas J. Nettles, 293–315. Cape Coral: Founders, 2012.

———. "Review of *Whosoever Will: A Biblical-Theological Critique of Five-Point Calvinism*." https://founders.org/reviews/whosoever-will-a-biblical-theological-critique-of-five-point-calvinism.

Nicole, Roger. "Covenant, Universal Call and Definite Atonement." *Journal of the Evangelical Theological Society* 38 (1995) 403–11.

———. "John Calvin's View of the Extent of the Atonement." *Westminster Theological Journal* 47 (1985) 197–225. Reprinted in *An Elaboration of the Theology of Calvin*, edited by Richard C. Gamble, 119–47. New York: Garland, 1992.

———. *Moyse Amyraut: A Bibliography with Special Reference to the Controversy on Universal Grace*. New York: Garland, 1981.

———. "Moyse Amyraut (1596–1664) and the The Controversy on Universal Grace: First Phase (1634–1637)." PhD diss., Harvard University, 1966.

———. "Particular Redemption." In *Our Savior God: Man, Christ, and the Atonement*, edited by James M. Boice, 165–78. Grand Rapids: Baker, 1980.

———. *Standing Forth: Collected Writings of Roger Nicole*. Fearn, UK: Christian Focus, 2002.

Niesel, Wilhelm. *The Theology of Calvin*. Translated by Harold Knight. Philadelphia: Westminster, 1956.

Nomura, Shin. "The Extent of the Atonement in Calvin's Concept of the Preaching of the Gospel." ThM thesis, Western Theological Seminary, 1991.

Orr, James. *Progress of Dogma*. London: Hodder and Stoughton, 1901.

Orrick, Jim Scott. *Mere Calvinism*. Phillipsburg, NJ: P&R, 2019.

Owen, John. *The Works of John Owen*, edited by William H. Goold. 16 vols. London: Johnston and Hunter, 1852.

Owen, Paul. "John Calvin and Penal Substitutionary Atonement." In *Celebrating the Legacy of the Reformation*, edited by Kevin L. King, Edward Hindson, and Benjamin K. Forrest, 65-78. Nashville: B&H Academic, 2019.

Packer, J. I. "Calvin the Theologian." In *John Calvin: A Collection of Essays*, edited by G. Duffield, 149-75. Grand Rapids: Eerdmans, 1966.

———. *Introductory Essay to John Owen's* The Death of Death in the Death of Christ. Choteau, MT: Gospel Mission, 1980.

———. "The Love of God: Universal and Particular." In *The Grace of God and the Bondage of the Will*, vol. 2: *Historical and Theological Perspectives on Calvinism*, edited by Thomas R. Schreiner and Bruce A. Ware, 413-27. Grand Rapids: Baker, 1995.

———. "Saved by His Precious Blood: An Introduction to John Owen's *The Death of Death in the Death of Christ*." In *In My Place Condemned He Stood*, edited by J. I. Packer and Mark Dever, 111-44. Wheaton, IL: Crossway, 2008.

———. "What Did the Cross Achieve? The Logic of Penal Substitution." *Tyndale Bulletin* 25 (1974) 3-45.

Partee, Charles. "Calvin's Central Dogma Again." *Sixteenth Century Journal* 18 (1987) 191-99.

———. "The Phylogeny of Calvin's Progeny: A Prolusion." In *Evangelical Calvinism: Essays Resourcing the Continuing Reformation of the Church*, edited by Myk Habets and Bobby Grow, 23-61. Eugene, OR: Pickwick, 2012.

———. *The Theology of John Calvin*. Louisville, KY: Westminster/John Knox, 2008.

Paul, Robert S. "The Reformers and Their Followers." In *The Atonement and the Sacraments*, 91-131. London: Hodder & Stoughton, 1961.

Penner, Myron. "Calvin, Barth, and the Subject of Atonement." In *Calvin, Barth, and Reformed Theology*, edited by Neil B. MacDonald and Carl Trueman, 118-45. Paternoster Theological Monographs. Milton Keynes: Paternoster, 2008.

Peterson, Robert A. *Calvin and the Atonement*. Rev. ed. Fearn, UK: Mentor, 1999.

———. "Calvin on Christ's Saving Work." In *A Theological Guide to Calvin's Institutes: Essays and Analysis*, edited by David W. Hall and Peter A. Lillback, 226-47. Phillipsburg, NJ: P&R, 2008.

———. *Calvin's Doctrine of the Atonement*. Phillipsburg, NJ: Presbyterian and Reformed, 1983.

———. *Salvation Accomplished by the Son: The Work of Christ*. Wheaton, IL: Crossway, 2012.

———. "To Reconcile to Himself All Things: Colossians 1:20." *Presbyterion* 36 (2010) 37-46.

Picirilli, Robert E. *Grace, Faith, Free Will. Contrasting Views of Salvation: Calvinism & Arminianism*. Nashville: Randall House, 2002.

Pieper, Francis. *Christian Dogmatics*. 4 vols. St. Louis: Concordia, 1951.

Pinnock, Clark H. *A Wideness in God's Mercy: The Finality of Jesus Christ in a World of Religions*. Grand Rapids: Zondervan, 1992.

Piper, John. "Are There Two Wills in God? Divine Election and God's Desire for All to Be Saved?" In *The Grace of God and the Bondage of the Will*, vol. 1: *Biblical and Practical Perspectives on Calvinism*, edited by Thomas R. Schreiner and Bruce A. Ware, 107-31. Grand Rapids: Baker, 1995.

———. *Does God Desire All to Be Saved?* Wheaton, IL: Crossway, 2013.

———. *Five Points: Towards a Deeper Experience of God's Grace*. Fearn, UK: Christian Focus, 2013.

———. "'My Glory I Will Not Give to Another': Preaching the Fullness of Definite Atonement to the Glory of God." In *From Heaven He Came and Sought Her: Definite Atonement in Historical, Biblical, Theological, and Pastoral Perspective*, edited by David Gibson and Jonathan Gibson, 633–67. Wheaton, IL: Crossway, 2013.

Pittsley, Jeremy. "To Purify a People: A Definite Design in the Death of Christ." ThM thesis, Detroit Baptist Theological Seminary, 2008.

Placher, William. *Domestication of Transcendence: How Modern Thinking about God Went Wrong*. Louisville, KY: Westminster/John Knox, 1996.

Ponter, David W. "A Brief History of Deviant Calvinism." MDiv paper. Reformed Theological Seminary, 2004.

———. "Calvin and Calvinism." http://calvinandcalvinism.com.

———. "Calvin and the Decree." MDiv paper. Reformed Theological Seminary, 2005.

———. "The Collegiate Suffrage of the Divines of Great Britain, Concerning the Five Articles Controverted at the Synod of Dort." http://calvinandcalvinism.com/?p=11317.

———. "For Whom Did Christ Die?" http://calvinandcalvinism.com/?page_id=7147.

———. "John Calvin and Tileman Heshusius." http://calvinandcalvinism.com?p=175.

———. "John Calvin (1509–1564) on Unlimited Expiation, Sin-Bearing, Redemption and Reconciliation." http://calvinandcalvinism.com?p=230.

———. "Peter Martyr Vermigli (1499–1563) on 1 Timothy 2:4." http://calvinandcalvinism.com/?p=79.

———. "Review Essay (Part One): John Calvin on the Death of Christ and the Reformation's Forgotten Doctrine of Universal Vicarious Satisfaction: A Review and Critique of Tom Nettles' Chapter in *Whomever He Wills*." *Southwestern Journal of Theology* 55 (2012) 138–58.

———. "Review Essay (Part Two): John Calvin on the Death of Christ and the Reformation's Forgotten Doctrine of Universal Vicarious Satisfaction: A Review and Critique of Tom Nettles' Chapter in *Whomever He Wills*." *Southwestern Journal of Theology* 55 (2012) 252–70.

———. "Robert Letham on the English Hypothetical Universalists at the Westminster Assembly." http://calvinandcalvinism.com/?s=amyraut&paged=9.

Prestwich, Menna, ed. *International Calvinism, 1541–1715*. Oxford: Clarendon, 1985.

Proctor, Lawrence. "The Theology of Moïse Amyraut Considered as a Reaction against Seventeenth-Century Calvinism." PhD diss., University of Leeds, 1952.

Pugh, Ben. *Atonement Theories: A Way through the Maze*. Eugene, OR: Cascade, 2014.

Purves, Andrew. *Exploring Christology and Atonement: Conversations with John McLeod Campbell H. R. Mackintosh and T. F. Torrance*. Downers Grove, IL: IVP Academic, 2015.

Quick, John. *Synodicon in Gallia Reformata*. 2 vols. London: Parkhurst and Robinson, 1692.

Rainbow, Jonathan H. "*Redemptor Ecclesiae, Redemptor Mundi*: An Historical and Theological Study of John Calvin's Doctrine of the Extent of Redemption." PhD diss., University of California Santa Barbara, 1986.

———. *The Will of God and the Cross: An Historical and Theological Study of John Calvin's Doctrine of Limited Redemption*. San Jose: Pickwick, 1990.

Rehnman, Sebastian. "A Particular Defense of Particularism." *Journal of Reformed Theology* 6 (2012) 24–34.

Reid, J. K. S. "Editor's Introduction." In *Concerning the Eternal Predestination of God.* Translated by J. K. S. Reid, 8–44. London: Clarke, 1961.

———. "The Office of Christ in Predestination." *Scottish Journal of Theology* 1 (1948) 5–19; 166–83.

Reid, W. Stanford. "The Transmission of Calvinism in the Sixteenth Century." In *John Calvin: His Influence in the Western World*, edited by W. Stanford Reid, 31–52. Grand Rapids: Zondervan, 1982.

Rex, Walter. *Essays on Pierre Bayle and Religious Controversy*. The Hague: Nijhoff, 1965.

Reymond, Robert L. "A Consistent Supralapsarian Perspective on Election." In *Perspectives on Election: Five Views*, edited by Chad Owen Brand, 150–94. Nashville: B&H Academic, 2006.

———. *A New Systematic Theology of the Christian Faith*. 2nd ed. Nashville: Thomas Nelson, 1998.

Rolston, Holmes, III. *John Calvin versus the Westminster Confession*. Richmond: John Knox, 1972.

———. "Responsible Man in Reformed Theology: Calvin versus the Westminster Confession." *Scottish Journal of Theology* 23 (1970) 129–56.

Rouwendal, P. L. "Calvin's Forgotten Classical Position on the Extent of the Atonement: About Sufficiency, Efficiency, and Anachronism." *Westminster Theological Journal* 70 (2008) 317–35.

Saito, Masahiko. "The Theory of the Atonement in the Theology of Luther and Calvin." MST thesis, Southern Methodist University, 1959.

Scaer, David. "The Nature and Extent of the Atonement in Lutheran Theology." *Bulletin of the Evangelical Theological Society* 10 (1967) 179–87.

Schaeffer, Harry. "The Doctrine of Atonement in the Writings of Luther and Calvin." PhD diss., University of Chicago, 1920.

Schaff, Philip. *The Creeds of Christendom, with a History and Critical Notes*. New York: Harper, 1887.

Sell, Alan. *The Great Debate: Calvinism, Arminianism, and Salvation*. Reprint, Eugene, OR: Wipf & Stock, 1998.

Shand, Mark. "The English Delegation to the Synod of Dort." *British Reformed Journal* 28 (1999) 37–39.

———. "John Davenant: A Jewel of the Reformed Churches or a Tarnished Stone." *Protestant Reformed Theological Journal* 31 (1998) 43–69; 32 (1998) 20–28.

Shedd, William G. T. *Dogmatic Theology*. Classic reprint edition. Grand Rapids: Zondervan, 1971.

Shepherd, Victor A. *The Nature and Function of Faith in the Theology of John Calvin*. NABPR Dissertation Series 2. Macon, GA: Mercer University Press, 1983.

Shultz, Gary L., Jr. "A Biblical and Theological Defense of a Multi-Intentioned View of the Extent of the Atonement." PhD diss., The Southern Baptist Theological Seminary, 2008.

———. "God's Purposes in the Atonement for the Nonelect." *Bibliotheca Sacra* 165 (2008) 145–63.

———. *A Multi-Intentioned View of the Extent of the Atonement*. Eugene, OR: Wipf & Stock, 2013.

———. "Why a Genuine Universal Gospel Call Requires an Atonement that Paid for the Sins of All People." *Evangelical Quarterly* 82 (2010) 111–23.

Sinnema, Donald. "Are the Canons of Dordt a True Reflection of Calvin's View of Reprobation?" *In die Skriflig* 52 (2018) 1–11.

———. "Calvin and the Canons of Dordt (1619)." *Church History & Religious Culture* 91 (2011) 87–103.

———. "Calvin's View of Reprobation." In *Calvin for Today*, edited by Joel R. Beeke, 115–36. Grand Rapids: Reformation Heritage, 2009.

Smit, Dirkie, "Justice and Divine Justice?" In *What Is Justification About? Reformed Contributions to an Ecumenical Theme*, edited by Michael Weinrich and John P. Burgess, 88–120. Grand Rapids: Eerdmans, 2009.

Smith, Scott A. "Pananastasism—A Penal Substitutionary Model of a Definite Universal Atonement: God's Gracious Substitution to Pay the Penalty Due Every Individual in Order to Righteously Resurrect All Mankind and Save a Particular People for Himself." PhD diss., Piedmont International University, 2015.

Snoddy, Richard. *The Soteriology of James Ussher: The Act and Object of Saving Faith*. Oxford Studies in Historical Theology. Oxford: Oxford University Press, 2014.

Snoeberger, Mark A. "Introduction." In *Perspectives on the Extent of the Atonement: Three Views*, edited by Andrew David Naselli and Mark A. Snoeberger, 1–17. Nashville: B&H Academic, 2015.

———. "The Logical Priority of Regeneration to Saving Faith in a Theological *Ordo Salutis*." *Detroit Baptist Seminary Journal* 7 (2002) 49–93.

Snyder, Darrin W. *Atonement, Justice, and Peace: The Message of the Cross and the Mission of the Church*. Grand Rapids: Eerdmans, 2011.

Stagg, John W. *Calvin, Twisse and Edwards on the Universal Salvation of Those Dying in Infancy*. Richmond, VA: Presbyterian Committee of Publication, 1902.

Steele, David N., et al. *The Five Points of Calvinism Defined, Defended, and Documented*. 2nd ed. Philadelphia: Presbyterian & Reformed, 2004.

Steinmetz, David. *Calvin in Context*. New York: Oxford University Press, 1995.

———. *Reformers in the Wings*. Philadelphia: Fortress, 1971.

———. "The Scholastic Calvin." In *Protestant Scholasticism: Essays in Reassessment*, edited by Carl R. Trueman and R. Scott Clark, 16–30. Carlisle, UK: Paternoster, 1999.

Stephens, W. Peter. "Bullinger and Zwingli on the Salvation of the Heathen." *Reformation & Renaissance Review* 7 (2005) 283–300.

Stewart, Kenneth J. "The Points of Calvinism: Retrospect and Prospect." *Scottish Bulletin of Evangelical Theology* 26 (2008) 187–203.

———. *Ten Myths about Calvinism: Recovering the Breadth of the Reformed Tradition*. Downers Grove, IL: IVP Academic, 2011.

Strange, Daniel. "Slain for the World? The 'Uncomfortability' of the 'Unevangelized' for a Universal Atonement." In *From Heaven He Came and Sought Her: Definite Atonement in Historical, Biblical, Theological, and Pastoral Perspective*, edited by David Gibson and Jonathan Gibson, 585–605. Wheaton, IL: Crossway, 2013.

Strehle, Stephen. "The Extent of the Atonement and the Synod of Dort." *Westminster Theological Journal* 51 (1989) 1–23.

———. "The Extent of the Atonement within the Theological Systems of the Sixteenth and Seventeenth Centuries." ThD diss., Dallas Theological Seminary, 1980.

———. "Universal Grace and Amyraldianism." *Westminster Theological Journal* 51 (1989) 345–57.

Strimple, Robert B. "St. Anselm's *Cur Deus Homo* and John Calvin's Doctrine of the Atonement." In *Anselm: Aosta, Bec and Canterbury*, edited by D. E. Luscombe and G. R. Evans, 248–60. Sheffield, UK: Sheffield Academic, 1996.

Strivens, Robert. *Philip Doddridge and the Shaping of Evangelical Dissent.* Ashgate Studies in Evangelicalism. Burlington, VT: Ashgate, 2015.

Strohm, Christoph. "Methodology in Discussion of Calvin and Calvinism." In *Calvinus Praeceptor Ecclesiae: Papers of the International Congress on Calvin Research, Princeton, August 20–24, 2002*, edited by Herman J. Selderhuis, 65–105. Geneva: Librairie Droz, 2004.

———. "Theologie und Zeitgeist: Beobachtungen zum Siegeszug der Methode des Petrus Ramus am Beginn der Moderne." *Zeitschrift für Kirchengeschichte* 110 (1999) 352–71.

Strong, Augustus Hopkins. *Systematic Theology: A Compendium Designed for the Use of Theological Students.* Westwood, NJ: Revell, 1907.

Suhany, Alan Michael. "John Calvin and the Extent of the Atonement Revisited." Paper presented at the 45th Annual Meeting of the Evangelical Theological Society (Washington, DC), November 20, 1993.

Sumner, Darren. "Theory and Metaphor in Calvin's Doctrine of the Atonement." *Princeton Theological Review* 13 (2007) 49–60.

Swinne, Axel Hilmar. *John Cameron, Philosoph und Theologe (1579–1625): Bibliographisch-kritische Analyse der Hand- und Druckschriften sowie der Cameron-Literatur.* Marburg: Elwert, 1968.

Tamburello, Dennis E. *Union with Christ: John Calvin and the Mysticism of St. Bernard.* Louisville, KY: Westminster John Knox, 1994.

Tay, Edwin E. M. *The Priesthood of Christ: Atonement in the Theology of John Owen (1616–1683).* Studies in Christian History and Thought. Milton Keynes. UK: Paternoster, 2014.

Thomas, G. Michael. "Calvin and English Calvinism: A Review Article." *Scottish Bulletin of Evangelical Theology* 16 (1998) 111–27.

———. *The Extent of the Atonement: A Dilemma for Reformed Theology from Calvin to the Consensus (1536–1675).* Carlisle, UK: Paternoster, 1997.

Thomas, Owen. *The Atonement Controversy in Welsh Theological Literature and Debate, 1707–1841.* Edinburgh: Banner of Truth, 2002.

Thompson, Mark D. "Calvin on the Cross of Christ." In *John Calvin and Evangelical Theology: Legacy and Prospect in Celebration of the Quincentenary of John Calvin*, edited by Sung Wook Chung, 107–27. Louisville, KY: Westminster John Knox, 2009.

———. "Calvin on the Mediator." In *Engaging with Calvin: Aspects of the Reformer's Legacy for Today*, edited by Mark D. Thompson, 106–35. Nottingham, UK: Apollos, 2009.

Thorson, Stephen. "Tensions in Calvin's View of Faith: Unexamined Assumptions in R. T. Kendall's *Calvin and English Calvinism to 1649*." *Journal of the Evangelical Theological Society* 37 (1994) 413–26.

Toon, Peter. *The Emergence of Hyper-Calvinism in English Nonconformity, 1689–1765.* Reprint, Eugene, OR: Wipf & Stock, 2011.

Torrance, James B. "The Concept of Federal Theology—Was Calvin a Federal Theologian?" In *Calvinus Sacrae Scripturae Professor: Calvin as Confessor of Holy Scripture*, edited by Wilhelm H. Neuser, 15–40. Grand Rapids: Eerdmans, 1994.

———. "The Incarnation and 'Limited Atonement.'" *Evangelical Quarterly* 55 (1983) 83–94.

———. "Strengths and Weaknesses of the Westminster Theology." In *The Westminster Confession in the Church Today*, edited by Alasdair I. C. Heron, 40–54. Edinburgh: Saint Andrew, 1982.

Torrance, Thomas F. *Atonement: The Person and Work of Christ.* Edited by Robert T. Walker. Milton Keynes, UK: Paternoster, 2009.

———. "The Atonement: The Singularity of Christ and the Finality of the Cross: The Atonement and the Moral Order." In *Universalism and the Doctrine of Hell*, edited by Nigel M. de S. Cameron, 225–56. Carlisle, UK: Paternoster, 1992.

———. *Scottish Theology: From John Knox to John Mcleod Campbell.* Edinburgh: T. & T. Clark, 1996.

Treat, Jeremy R. "Expansive Particularity: Calvin's Way of Avoiding 'Either/Or' Reductionism and 'Both/And' Homogeneity." *Trinity Journal* 34 (2013) 45–59.

Troxel, A. Craig. "Amyraut 'at' the Assembly: The Westminster Confession of Faith and the Extent of the Atonement." *Presbyterion* 22 (1996) 43–55.

Trueman, Carl R. "Atonement and the Covenant of Redemption: John Owen on the Nature of Christ's Satisfaction." In *From Heaven He Came and Sought Her: Definite Atonement in Historical, Biblical, Theological, and Pastoral Perspective*, edited by David Gibson and Jonathan Gibson, 201–23. Wheaton, IL: Crossway, 2013.

———. "Calvin and Calvinism." In *The Cambridge Companion to John Calvin*, edited by Donald K. McKim, 225–44. Cambridge: Cambridge University Press, 2004.

———. *The Claims of Truth: John Owen's Trinitarian Theology.* Carlisle, UK: Paternoster, 1998.

———. "Election: Calvin's Theology and Its Early Reception." In *Calvin's Theology and Its Reception: Disputes, Developments, and New Possibilities*, edited by J. Todd Billings and I. John Hesselink, 97–120. Louisville, KY: Westminster John Knox, 2012.

———. "From Calvin to Gillespie on Covenant: Mythological Excess or an Exercise in Doctrinal Development?" *International Journal of Systematic Theology* 11 (2009) 378–97.

———. "The Necessity of the Atonement." In *Drawn into Controversie: Reformed Theological Diversity and Debates within Sixteenth-Century British Puritanism*, edited by Michael A. G. Haykin and Mark Jones, 204–22. Göttingen: Vandenhoeck & Ruprecht, 2011.

———. "The Reception of Calvin: Historical Considerations." *Church History and Religious Culture* (2011) 19–27.

Trueman, Carl R., and R. Scott Clark, eds. *Protestant Scholasticism: Essays in Reassessment.* Carlisle, UK: Paternoster, 1999.

Ursinus, Zacharius. *The Commentary of Dr. Zacharius Ursinus on the Heidelberg Catechism.* Phillipsburg, NJ: P&R, 1994.

Vail, William H. "The Five Points of Calvinism Historically Considered." *The Outlook* 104 (June 21, 1913) 394.

van Asselt, Willem J. "Christ's Atonement: A Multi-Dimensional Approach." *Calvin Theological Journal* 38 (2003) 52–67.

van Asselt, Willem J., and Eef Dekker. *Reformation and Scholasticism: An Ecumenical Enterprise.* Grand Rapids: Baker, 2001.

van Buren, Paul Matthews. *Christ in Our Place: The Substitutionary Character of Calvin's Doctrine of Reconciliation.* Edinburgh: Oliver and Boyd, 1957.

Van Dixhoorn, C. B. "Reforming the Reformation: Theological Debate at the Westminster Assembly 1642–1652." PhD diss., University of Cambridge, 2004.

Van Dyk, Leanne. *The Desire of Divine Love: John McLeod Campbell's Doctrine of the Atonement.* Studies in Church History 4. New York: Lang, 1995.

———. "How Does Jesus Make a Difference?" In *Essentials of Christian Theology*, edited by William C. Placher, 205–20. Louisville, KY: Westminster John Knox, 2000.
van Stam, Frans Pieter. *The Controversy over the Theology of Saumur, 1635–1650: Disrupting Debates among the Huguenots in Complicated Circumstances*. Amsterdam: APA-Holland University Press, 1988.
Venema, Cornelis. "Union with Christ, the 'Twofold Grace of God,' and the 'Order of Salvation' in Calvin's Theology." In *Calvin for Today*, edited by Joel R. Beeke, 91–114. Grand Rapids: Reformation Heritage, 2009.
Waldron, Sam. "The Biblical Confirmation of Particular Redemption." In *Calvinism: A Southern Baptist Dialogue*, edited by E. Ray Clendenen and Brad J. Waggoner, 139–52. Nashville: B&H Academic, 2008.
Wallace, Ronald S. *The Atoning Death of Christ*. Westchester, IL: Crossway, 1981.
Ware, Bruce A. "*Cur Deus Trinus*? The Relation of the Trinity to Christ's Identity as Savior and to the Efficacy of His Atoning Death." *Southern Baptist Journal of Theology* 10 (2006) 48–56.
———. "Extent of the Atonement: Outline of the Issue, Positions, Key Texts, and Key Theological Arguments." http://mydigitalseminary.com/wp-content/uploads/2013/05/Ware-Extent-of-the-Atonement.pdf.
Warfield, Benjamin B. *Calvin and Augustine*. Philadelphia: Presbyterian & Reformed, 1956.
———. *Calvin and Calvinism*. New York: Oxford University Press, 1931.
———. *The Plan of Salvation*. Reprint, Eugene, OR: Wipf & Stock, 2001.
Wax, Trevin. "Why Calvin Is More Biblical Than Some Calvinists." https://blogs.thegospelcoalition.org/trevinwax/2009/08/11/why-calvin-is-more-biblical-than-some-calvinists.
Weber, Hans Emil. *Reformation, Orthodoxie, und Rationalismus*. Beiträge zur Förderung christlicher Theologie 35, 45, 51. Gütersloh: Bertelsmann, 1937–51.
Wells, David R. "*Decretum Dei Speciale*: An Analysis of the Content and Significance of Calvin's Doctrine of Soteriological Predestination." ThM thesis, Trinity Evangelical Divinity School, 1967.
Wells, Paul. *Cross Words: The Biblical Doctrine of the Atonement*. Fearn, UK: Christian Focus, 2006.
Wendel, François. *Calvin: Origins and Development of His Religious Thought*. New York: Harper & Row, 1963.
Wenger, Thomas. "The New Perspective on Calvin: Responding to the Recent Calvin Interpretations." *Journal of the Evangelical Theological Society* 50 (2007) 311–28.
———. "Theological Spectacles and a Paradigm of Centrality: A Reply to Marcus Johnson." *Journal of the Evangelical Theological Society* 51 (2008) 559–72.
Wenkel, David H. "Amyraldianism: Theological Criteria for Identification and Comparative Analysis." *Chafer Theological Journal* 11 (2005) 83–96.
———. "John Bunyan's Soteriology during His Pre-Prison Period (1656–1659): Amyraldian or High-Calvinist?" *Scottish Journal of Theology* 3 (2005) 333–52.
———. "John Bunyan's Theory of Atonement in His Early Doctrinal and Polemical Works: Amyraldian or Particular?" ThM thesis, Trinity International University, 2004.
Wiley, David N. "Calvin's Doctrine of Predestination: His Principal Soteriological and Polemical Doctrine." PhD diss., Duke University, 1971.

Williams, Garry J. "The Definite Atonement of Penal Substitutionary Atonement." In *From Heaven He Came and Sought Her: Definite Atonement in Historical, Biblical, Theological, and Pastoral Perspective*, edited by David Gibson and Jonathan Gibson, 461–82. Wheaton, IL: Crossway, 2013.

———. "Karl Barth and the Doctrine of the Atonement." In *Engaging with Barth: Contemporary Evangelical Critiques*, edited by David Gibson and Daniel Strange, 249–70. Milton Keynes, UK: Paternoster, 2012.

———. "Punishment God Cannot Twice Inflict: The Double Payment Argument *Redivivus*." In *From Heaven He Came and Sought Her: Definite Atonement in Historical, Biblical, Theological, and Pastoral Perspective*, edited by David Gibson and Jonathan Gibson, 483–518. Wheaton, IL: Crossway, 2013.

Williams, Jarvis J. *For Whom Did Christ Die? The Extent of the Atonement in Paul's Theology*. Paternoster Biblical Monographs. Milton Keynes, UK: Paternoster, 2012.

Williams, Timothy A. *The Heart of Piety: An Encouraging Study in Calvin's Doctrine of Assurance*. Woodstock, NY: Heritage, 2011.

Wisse, Maartin, et al., eds. *Scholasticism Reformed: Essays in Honour of Willem van Asselt*. Studies in Theology and Religion 14. Leiden: Brill, 2010.

Witsius, Herman. *The Economy of the Covenants*. Translated by William Crookshank. 2 vols. 1822. Escondido: Den Dulk Christian Foundation, 1990.

Wolterstorff, Nicholas. "The Assurance of Faith." In *Selected Essays*, vol. 2: *Practices of Belief*, edited by Terence Cuneo, 289–312. Cambridge: Cambridge University Press, 2010.

Wright, David F. "The Atonement in Reformation Theology." *European Journal of Theology* 8 (1999) 37–48.

———. "Calvin's Accommodating God." In *Calvinus sincerioris religionis vindex*, edited by Wilhelm H. Neuser and Brian G. Armstrong, 3–19. Kirksville: Sixteenth Century Journal, 1997.

———. "Calvin's 'Accommodation' Revisited." In *Calvin as Exegete*, edited by Peter de Klerk, 171–90. Grand Rapids: CRC, 1995.

Zemek, George J. *A Biblical Theology of the Doctrines of Sovereign Grace: Exegetical Considerations of Key Anthropological, Hamartiological, and Soteriological Terms and Motifs*. Little Rock, AR: BTDSG, 2002.

Name Index

Allen, David L., 5, 14, 136n51, 147n100, 159n154
Ames, William, 24
Amyraut, Moïse, 14–15, 14n34, 23, 77n91, 82n111, 84, 85n2, 116n145, 148
Aquinas, Thomas, 18n48, 90, 100n64
Archbald, Paul, 51n116
Armstrong, Brian, 91–92, 92n25, 92n29, 93n32, 95, 95–96n40, 99n59, 104–6, 104n75
Arrowsmith, John, 108n91, 117n153
Augustine of Hippo, 59n2, 77, 99n57

Balcanqual, Walter, 120nn165
Baron, Robert, 109
Battles, Ford Lewis, 154n129
Baxter, Richard, 109, 117–18
Bayle, Pierre, 92n27
Beeke, Joel, 22n66
Bell, Charles, 13, 37n62, 40n75, 61n11
Bellamy, Joseph, 96n44
Berkhof, Louis, 89n18, 146n94
Beza, Theodore, 14, 48n107, 50n110, 83n112, 89n16, 107n83, 148
Blacketer, Raymond, 4, 4n19, 5n27, 18n48, 56n141, 66n41, 86n5
Blocher, Henri, 40n75, 61n11, 117n150, 137n53, 150n112, 160–61
Blunt, David, 117n151

Boersma, Hans, 15–16n39, 15–17, 15n38, 16n40, 61
Boettner, Loraine, 113n126, 128n20
Bolsec, Jerome, 49n108
Bradwardine, Thomas, 59n2
Bucanus, Gulielmus, 18n49
Bucer, Martin, 23
Bullinger, E. W., 82n111
Bullinger, Heinrich, 152, 152n122
Burman, Franz, 93n31
Byl, Bart, 113n126

Calamy, Edmund, 108, 108n91, 117n151, 117n153, 130n26
Cameron, John, 23, 91, 92n29, 93–94n32, 93n31, 95n40, 107, 116n145
Campbell, John McLeod, 55n135
Cappel, Louis, 116n145
Carleton, George, 120nn165
Carson, D. A., 127n13
Cartwright, Thomas, 124
Charnock, Stephen, 96n44
Clark, Gordon, 127n13
Clifford, Alan, 14, 15n38, 22n64, 51n115, 56n140, 81n110
Cocceius, Johannes, 93n31
Coppenger, Mark, 147n96
Costley, Stephen L., 63n22
Crisp, Oliver, 3n15, 89n18, 110n102, 120–21, 136n51, 142
Crisp, Tobias, 33n41
Cunningham, William, 11, 11n18, 24–25, 25n75, 61

NAME INDEX

Dabney, Robert L., 132n33, 141, 144, 144n80, 144n86
Daniel, Curt, 13–14, 14n29, 23n71, 51n114, 60n5, 62, 86n4, 88n15, 135, 137, 137n54
Davenant, John, 81–82n111, 89n18, 98n51, 100, 100n65, 107, 109n95, 110n102, 118–23, 120nn165, 121nn172, 133n38, 139n59, 147, 148
Demarest, Bruce, 55n136, 94n34, 107n83
Denlinger, Aaron Clay, 109n99, 121
Djaballah, Amar, 105n79, 108n89
Doddridge, Philip, 96n46
Douty, Norman, 144n79
Doyle, Robert Colin, 126n9
Du Moulin, Pierre, 92, 105n82, 120nn166, 123, 142n70, 148

Eaton, John, 33n41

Ferguson, Sinclair, 137n54
Ferguson, William Stark, 37n62
Foord, Martin, 4n18, 47n101, 70–72, 71n57, 77, 79, 100n64, 115n136
Ford, Thomas, 108n91, 117n153
Fraser, James, 113n122
Fuller, Morris J., 141

Garcia, Mark A., 33n41, 111n104
Gatiss, Lee, 33n41, 107, 121, 121nn172, 134n42, 141
George, Timothy, 59–60n2
Georgius, 65
Gerstner, John, 37n62
Gibson, Jonathan, 54n135, 137n54
Goad, Thomas, 120nn165
Godfrey, W. Robert, 11, 18n49
Golding, Arthur, 45n91
Gomarus, Franciscus, 89n16
Gootjes, Albert, 121
Gottschalk of Orbais, 23, 59n2
Greenbury, James, 59n2
Grow, Bobby, 126n8, 156n137

Hall, Basil, 3n17, 103n72

Hall, Joseph, 107
Hammett, John, 137–38
Harding, Matthew, 5, 14, 127
Helm, Paul, 2n14, 4, 5, 12, 22n66, 40n75, 48n107, 54, 83n115, 86n4, 87n9, 128n20, 149–50, 162n165
Hesselink, John, 22n63
Hildebrand, Herman, 107
Hodge, Archibald Alexander, 15n37, 44n87
Hodge, Charles, 143–44n79, 155
Holmes, Stephen, 6n29, 126–27n12
Horton, Michael, 125, 142, 145n91
Huber, Samuel, 90, 90n21

Jeffery, Steve, 98n52
John of Damascus, 100n64
Johnson, Jeffrey, 130n23, 155n135
Jurieu, Pierre, 124

Kendall, R. T., 13, 13n26
Kennedy, Kevin, 1, 1n1, 5, 10n5, 115, 135n44
Kieser, Ty, 54n129
Kimedoncius, Jacob, 18n49, 68, 71n57
Kuiper, Rienk, 48n107, 130n26, 133n38, 134, 134–35n44, 146, 146n94, 154–55
Kuyper, Abraham, 2

Lane, Anthony, 4n21, 13, 13–14n28, 33, 33n42, 57n144, 83n116, 103–4, 103n73, 126, 150
Latham, Bob, 117n152
Leahy, Frederick, 19n51, 60
Letham, Robert, 21–22, 21–22n63, 23, 54, 124nn184, 136n50
Lombard, Peter, 18n48, 90
Luther, Martin, 48n107, 126n12
Lynch, Michael, 107, 117n151, 118, 121–22, 129n21, 140–41, 140–41n64, 141n65

Macleod, Donald, 87n9, 98n51
Manton, Thomas, 96n44
Martinius, Matthias, 118

McAfee, Cleland Boyd, 113n126
McGowan, Andrew T. B., 10–11, 115n140, 125
McNeill, J. T., 134n43
Miller, Perry, 124
Moore, Jonathan, 2, 2n10, 116–17, 117n150, 117n152, 121, 121nn172
Muller, Richard, 1n1, 2, 3n17, 42n78, 59n2, 68, 77, 81–82n111, 87–88n12, 90, 93n31, 93n32, 94n32, 94n34, 100n64, 106n83, 107, 110–11n103, 111, 111n104, 114, 114n134, 118, 120, 120–21nn172, 120nn166, 120nn169, 141, 142n71, 148–49, 149n104, 151, 152, 153n128, 157n140, 159–60, 159n151, 159n152
Murray, John, 12n24, 48n107, 135n44
Musculus, Wolfgang, 68, 152

Naselli, Andrew, 145–46n92
Nettles, Thomas, 5, 11, 132n33
Nicole, Roger, 7n36, 10, 24n73, 37n63, 53n129, 65–66n36, 86n5, 103n73, 110n102, 128n20, 136, 145n92

Orrick, Jim Scott, 145n88
Ovey, Michael, 98n52
Owen, John, 24, 68n46, 84, 89n18, 96n40, 100, 100–101n65, 148n102

Paraeus, David, 18, 130n26
Partee, Charles, 9n3, 126n8
Penner, Myron, 21, 21n60
Perkins, William, 24
Peterson, Robert, 6, 9, 9n1, 21, 22–23, 22n64, 22n65, 23n71, 27, 28, 54, 63–64, 127n14
Piper, John, 99n53, 145–47, 145n89, 146n95, 147n98, 147n100
Placher, William, 103–4n73

Ponter, David, 5, 5n27, 43n83, 47n101, 60n5, 65n32, 68n46, 85n2, 88n15, 90–91n22, 91n24, 117n153, 118, 121, 121n175
Preston, John, 13n26, 107, 146n92
Pugh, Ben, 151n119
Purves, Andrew, 55n135

Quick, John, 20n57, 97, 101–2

Rainbow, Jonathan, 23, 33n39, 40n75, 43n83, 48n107, 60n5, 98n51
Reid, J.K.S., 127, 127n16, 139–40n63
Reid, W. Stanford, 103n73
Reymond, Robert L., 102n69
Reynolds, Edwards, 117n153
Rivet, Andre, 107
Roberts, Francis, 93n31
Rous, Francis, 108n91, 117n153
Rouwendal, P. L., 4, 7n36, 17–21, 18–19n50, 18n49, 19n51, 20n55, 24–25n74, 51n116, 61, 79n103, 88

Sach, Andrew, 98n52
Schaff, Philip, 106n82
Seaman, Lazarus, 108n91, 117n153
Sell, Alan, 142n74
Shedd, William, 143
Shultz, Gary L., Jr., 86n7, 138
Sinnema, Donald, 119, 142
Spellman, Ched, 113n126
Stewart, Kenneth J., 1–2, 1n1, 113n126, 142
Strehle, Stephen, 47n101, 83n115, 102, 115n140
Strohm, Christoph, 1–2, 2n8
Strong, A. H., 55n136

Tay, Edwin E. M., 158n149
Thomas, G. Michael, 17, 18n49, 57n144, 79n103, 85, 92n29, 95, 98n52, 106n82, 133n35
Thomas Aquinas, 18n48, 90, 100n64
Thompson, Mark D., 3n17

Toon, Peter, 16n41
Torrance, James B., 54–55n135
Torrance, Thomas F., 55n135, 130n25
Treat, Jeremy, 19n54
Troxel, A. Craig, 117n153, 118
Trueman, Carl, 2–3, 3n15, 54n135, 64–65, 87n9, 108n92, 111, 114–15, 125–26
Turretin, Francis, 93n32
Twisse, William, 108n91, 117n153

Ursinus, Zacharius, 18n49, 152
Ussher, James, 107

Vail, William, 113n126
van Buren, Paul Matthews, 139n61
van Til, Cornelius, 127n13
Vermigli, Peter Martyr, 71n57, 77
Vines, Richard, 108n91, 117n153

Waldon, Sam, 151n118
Walker, George, 108n91, 117n153
Ward, Samuel, 82n111, 118–19, 120nn165
Ware, Bruce, 54n129
Warfield, B. B., 102n69
Westhead, Nigel, 65
Whitgift, John, 124
Williams, Garry, 132n33, 136n51, 141, 149n106
Williams, Timothy, 105n77
Witsius, Herman, 93n31, 110n102

Zanchi, Girolamo, 68, 152
Zwingli, Huldrych, 82n111, 96n46

Subject Index

accommodation, concepts of, 16,
    16n40, 32n35
Act of the Associate Synod at
    Edinburgh (1754), 121n172
Alençon Synod, 97n49, 98n52
Amyraldian theology
    Calvin and, 14, 91
    as a Calvinist, 123
    "classical" view, 20n57, 97n50
    covenant of grace, 94n34
    term usage, 3n17, 4, 111
    treatises of, 91–110
    on unconditional election,
        91n23, 97n50, 105, 107
antecedent will, 71n57, 100n64, 153,
    153n126
apokatastasis doctrine (Origen),
    64n28, 69n51
assurance of salvation, 40–41n75
atonement
    conflicting tensions on, 15–25,
        86–91
    definite atonement, 7n36, 11–12,
        89n18, 140–41
    empty atonement, 37–38n63
    generally, 4–6, 87–88n12
    limited atonement (*See* limited
        atonement)
    substitutionary atonement,
        33n41
    universal atonement, 89n18, 91
    unlimited atonement (*See*
        unlimited atonement)
Augsburg Confession of Faith,
    106n84, 161n163

Bay of Guanabara, Brazil, mission,
    45n92
belief
    Christ's work on the cross and,
        29–30, 32–37, 39n68
    why everyone does not believe,
        29–30
Book of Common Prayer Catechism
    of the Anglican tradition,
    120

Calvin, John
    1 John 2:2 as evidence, 63–68
    1 Timothy 2:4 as evidence,
        68–84
    ambiguity of his position, 158
    assurance of salvation, 40–
        41n75
    on atonement generally, 5–6
    Augsburg Confession of Faith,
        106n84
    Christ's redemption of the whole
        world, 30n28, 34–37, 62n18
    Christ's work on the cross and
        belief, 29–30, 32–37, 39n68
    complex-intentioned approach,
        37–38n63, 128–40, 160–61
    conflicting tensions on
        atonement, 15–25
    covenant relationships, 93n32,
        94–95
    definite atonement and, 7n36,
        11–12

Calvin, John (*continued*)
  distinction of specific
    individuals, 30–31
  on the elect and election, 32–37,
    40n74, 51–53
  general provision, language used
    by, 157–58
  God's love, 32n35, 37n60
  grace offered to unbelievers,
    45–47, 45n94, 52, 153
  limited atonement and, 10–12,
    156–57
  on Lord's Supper, 61–63, 62n18
  on ministry of evangelism,
    42–45, 74, 75n81
  multiple intentions approach,
    37–38n63, 112–13n122
  on offer of the gospel, 27–28,
    34–37
  on prayer, 28
  reflections on, 125–28, 149–55
  Reformed mission, Bay of
    Guanabara, Brazil, 45n92
  "Reply to Heshusius" as
    evidence, 60–63
  second approach, 12–15, 91
  theological contribution, 111–
    13, 158–59
  third approach, 15–25, 86–91
  on unity of the Trinity, 53–58,
    56n140
  universal offer of salvation,
    30–31n30, 37–38n63, 37–41,
    37n62
  on universalist view, 27, 57n144
  unlimited atonement and, 12–
    15, 18, 19n50, 23, 60
  why everyone does not believe,
    29–30
  will of God (*See* secret decree
    versus revealed will of God)
Calvin and the Calvinists debate,
  111n104, 158n149
Calvin-Amyraut' outlook, 99
Calvinism
  confessionalism, 3n15
  five-point Calvinism, 3, 69,
    78, 84, 113n126, 124, 142,
    145–46
  four-point Calvinism, 3n17, 14,
    67, 84, 110, 142
  high orthodox, 24n73
  limited atonement and, 3–5
  term usage, 1–7, 1n2, 111–12,
    123–24
Canons of Dort (1619), 3n15,
  93–94n32, 114, 116, 118–22,
  147n101, 148, 151n118
Catechism of the Anglican *Book of
  Common Prayer*, 120
Colloquy of Montbéliard (1586),
  107n84
complex-intentioned approach,
  37–38n63, 128–40, 160–61
conditional will of God, 20, 91, 100,
  104–5
Confession of Thorn, 106n82
confessionalism, 3n15, 3n17
consequent will, 71n57, 100n64,
  153, 153n126
Council of Trent, 24n74
covenant
  term usage, 91n23
  three-fold scheme of, 93–95,
    94n34

decretal will, 128, 153
definite atonement, 7n36, 11–12,
  89n18, 140–41
divine intention and sufficiency,
  144–49
double payment argument, 101n65,
  135n44, 136n51, 148n102
duplex persona ("twofold character")
  of God, 16n40, 98n52
Dutch Reformed Church, term
  usage in Calvinism, 2

election and the elect
  Christ's redemption of the whole
    world, 30n28, 34–37, 62n18
  Christ's work on the cross and
    belief, 29–30, 32–37, 39n68
  Davenant's third element, 122

distinction of specific
   individuals, 30–31
God's chosen people, 31n32
redemption for all, 30n28, 51–53
sufficient for all but efficient for
   the elect, 21n60, 88–90
universal offer of salvation,
   30–31n30, 37–38n63, 37–41,
   37n62
empty atonement, 37–38n63
epistemic condition, language of,
   128n20
eternal justification, 33n41
eternal plan of salvation, historical
   moments in human history,
   81–82
Eucharist, 61–63, 62n18
evangelism, ministry of, 42–45, 74,
   75n81
expiation of sins
   Calvin on, 68n46, 87–88n12,
      88n15, 100
   Dabney on, 144

fairness, 82–83n114
faith
   assurance and, 40–41n75
   the illumination of God, 30–
      31n30
   relational trust in God's
      promises, 38
false teachers/prophets, 53, 53n125
federalism, 24n73, 91–92n24, 102
five-point Calvinism, 3, 69, 78, 84,
   113n126, 124, 142, 145–46
forensic satisfaction, 132n33
Formula Consensus Helvetica,
   116n149
four-point Calvinism, 3n17, 14, 67,
   84, 110, 142
free will
   of God, 101
   of people, 31

God
   conditional will of, 20, 91, 100,
      104–5
   degrees of His love shown in
      Christ, 81
   duplex persona ("twofold
      character") of, 16n40, 98n52
   four key moments in saving
      work, 54n135
   illumination of, 30–31n30
   love of, 32n35, 37n60, 98n51,
      137–38n54
   moral will of, 98n52
   paternal benevolence of, 77
   revealed will of (See secret
      decree versus revealed will
      of God)
   secret decree of (See secret
      decree versus revealed will
      of God)
   will of, 98–99
   wrath of, 126n9
gospel, offer of to all, 27–28, 34–37
grace
   covenant of, 81–82n111
   limitation of, 81–82n111
   objective grace, 96n43
   offered to unbelievers, 45–47,
      45n94, 52, 153
   subjective grace, 96n43

Heidelberg Catechism (1563), 119
Helvetic Consensus Formula (1675),
   96–97n43
hypothetical universalism
   as alternative forms of limited
      atonement, 90n21
   conditional, covenantal
      framework, 100, 100n65
   covenant and, 93–94n32
   Crisp on, 110n102
   definite-atonement and
      universal-atonement, 89n18
   diverse forms of, 116–18
   essential elements, 122
   grace for all men, 107n84,
      107n85
   historical scholarship needed,
      121
   Muller on, 114

hypothetical universalism (*cont.*)
    non-speculative forms of, 101n66, 120
    Preston as, 13
    version of uniting, 107–9
    Westminster Confession of Faith, 3n15

illumination of God, 30–31n30
inefficacious intentionality, 48n107
intentionality
    complex-intentioned approach, 37–38n63, 128–40, 160–61
    complexity of, 128–40
    divine intention and sufficiency, 144–49
    inefficacious intentionality, 48n107
    multiple intentions approach, 37–38n63, 112–13n122, 130, 131, 138

lapsarian schemes, 24n73, 102, 102n68, 103n72
limited atonement
    Calvin on, 10–12, 156–57
    Calvinism and, 3–5
    hypothetical universalism and, 90n21
    Muller on, 141
    "Reply to Heshusius" evidence, 60–63
    Trinitarian harmony and, 54
limited redemption, 40n75, 58, 60, 61n11, 143
Lombardian formula, 18n48, 89–90n18, 89n16, 123, 143, 145
Lord's Supper, 61–63, 62n18
Lutheranism, 106n82, 107n84, 141n66

metaphor, label of, 5n29
middle positions, 109, 118
moral ability, 96
moral will, 98n52
multiple intentions approach, 37–38n63, 112–13n122, 130, 131, 138

natural ability, 96
non-speculative, term usage, 101n66

objective grace, 96n43

paradox, language of, 127n13
pardoned thief on the cross, 52
particular predestination, 17
particular redemption
    double payment argument and, 136n51
    Owen on, 24
    Reformed theologians on, 121n172, 143–44, 145n92
    term usage, 4
    Westminster Calvinism and, 117n151
pecuniary satisfaction, 132n33
prayer
    for all, 28, 42–43n83, 67–68n46
    Trinitarian prayer, 56–57, 72–73
    for unbelievers, 72–76
predestination (*See* election and the elect)
preterition and predamnation, 85n1
Protestant unity, 161, 161n163
purchased redemption, 81–82, 122

quodammodo, scripture, use of, 85n1

Ramist methodology, 104n73
redemption
    limited redemption, 40n75, 58, 60, 61n11, 143
    particular redemption (*See* particular redemption)
    purchased redemption, 81–82, 122
    unlimited redemption, 107
Reformation theology
    on Calvinism, 2, 3n17
    creeds, 15n37
    diversity of, 112–16, 120, 143–44
    Westminster Confession of Faith, 3n15, 116–17, 122
Reformed Scholasticism, 102n71

regeneration, 95
repentance, 81–82n111
"Reply to Heshusius" Calvin, 60–63
revealed will versus secret decree of God (*See* secret decree versus revealed will of God)

scholasticism, term usage, 110–10n103
scripture, use of *quodammodo*, 85n1
second approach, unlimited atonement, 12–15, 91
secret decree versus revealed will of God, 16, 20, 31, 47–51, 77–78, 98–99, 104
souls in peril, 52
sovereign will, 98n52
speculative, term usage, 102n68
subjective grace, 96n43
substitutionary atonement, 33n41
sufficiency and divine intention, 144–49
Synod of Dort (1618-19), 114n134, 122n181 (*See also* Canons of Dort (1619))

third approach, conflicting tensions on atonement, 15–25, 86–91
Thirty-Nine Articles (1571), 119
Trinitarian prayer, 56–57, 72–73
Trinity
    approach to redemptive history, 95–96
    unity of, 53–58, 56n140, 136–39, 137n54
TULIP
    acronym meaning, 113n125
    inadequacy of, 140–43
    origin of, 113, 113n126
"twofold character" (*duplex persona*) of God, 16n40, 98n52

unbelievers
    double culpability of, 151
    Eucharist and, 61–63, 62n18
    grace offered to, 45–47, 45n94, 52, 153
    prayer for, 72–73, 75–76
    price of redemption for, 157n144
unconditional election
    Amyraldian theology, 91n23, 97n50, 105, 107
    Calvin on, 5, 12, 30, 59, 83, 83n115, 88, 91, 161
    Confessional Lutheran's, 141n66
    hypothetical universalism and, 107n85
    middle way positions, 109
    multiple intentions and, 130, 131, 138
universal atonement, 89n18, 91
universal offer of salvation, 30–31n30, 37–38n63, 37–41, 37n62
universalist view (all will be saved), 27, 57n144, 75, 90
unlimited atonement
    Amyraut on, 23
    Anglican *Book of Common Prayer*, 120
    Calvin on, 12–15, 18, 19n50, 23, 60
    Cameron on, 23
    limited atonement vs., 155
    second approach, 12–15, 91
    Shedd on, 143
    term usage, 90, 109, 159n151
unlimited expiation, 88n15, 144
unlimited redemption, 107

velleity, 48n107

Westminster Confession of Faith, 3n15, 94n32, 116–17, 122

Scripture Index

OLD TESTAMENT

Deuteronomy
5:11	48n106
22:2–4	43n85

Psalms
19:1–4	137n54
81:13	32n35
119	39

Isaiah
22:4	44n88
42:6	36n59
53	51
53:10	26n1
53:12	36n55, 70n56

Jeremiah
14:22	28n18
31:31–34	146n95

Lamentations
	3:33, 32n35

Ezekiel
18:1–4	41n77
18:23	50, 76, 78, 104n75
18:32	16n40
33:11	78
48:23	104n75

Hosea
	13:14, 45n93

Jonah
	4:2, 51n113

∽

NEW TESTAMENT

Matthew
1:1–17	38n65
11:21	71n57
13:44	131n31
14:24	62n18
15:13	29n23
18:12	27–28n11
20:28	62n18, 79n103
23:37	32n35, 47n101, 48n107, 49–50, 50n110, 76n89, 105n77, 150n113, 151n114
26:24	100n61
26:39	36n54

Mark
	14:24, 63n22, 79n103

Luke
2:10	47n100
3:23–38	38n65
22:19	59n1, 62n18

John

1:9	71n57
1:29	119n165
3:16	30, 30n28, 40–41, 41n77, 98n51, 99, 119n165
3:16–17	32n35, 38n67, 40n73, 48n104
3:17	46n95, 47
4:42	119n165
5:34	47n103
6:9–10	54n132
6:33	119n165
6:45	79n103
6:51	119n165
10:11	64n27
10:15	131n30
10:16	31n32
12:32	60n5
12:47	27n11, 28n13, 47n103
14:16	56n138
14:30	54n134
14:30–31	100n60
14:31	54n133
15:9	40n74
16:33	68, 68n47
17:2	54n132
17:9	66n38, 67, 67n45
17:21	67, 67n45
18:11	30n28
19	54n132
19:12	40n75
24	54n132

Acts

2:21	28n16
5:12	47n103
10	83n116
10:28	131n29
14:16	80
16:6–7	80
20:28	43n86, 131n29

Romans

1:16	28n14, 31n25
3:25	33, 33n40

5:15	29n20, 62n18, 65, 79n103
5:18	29n19, 35n46, 65n34, 65n35, 158n146
8:18–22	130n25
8:32	131n29
9:1–3	57
9:1–5	72n66
10:1	57
10:1–2	72n66
10:1–3	28n18
10:1–4	72
10:16	31n26

1 Corinthians

11	61
11:24	59n1
15:3	59n1
15:24–28	130n25
15:28	135n47

2 Corinthians

5	48
5:18	30, 33n41, 65n32
5:18–21	130n25
5:19	37n60
5:20	48n105

Galatians

2:20	32n36, 39, 59n1
3:13	59n1
5:12	33–34n45

Ephesians

1	31
1:3–13	129n21
1:3–14	54n132
1:4–6	31n33
2:1–7	32n35
2:1–13	136n51
5:1	6n31
5:2	59n1
5:25	131n29
5:25–27	131n29
6:18–19	42n83

Philippians
2:9–11, 130n25

Colossians
1:14   35n51
1:19–20   130, 135n47

1 Thessalonians
5:10, 59n1

1 Timothy
2   70n56
2:1–6   74
2:1–7   72
2:3   28n15
2:3–5   29n21, 29n22, 69–70
2:4   68, 68n50, 69, 71, 99
2:4–5   70n55
2:5   28n18, 70n56, 71n57
2:6   27n6
4:10   98n51, 147
6:13–16   56–57n142

2 Timothy
1:9–10, 40n74

Titus
1:11   44n89
2:11   27n6, 80n106

Hebrews
5:9   79n103
8:2   35n53
9:27   29n20
9:28   79n103
12:22–24   131n29

James
2   83n116
5:20   43n86

1 Peter
1:1–2   54n132
1:18   34n43
1:20   100n61
2:22   60n5
2:24   58n146

2 Peter
2:1   43n83, 53, 53n125, 53n126, 151n115
3:9   32n35, 49n108

1 John
2   83–84
2:2   18n48, 22n64, 27n6, 63–68, 64n27, 67n42, 78, 89n17, 99, 99n55, 119n165, 132n32
4:9–10   119n165, 132n32
5:16   44n90, 151n115

Jude
4, 43n83, 53

Revelation
5:9   131n29
5:9–10   79n105
7:9–10   79n105

www.ingramcontent.com/pod-product-compliance
Lightning Source LLC
Chambersburg PA
CBHW032059230426
43662CB00035B/719